THE POETS AND THEIR CRITICS

THE POETS AND THEIR CRITICS

THE POETS
AND THEIR CRITICS

Chaucer to Collins

———◆———

HUGH SYKES DAVIES

Fellow of St. John's College
Cambridge

HUTCHINSON EDUCATIONAL

HUTCHINSON EDUCATIONAL LTD
178–202 Great Portland Street, London W1

London Melbourne Sydney
Auckland Bombay Toronto
Johannesburg New York

★

First published by Penguin Books 1943
Revised edition published 1960
Reprinted 1969

This book has been set in Times, printed in Great Britain
on Antique Wove paper by Anchor Press, and
bound by Wm. Brendon, both of Tiptree, Essex

09 057292 0

Contents

Acknowledgements

For permission to use copyright material, acknowledgements are due to:

George Allen & Unwin (John Ruskin, *The Stones of Venice* and *Lectures on Art*)

Edward Arnold (Sir Walter Raleigh, *Milton*)

The Cambridge University Press (Lytton Strachey, *Pope*)

Cassell & Co. (Hilaire Belloc, *Milton*)

Chatto & Windus (E. M. W. Tillyard, *The English Epic and its Background*; William Empson, *Seven Types of Ambiguity*)

The Clarendon Press (H. J. C. Grierson, *The Poems of John Donne*; C. S. Lewis, *The Allegory of Love*)

T. S. Eliot (*A Note on the Verse of John Milton*, from *Essays and Studies*)

Faber & Faber (T. S. Eliot, *On Poetry and Poets*)

The Harvard University Press (T. S. Eliot, from *A Garland for John Donne*)

William Heinemann (Sir Edmund Gosse, *The Life and Letters of John Donne*; A. C. Swinburne, *Collins, A Century of English Poetry*, *Study of Ben Jonson*)

The Hogarth Press (T. S. Eliot, *Homage to John Dryden*)

Macmillan & Co. (W. P. Ker, *Form and Style in Poetry*; Leslie Stephen, *Pope*)

Houghton Mifflin Co. (J. L. Lowes, *Geoffrey Chaucer*)

John Murray (Leslie Stephen, *Gray and His School*, from *Hours in a Library*)

The Oxford University Press (Middleton Murry, *The Poetry of W. Collins*; Charles Williams, *Introduction to the English Poems of John Milton*)

George Routledge (George Saintsbury, *Introduction* to Chambers' edition of Donne's *Poems*; J. Dowden, *The Poetry of John Donne*)

Preface to the Second Edition

The first edition was published as a Pelican in the middle of the last hot war, and some of those who found it useful are no longer consoled for the tattered state of their copies by the grey nostalgia of ageing austerity paper. It is hoped that this new edition will be a more robust replacement, and that it may perhaps find some new users as well. On the whole, experience has shown that the book has its uses, and that its abuses, besides being detectable, demand a certain intelligence in their practitioner. And I have been the readier to bother with a new edition because it gives me the chance to complete the original plan, by adding a second volume, arranged in the same general manner, on the Romantics and the two Great Victorians—the arrangement seems to me not worth pursuing after Tennyson and Browning, because the historical perspective becomes too short.

At first I hoped that it would be possible to make many splendid additions to the first volume, and the search for them was carried through many books, old and new. But it now seems that, so far as the older critics are concerned, I had already found what I needed, while with the more recent critics, the rather testy expression of opinion in the first Preface about the relation between learning and criticism has turned out to be more prophetic than it deserved. There has been, in the last twenty years, a staggering proliferation of learned study of these poets, and some of it has been profitable. But the over-all *critical* results are small, in the sense that most of them hold much the same place in the procession of English literature that they held a generation ago. Thus Chaucer and Spenser can now be studied with a better understanding of the complexity of their intentions and technique, but, while we may perhaps be persuaded to think them better poets, we have been given no strong reason for thinking them to be any different in kind. One passage has been added to the section on Spenser, because it seemed a very good example of what can be achieved by the modern combination of learning with criticism.

The most interesting and considerable changes seem to me to have been in the development of opinion about Milton and Pope. Mr Eliot has carried much further the reflections represented in the last extract of the section on Milton in the first edition—so much further that, here and there, one might almost say that he has changed his mind. Some of these new thoughts have been added in this edition. I have also added, partly because Mr Eliot commends it, a criticism mainly directed to *Comus* by a distinguished exponent of the new school which finds, or makes, Milton's doctrine congenial.

To the section on Pope have been added two passages from Professor Empson's *Seven Types of Ambiguity*, a book with which I was very familiar when the first edition was prepared, but from which I lacked the wit to levy this contribution. It is, I believe, typical of (and in some ways central to) the enhanced position which Pope now holds in critical opinion.

Three apologies (with appropriate excuses) remain to be made. The first is to readers who find much poor stuff in the book; they are asked to suppose that many and greater fatuities have been kept out of it. The second is to those who feel that very good things are omitted; they are reminded that often it has seemed pointless to include extracts from writings which are not only readily available, but also (to the best of my knowledge) very often in the hands of the modern student of English literature. The third is to the authors, past and present, whose careful arguments I have been compelled (and allowed) to shiver into splinters for the present purpose. I hope that most of the splinters are pointed, at least at one end, and by them a few readers may, after all, be stimulated to seek out the originals, and see what they really meant and said.

Preface to the Original Edition

Each piece in this collection has been included for one, or for more than one, of these reasons:

Because it seemed to be a good criticism of the author concerned.

Because, though not in itself a good criticism, it illustrated a significant variation in the author's reputation.

Because, though only moderately important for either of these reasons, it comes from some book which is not easily got at by the ordinary reader.

The reasons for which pieces have been excluded are roughly the opposite of these. Thus I hope there are no absolutely worthless criticisms; I hope there are none which are mere echoes, not real modifications, of prevailing fashions. And there should be only a few from books (such as the stock *Histories of English Literature*) which are to be found in most libraries, private or public.

Further, I have excluded anything which seemed to be rather a work of learning than of criticism. Whether learning is better or worse than criticism, I do not know. Though, as I have put these pieces together, I have come to the strong conclusion that, while there is ample scope for profitable learned study of the English poets, there is little need for any further criticism of them.

The uses and abuses to which the collection may be put are perhaps obvious enough; and if the uses may not be very great, at least the abuses should be easy to detect.

Chaucer

Chaucerian criticism, of course, covers a longer period than any other section of this book, and the earlier specimens of it come down from a time when English was both spoken and spelt in a way to which we are not accustomed. I have left this as it is, so that the ordinary reader may see what the old spelling is really like: outside the words which he already knows, such as Ye Olde Tea Shoppe.

The most striking thing about the development of Chaucerian criticism is that the earlier critics did not like him for qualities which the modern reader seems to find in him. They were mainly concerned with his poetry as language, *as artful diction; and the greatest compliment they pay him is that of being a great rhetorician. Modern scholarship confirms their view amply; but it is doubtful if many people have the time to become masters of modern scholarship in order to agree with Lydgate.*

After the Reformation, Chaucer enjoyed an undeserved respect as a forerunner of religious revolution; and it was said, on the great authority of Foxe (of the Martyrs), that he had been a Wycliffite.

It was Dryden who first firmly stated the modern reading of Chaucer's work, drawing attention to his characterization and humanity. It was Dryden, too, who gave the great authority of his name to the view that Chaucer's language was uncouth and irregular, like his versification. And it was Dryden who started the fashion of rescuing Chaucer from his worse self by translating him from his own language into a better one.

In the eighteenth century Chaucerian scholarship commenced, and soon disposed of the long-established traditions concerning Chaucer's language and versification. Chaucer was

*treated with steadily increasing respect, and read with better
understanding, until he emerged with a blaze of glory among the
Romantics. Nearly all the early nineteenth-century critics have
a go at him; but Hunt deserves special attention for his life-
long devotion, rewarded at last by a very fine understanding.*

*In England, Matthew Arnold's attempt to put Chaucer a
little below the highest in poetry still colours critical fashion.
But in America, from the time of Lowell onwards, Chaucer
has continued to find both whole-hearted champions and admirable scholars. Indeed, the modern development of Chaucerian
criticism is an American rather than an English phenomenon.*

LYDGATE

And eke my master Chauceris nowe is grave
The noble rethor Poete of breteine
That worthy was the laurer to have
Of poetrie and the palme atteine
That made firste to distille and reyne
The golde dewe droppis of speche and eloquence
In-to oure tounge thourgh his excellence
And founde the flourys first of rethoryk
Oure rude speche oonly to enlumyne
That in oure tunge was never noon him like. . . .

The Life of our Lady 1409–11?

HOCCLEVE

O, maister deere, and fadir reverent!
Mi maister Chaucer, flour of eloquence,
Mirour of fructuous entendement,
O, universel fadir in science! . . .

Also, who was hier in philosophie
To Aristotle, in our tonge, but thow?
The steppes of virgile in poesie
Thou filwedist eeke, men wot wel y-now. . . .

The firste fyndere of our faire langage . . .

The Regement of Princes 1412

ANON

Redith his werkis ful of plesaunce
  Clere in sentence in langage excellent
Briefly to wryte suche was his suffysance
  Whatever to saye he toke in his entente
  His langage was so fayr and pertynente
    It semeth unto mannys heerynge
    Not only the worde but verely the thynge.

The Book of Curtesye 1477?

CAXTON

. . . we ought to gyve a synguler laude unto that noble &
grete philosopher Gefferey chaucer the whiche for his ornate
wrytyng in our tongue maye wel have the name of laureate
poete. For to fore that he by his labour embelysshyd ornated
and made faire our englisshe in thys Royame was had rude
speche & Incongrue as yet it appiereth by olde bookes whyche
at thys day ought not to have place ne be compared emong
ne to his beauteuous volumes and aournate writynges of whom
he made many bokes and treatyces of many a noble historye
as wel in metre as in ryme and prose and them so craftyly
made that he comprehended hys maters in short quyck and hye
sentences eschewyng prolyxyte castyng away the chaf of
superfluyte and shewyng the pyked grayn of sentence uttered
by crafty and sugred eloquence. . . .

Prohemye to Canterbury Tales 1483?

DUNBAR

O reverend Chaucere, rose of rethoris all,
As in oure tong ane flour imperiall
That raise in Britane ewir, quho redis rycht,
Thou beris of makaris the tryumph riall;
Thy fresch anamalit termes celicall
This mater coud illumynit have full brycht:

The Golden Targe 1503

GAVIN GOUGLAS

Hevinlie trumpat, horleige and reguleir,
In eloquence balmy, condit, and diall,
Mylky fountane, cleir strand, and rose riall,
Of fresch endite, throw Albion iland braid.

The Palis of Honoure   1513

SKELTON

In Chauser I am sped,
His tales I have red:
His mater is delectable
Solacious and commendable;
His englishe wel alowed,
So as it is enprowed,
For as it is enployed
There is no englyshe voyd—
At those days moch commended,
And now men wold have amended
His english, where at they barke,
And marre all they warke:
Chaucer, that famous Clarke,
His tearmes were not darcke,
But pleasaunt, easy, and playne;
No worde he wrote in vayne.

Book of Phillip Sparrow   1507?

THYNNE'S EDITION

. . . that noble & famous clerke Geffray Chaucer in whose workes is so manyfest comprobacion of his excellent lernyng in all kyndes of doctrynes and sciences such frutefulnesse in wordes wel accordynge to the mater and purpose so swete and plesaunt sentences suche perfectyon in metre the composycion so adapted suche fresshnesse of invencion compendyousnesse in narration such sensyble and open style lackyng neither maiestie ne mediocritie covenable in disposycion and suche sharpnesse or quycknesse in conclusyon that it is moche to be marveyled howe in his tyme whan doutlesse all good letters were layde a slepe through out the worlde ... suche an excellent poete in our tonge shulde, as it were (nature repugnyng) spryng and aryse. ...

Written by Sir Brian Tuke. Dedication to Henry VIII, prefixed to Thynne's edition of Chaucer's works 1532

FOXE

... but muche more I mervell to consider this, how that the Bishoppes condemnyng and abolishyng al maner of Englishe bookes and treatises, which might bryng the people to any light of knowledge, did yet authorise the woorkes of Chaucer to remayne still & to be occupyed: Who (no doubt) saw in Religion as much almost, as even we do now, and uttereth in hys worke no lesse, and semeth to be a right Wiclevian, or els was never any, and that all his workes almost, if they be throughly advised will testifie (albeit it bee done in myrth, & covertly). ...

Eccleciasticall History 1570

SIDNEY

Chaucer undoubtedly did excellently in hys *Troilus and Cresseid*; of whom, truly I know not, whether to mervaile more, either that he, in that mistie time, could see so clearly, or that we, in this cleare age, walke so stumblingly after him. Yet had he great wants, fit to be forgiven in so reverent antiquity.

An Apologie for Poetrie 1581?

WEBBE

Chawcer, who for that excellent fame which he obtayned in his Poetry was alwayes accounted the God of English Poets

(such a tytle for honours sake hath beene given him) . . . hath
left many workes, both for delight and profitable knowledge,
farre exceeding any other that as yet ever since hys time
directed theyr studies that way. Though the manner of hys
stile may seeme blunte and course to many fine English eares
at these dayes, yet in trueth, if it be equally pondered, and with
good judgement advised, and confirmed with the time wherein
he wrote, a man shall perceive thereby even a true picture or
perfect shape of a right Poet. He by his delightsome vayne, so
gulled the eares of men with his devises, that, although corruption bare such sway in most matters, that learning and truth
might skant bee admitted to shewe it selfe, yet without con-
trollment, myght hee gyrde at the vices and abuses of all
states, and gawle with very sharp and eger inventions, which
he did so learnedly and pleasantly, that none therefore could
call him into question. For such was his bolde spyrit, that
what enormities he saw in any, he would not spare to pay
them home, eyther in playne words, or els in some pretty and
pleasant covert, that the simplest might espy him.

A Discourse of English Poetrie 1586

SPENSER

. . . Dan *Chaucer*, well of Englishe undefyled,
On Fames eternall beadroll worthie to be fyled.

But wicked Time that all good thoughts doth waste,
  And workes of noblest wits to nought out weare,
That famous moniment hath quite defaste,
  And robd the world of treasure endlesse deare,
  The which mote have enriched all us heare. . . .

The Faerie Queene 1590

PEACHAM

Of English Poets of our owne Nation, esteeme Sir *Geoffrey
Chaucer* the father; although the stile for the antiquitie may

distaste you, yet as vnder a bitter and rough rinde there lyeth a delicate kernell of conceit and sweete inuention. What Examples, Similitudes, Times, Places, and aboue all, Persons with their speeches and attributes, doe, as in his *Canterburie-tales*, like these threds of gold and rich *Arras*, beautifie his Worke quite thorough! And albeit diuers of his workes are but meerely translations out of *Latine* and *French*, yet he hath handled them so artificially that thereby he hath made them his owne, as his *Troilus* and *Cresseid*. The Romant of the Rose was the Inuention of *Iehan de Mehunes*, a French Poet, whereof he translated but onely the one halfe; his *Canterburie*-tales without question were his owne inuention, all circumstances being wholly English. Hee was a good Diuine, and saw in those times without his spectacles, as may appeare by the Plough-man and the Parsons tale; withall an excellent Mathematician, as plainly appeareth by his discourse of the Astrolabe to his little sonne *Lewes*. In briefe, account him among the best of your English bookes in your librarie.

The Compleat Gentleman 1622

DRYDEN

In the first place, as he is the father of English poetry, so I hold him in the same degree of veneration as the Grecians held Homer, or the Romans Virgil. He is a perpetual fountain of good sense; learn'd in all sciences; and, therefore, speaks properly on all subjects. As he knew what to say, so he knows also when to leave off; a continence which is practised by few writers, and scarcely by any of the ancients, excepting Virgil and Horace. . . .

Chaucer followed Nature everywhere, but was never so bold to go beyond her; and there is a great difference of being *poeta* and *nimis poeta*, if we may believe Catullus, as much as betwixt a modest behaviour and an affectation. The verse of Chaucer, I confess, is not harmonious to us; 'tis but like the eloquence of one whom Tacitus commends, it was *auribus istius temporis accomodata*: they who lived with him, and some time after him, thought it musical; and it continues so, even

in our judgment, if compared with the numbers of Lidgate
and Gower, his contemporaries: there is the rude sweetness of
a Scotch tune in it, which is natural and pleasing, though not
perfect. 'Tis true, I cannot go so far as he who published the
last edition of him; for he would make us believe the fault is
in our ears, and that there were really ten syllables in a verse
where we find but nine: but this opinion is not worth con-
futing. . . .

He must have been a man of a most wonderful comprehensive nature, because, as it has been truly observed of him,
he has taken into the compass of his *Canterbury Tales* the
various manners and humours (as we now call them) of the
whole English nation, in his age. Not a single character has
escaped him. All his pilgrims are severally distinguished from
each other; and not only in their inclinations, but in their
very physiognomies and persons. Baptista Porta could not
have described their natures better, than by the marks which
the poet gives them. The matter and manner of their tales, and
of their telling, are so suited to their different educations,
humours, and callings, that each of them would be improper
in any other mouth. Even the grave and serious characters are
distinguished by their several sorts of gravity: their discourses
are such as belong to their age, their calling, and their breeding;
such as are becoming of them, and of them only. Some of his
persons are vicious, and some virtuous; some are unlearn'd, or
(as Chaucer calls them) lewd, and some are learn'd. Even the
ribaldry of the low characters is different: the Reeve, the
Miller, and the Cook, are several men, and distinguished
from each other as much as the mincing Lady-Prioress and the
broad-speaking, gap-toothed Wife of Bath. But enough of this;
there is such a variety of game springing up before me, that I
am distracted in my choice, and know not which to follow.
'Tis sufficient to say, according to the proverb, that *here is
God's plenty*. We have our forefathers and great-grand-dames
all before us, as they were in Chaucer's days: their general
characters are still remaining in mankind, and even in England,
though they are called by other names than those of Monks,
and Friars, and Canons, and Lady Abbesses, and Nuns; for

mankind is ever the same, and nothing lost out of Nature,
though everything is altered. . . .

Preface to the Fables 1700

T. WARTON

I cannot dismiss this section without a wish, that this
neglected author whom Spenser proposed in some measure
as the pattern of his language, and to whom he is not a little
indebted for many noble strokes of poetry, should be more
universally and attentively studied. Chaucer seems to be regarded rather as an old poet, than as a good one, and that he
wrote English verses four hundred years ago seems more
frequently to be urged in his commendation, than that he
wrote four hundred years ago with taste and judgment. We
look upon his poems rather as venerable relics, than as finished
patterns; as pieces calculated rather to gratify the antiquarian
than the critic. When I sat down to read Chaucer with the
curiosity of knowing how the first English poet wrote, I left
him with the satisfaction of having found what later and more
refined ages could hardly equal in true humour, pathos, or
sublimity.

Observations on the Faerie Queene of Spenser 1754

But Chaucer's vein of humour, although conspicuous in
the *Canterbury Tales*, is chiefly displayed in the Characters
with which they are introduced. In these his knowledge of the
world availed him in a peculiar degree, and enabled him to give
such accurate pictures of antient manners, as no contemporary
nation has transmitted to posterity. It is here that we view the
pursuits and employments, the customs and diversions, of our
ancestors, copied from the life, and represented with equal
truth and spirit, by a judge of mankind, whose penetration
qualified him to discern their foibles or discriminating peculiarities; and by an artist, who understood that proper selection
of circumstances, and those predominant characteristics, which
form a finished portrait. We are surprised to find, in so gross

and ignorant an age, such talents for satire, and for observation on life; qualities which usually exert themselves at more civilised periods, when the improved state of society, by subtilising our speculations, and establishing uniform modes of behaviour, disposes mankind to study themselves, and renders deviations of conduct, and singularities of character, more immediately and necessarily the objects of censure and ridicule. These curious and valuable remains are specimens of Chaucer's native genius, unassisted and unalloyed. The figures are all British, and bear no suspicious signatures of Classical, Italian, or French imitation. The characters of Theophrastus are not so lively, particular, and appropriated. . . .

We are surprised to find, in a poet of such antiquity, numbers so nervous and flowing. . . .

The History of English Poetry 1781

JOHNSON

The history of our language is now brought to the point at which the history of our poetry is generally supposed to commence, the time of the illustrious *Geoffry Chaucer*, who may perhaps, with great justice, be stiled the first of our versifiers who wrote poetically. He does not however appear to have deserved all the praise which he has received, or all the censure that he has suffered. Dryden, who mistaking genius for learning, and in confidence of his abilities, ventured to write of what he had not examined, ascribes to *Chaucer* the first refinement of our numbers, the first production of easy and natural rhymes, and the improvement of our language, by words borrowed from the more polished languages of the Continent . . . but the works of *Gower* and *Lydgate* sufficiently evince that his diction was in general like that of his contemporaries: and some improvements he undoubtedly made by the mixture of different numbers, in which he seems to have been happy and judicious.

The History of the English Language:
Johnson's Dictionary 1755

J. WARTON

But whatever Chaucer might copy from the Italians, yet the artful and entertaining plan of his *Canterbury Tales* was purely original, and his own. This admirable piece, even exclusive of its poetry, is highly valuable, as it preserves to us the liveliest and exactest picture of the manners, customs, characters, and habits, of our forefathers, whom he has brought before our eyes acting as on a stage, suitably to their different orders and employments. With these portraits the driest antiquary must be delighted: by this plan he has more judiciously connected these stories which the guests relate, than Boccace has done his novels; whom he has imitated, if not excelled, in the variety of the subjects of his tales. It is a common mistake, that Chaucer's excellence lay in his manner of treating light and ridiculous subjects; for whoever will attentively consider the noble poem of *Palamon and Arcite*, will be convinced, that he equally excels in the pathetic and the sublime. . . .

An Essay on the Genius and Writings of Pope   1782

BLAKE

The characters of Chaucer's Pilgrims are the characters which compose all ages and nations. As one age falls, another rises, different to mortal sight, but to immortals only the same; for we see the same characters repeated again and again, in animals, vegetables, minerals, and in men. Nothing new occurs in identical existence; Accident ever varies, Substance can never suffer change nor decay.

Of Chaucer's characters, as described in his *Canterbury Tales*, some of the names or titles are altered by time, but the characters themselves for ever remain unaltered; and consequently they are the physiognomies or lineaments of universal human life, beyond which Nature never steps. Names alter, things never alter. I have known multitudes of those who would have been monks in the age of monkery, who in this deistical age are deists. As Newton numbered the stars, and as

Linnaeus numbered the plants, so Chaucer numbered the classes of men. . . .

It is necessary here to speak of Chaucer's own character, that I may set certain mistaken critics right in their conception of the humour and fun that occur on the journey. Chaucer is himself the great poetical observer of men, who in every age is born to record and eternize its acts. This he does as a master, as a father and superior, who looks down on their little follies from the Emperor to the Miller, sometimes with severity, oftener with joke and sport. . . .

Chaucer's characters live age after age. Every age is a Canterbury Pilgrimage; we all pass on, each sustaining one of these characters; nor can a child be born who is not one or other of these characters of Chaucer. The Doctor of Physic is described as the first of his profession, perfect, learned, completely Master and Doctor in his art. Thus the reader will observe that Chaucer makes every one of his characters perfect in his kind; every one is an Antique Statue, the image of a class and not of an imperfect individual. . . .

The character of Women Chaucer has divided into two classes, the Lady Prioress and the Wife of Bath. Are not these leaders of the ages of men? The Lady Prioress in some ages predominates; and in some the Wife of Bath, in whose character Chaucer has been equally minute and exact; because she is also a scourge and a blight. I shall say no more of her, nor expose what Chaucer has left hidden; let the young reader study what he has said of her; it is useful as a scarecrow. There are of such characters born too many for the peace of the world.

Descriptive Catalogue, No. III   1809

COLERIDGE

I take unceasing delight in Chaucer. His manly cheerfulness is especially delicious to me in my old age. How exquisitely tender he is, and yet how perfectly free from the least touch of sickly melancholy or morbid drooping! The sympathy of the poet with the subjects of his poetry is particularly remarkable in Shakespeare and Chaucer; but what the first effects by a strong act of imagination and mental metamorphosis, the last does without any effort, merely by the inborn kindly joyousness of his nature. How well we seem to know Chaucer! How absolutely nothing do we know of Shakespeare!

I cannot in the least allow any necessity for Chaucer's poetry, especially the *Canterbury Tales*, being considered obsolete. Let a few plain rules be given for sounding the final *e* of syllables, and for expressing the termination of such words as *ocean*, and *nation*, etc., as dissyllables—or let the syllables to be sounded in such cases be marked by a competent metrist. This simple expedient would, with a very few trifling exceptions, where the errors are inveterate, enable any reader to feel the perfect smoothness and harmony of Chaucer's verse. As to understanding his language, if you read twenty pages with a good glossary, you surely can find no further difficulty, even as it is; but I should have no objection to see this done: Strike out those words which are now obsolete, and I will venture to say that I will replace every one of them by words still in use out of Chaucer himself, or Gower his disciple. I don't want this myself: I rather like to see the significant terms which Chaucer unsuccessfully offered as candidates for admission into our language; but surely so very slight a change of text will be pardoned, even by black-*letterati*, for the purpose of restoring so great a poet to his ancient and most deserved popularity.

Table Talk   March 15, 1834

Chaucer must be read with an eye to the Norman-French *Trouvères*, of whom he is the best representative in English. As in Shakespeare, his characters represent classes, but in a different manner; Shakespeare's characters are the representatives of the interior nature of humanity in which some element has become so predominant as to destroy the health of the mind; whereas Chaucer's are rather representatives of classes of manners. He is therefore more led to individualize in a mere personal sense. Observe Chaucer's love of nature; and how

happily the subject of his main work is chosen. When you
reflect that the company in the *Decameron* have retired to a
place of safety from the raging of a pestilence, their mirth provokes a sense of their unfeelingness; whereas in Chaucer
nothing of this sort occurs, and the scheme of a party on a
pilgrimage, with different ends and occupations, aptly allows
of the greatest variety of expression in the tales.

Notes of Lectures 1818

HAZLITT

.... while Chaucer's intercourse with the busy world, and
collision with the actual passions and conflicting interests of
others, seemed to brace the sinews of his understanding, and
give to his writings the air of a man who describes persons and
things that he had known and been intimately concerned in;
the same opportunities, operating on a differently constituted
frame, only served to alienate Spenser's mind the more from
the 'close-pent up' scenes of ordinary life, and to make him
'rive their concealing continents', to give himself up to the
unrestrained indulgence of 'flowery tenderness'. . . .

It is not possible for any two writers to be more opposite in
this respect. Spenser delighted in luxurious enjoyment; Chaucer,
in severe activity of mind. As Spenser was the most romantic
and visionary, Chaucer was the most practical of all the great
poets, the most a man of business and the world. His poetry
reads like history. Everything was a downright reality; at least
in the relator's mind. A simile, or a sentiment, is as if it were
given in upon evidence. . . .

The strokes of his pencil always tell. He dwells only upon
the essential, upon that which would be interesting to the
persons really concerned; yet as he never omits any material
circumstance, he is prolix from the number of points on which
he touches, without being diffuse on any one; and is sometimes tedious from the fidelity with which he adheres to his
subject, as other writers are from the frequency of their digressions from it. . . .

Chaucer's descriptions of natural scenery possess the same

sort of characteristic excellence, or what might be termed *gusto*. . . .

Nature is the soul of art: there is a strength as well as a simplicity in the imagination that reposes entirely on nature, that nothing else can supply. It was the same trust in nature, and reliance on his subject which enabled Chaucer to describe the grief and patience of Griselda; the faith of Constance; and the heroic perseverance of the little child, who, going to school through the streets of Jewry,

> 'Oh *Alma Redemptoris mater*, loudly sung',

and who after his death still triumphed in his song. Chaucer has more of this deep, internal, sustained sentiment, than any other writer, except Boccaccio. In depth of simple pathos, and intensity of conception, never swerving from his subject, I think no other writer comes near him, not even the Greek tragedians.

Lectures on the English Poets 1818

LEIGH HUNT

When Chaucer is free from this taint of his age (i.e. coarseness), his humour is of a description the most thoroughly delightful; for it is at once entertaining, profound, and goodnatured. If this last quality be thought a drawback by some, as wanting the relish of personality, they may supply even that (as some have supplied it), by supposing that he drew his characters from individuals, and that the individuals were very uncomfortable accordingly. I confess I see no ground for the supposition beyond what the nature of the case demands. Classes must of course be drawn, more or less, from the individuals composing them; but the unprofessional particulars added by Chaucer to his characters (such as the Merchant's uneasy marriage, and the Franklin's prodigal son) are only such as render the portraits more true, by including them in the general category of mankind. The gangrene which the Cook had on his shin, and which has been considered as a

remarkable instance of the gratuitous, is, on the contrary
(besides its masterly intimation of the perils of luxury in
general), painfully in character with a man accustomed to
breathe an unhealthy atmosphere, and to be encouraging bad
humours with tasting sauces and syrups. Besides, the Cook
turns out to be a drunkard.

Chaucer's comic genius is so perfect, that it may be said to
include prophetic intimations of all that followed it. . . . One
of its characteristics is a certain tranquil detection of particulars, expressive of generals; as in the instance just mentioned
of the secret infirmity of the Cook. Thus the Prioress speaks
French; but it is 'after the school of Stratford at Bow'. Her
education was altogether more showy than substantial. The
Lawyer was the busiest man in the world, and yet he 'seemed
busier than he was'. He made something out of nothing, even
in appearances. . . .

The third great quality of Chaucer's humour is its fair
play—the truth and humanity which induces him to see
justice done to good and bad, to the circumstances which make
men what they are, and the mixture of right and wrong, of
wisdom and folly, which they consequently exhibit. His worst
characters have some little saving grace of good-nature, or at
least of joviality and candour. Even the Pardoner, however
impudently, acknowledges himself to be a 'vicious man'. His
best people, with one exception, betray some infirmity. The
good Clerk of Oxford, for all his simplicity and singleness of
heart, has not escaped the pedantry and pretension of the
college. The Good Parson seems without a blemish, even in his
wisdom; yet when it comes to his turn to relate a story, he
announces it as a 'little' tale, and then tells the longest and
most prosing in the book—a whole sermonizing volume. . . .

The father of English poetry was essentially a modest
man. He sits quietly in a corner, looking down for the most
part and meditating; at other times eyeing everything that
passes, and sympathising with everything; chuckling heartily
at a jest, feeling his eyes fill with tears at sorrow, reverencing
virtue, and not out of charity with vice. When he ventures to
tell a story himself, it is as much under correction of the Host

as the humblest man in the company; and it is no sooner objected to, than he drops it for one of a different description.

Wit and Humour 1846

RUSKIN

For there is one strange, but quite essential, character in us—ever since the Conquest, if not earlier—a delight in the forms of burlesque which are connected in some degree with the foulness of evil. I think the most perfect type of a true English mind in its best possible temper, is that of Chaucer; and you will find that, while it is for the most part full of thoughts of beauty, pure and wild like that of an April morning, there are, even in the midst of this, sometimes momentarily jesting passages which stoop to play with evil—while the power of listening to and enjoying the jesting of entirely gross persons, whatever the feeling may be which permits it, afterwards degenerates into forms of humour which render some of quite the greatest, wisest, and most moral of English writers now almost useless for our youth. And yet you will find that whenever Englishmen are wholly without this instinct, their genius is comparatively weak and restricted

Lectures on Art 1870

JAMES RUSSELL LOWELL

Chaucer is the first who broke away from the dreary traditional style, and gave not merely stories, but lively *pictures* of real life as the ever-renewed substance of poetry. He was a reformer, too, not only in literature, but in morals. But as in the former his exquisite tact saved him from all eccentricity, so in the latter the pervading sweetness of his nature could never be betrayed into harshness and invective. . . . There is no touch of cynicism in all he wrote. Dante's brush seems sometimes to have been smeared with the burning pitch of his own fiery lake. Chaucer's pencil is dipped in the cheerful colour-box of the old illuminators, and he has their patient delicacy of touch, with a freedom far beyond their somewhat mechanic brilliancy. . . .

One of the world's three or four great story tellers, he was also one of the best versifiers that ever made English trip and sing with a gaiety that seems careless, but where every foot beats time to the tune of thought. By the skilful arrangement of his pauses he evaded the monotony of the couplet, and gave to the rhymed pentameter, which he made our heroic measure, something of the architectural repose of blank verse. He found our language lumpish, stiff, unwilling, too apt to speak Saxonly in grouty monosyllables; he left it enriched with the longer measure of the Italian and Provençal poets. . . .

Chaucer is a great narrative poet. The power of diffusion without being diffuse would seem to be the highest merit of narration, giving it that easy flow which is so delightful. Chaucer's descriptive style is remarkable for its lowness of tone—for that combination of energy with simplicity which is among the rarest gifts in literature. . . .

Not that Chaucer cannot be intense, too, on occasion; but it is with a quiet intensity of his own, that comes in as it were by accident. . . .

With Chaucer it is always the thing itself and not the description of it that is the main object. His picturesque bits are incidental to the story, glimpsed in passing; they never stop the way. His key is so low that his high lights are never obtrusive. . . .

Chaucer never shows signs of effort, and it is a main proof of his excellence that he can be so inadequately sampled by detached passages—by single lines taken away from the connection in which they contribute to the general effect. He has that continuity of thought, that evenly prolonged power, and that dignified equanimity, which characterize the higher orders of mind. There is something in him of the disinterestedness that made the Greeks masters in art. His phrase is never importunate. His simplicity is that of elegance, not of poverty. The quiet unconcern with which he says his best things is peculiar to him among English poets, though Goldsmith, Addison, and Thackeray have approached it in prose. . . .

Chaucer seems to me to have been one of the most purely original of poets, as much so in respect of the world that is about us as Dante in respect of that which is within us. There had been nothing like him before, there has been nothing since. He is original, not in the sense that he thinks and says what nobody ever thought and said before, and what nobody can ever think and say again, but because he is always natural; because, if not always absolutely new, he is always delightfully fresh, because he sets before us the world as it honestly appeared to Geoffrey Chaucer, and not a world as it seemed proper to certain people that it ought to appear.

In spite of some external stains, which those who have studied the influence of manners will easily account for without imputing them to any moral depravity, we feel that we can join the pure-minded Spenser in calling him 'most sacred, happy spirit'. If character may be divined from works, he was a good man, genial, sincere, hearty, temperate of mind, more wise, perhaps, for this world than the next, but thoroughly humane, and friendly with God and men. I know not how to sum up what we feel about him better than by saying (what would have pleased most one who was indifferent to fame) that we love him more even than we admire.

Chaucer 1870

ARNOLD

If we ask ourselves wherein consists the immense superiority of Chaucer's poetry over the romance-poetry—why it is that in passing from this to Chaucer we suddenly feel ourselves to be in another world, we shall find that his superiority is both in the substance of his poetry and in the style of his poetry. His superiority in substance is given by his large, free, simple, clear yet kindly view of human life—so unlike the total want, in the romance-poets, of all intelligent command of it. Chaucer has not their helplessness; he has gained the power to survey the world from a central, a truly human point of view. We have only to call to mind the Prologue to *The Canterbury Tales*. The right comment upon it is Dryden's: 'It is sufficient to say,

according to the proverb, that *here is God's plenty.*' And
again: 'He is a perpetual fountain of good sense.' It is by a
large, free, sound representation of things, that poetry, this
high criticism of life, has truth of substance; and Chaucer's
poetry has truth of substance.

Of his style and manner, if we think first of the romance-
poetry and then of Chaucer's divine liquidness of diction, his
divine fluidity of movement, it is difficult to speak temperately.
They are irresistible, and justify all the rapture with which his
successors speak of his 'gold dew-drops of speech'. . . . Chaucer
is the father of our splendid English poetry; he is our 'well of
English undefiled,' because by the lovely charm of his diction,
the lovely charm of his movement, he makes an epoch and
founds a tradition. In Spenser, Shakespeare, Milton, Keats, we
can follow the tradition of the liquid diction, the fluid movement, of Chaucer; at one time it is his liquid diction of which
in these poets we feel the virtue, and at another time it is his
fluid movement. And the virtue is irresistible.

Bounded as is my space, I must yet find room for an example of Chaucer's virtue, as I have given examples to show
the virtue of the great classics. I feel disposed to say that a
single line is enough to show the charm of Chaucer's verse;
that merely one line like this:

'O martyr souded in virginitee!'

has a virtue of manner and movement such as we shall not
find in all the verse of romance-poetry—but this is saying
nothing. The virtue is such as we shall not find, perhaps, in all
English poetry, outside the poets whom I have named as the
special inheritors of Chaucer's tradition. A single line, however,
is too little if we have not the strain of Chaucer's verse well in
our memory. . . .

And yet Chaucer is not one of the great classics. His poetry
transcends and effaces, easily and without effort, all the
romance-poetry of Catholic Christendom; it transcends and
effaces all the English poetry contemporary with it, it transcends
and effaces all the English poetry subsequent to it down to the

age of Elizabeth. Of such avail is poetic truth of substance, in its natural and necessary union with poetic truth of style. And yet, I say, Chaucer is not one of the great classics. He has not their accent. What is wanting to him is suggested by the mere mention of the name of the first classic of Christendom, the immortal poet who died eighty years before Chaucer—Dante. The accent of such verse as

'In la sua volontade è nostra pace . . .'

is altogether beyond Chaucer's reach; we praise him, but we feel that this accent is out of the question for him. It may be said that it was necessarily out of the reach of any poet in the England of that stage of growth. Possibly; but we are to adopt a real, not a historic, estimate of poetry. However we may account for its absence, something is wanting, then, to the poetry of Chaucer, which poetry must have before it can be placed in the glorious class of the best. And there is no doubt what that something is. It is the $\sigma\pi o\upsilon\delta\alpha\iota'\tau\eta s$, the high and excellent seriousness, which Aristotle assigns as one of the grand virtues of poetry. The substance of Chaucer's poetry, his view of things and his criticism of life, has largeness, freedom, shrewdness, benignity; but it has not this high seriousness. Homer's criticism of life has it, Dante's has it, Shakespeare's has it.

The Study of Poetry 1880

LOWES

Finally, I am not concerned about Chaucer's alleged defect of 'the $\sigma\pi o\upsilon\delta\alpha\iota\acute{o}\tau\eta s$, the high and excellent seriousness, which Aristotle assigns as one of the grand virtues of poetry'. The poet who wrote the closing stanzas of the *Troilus*, and the Invocation to the Virgin, in the Prologue of the Second Nun, and the Prioress's Prologue and Tale, and the noble balade *Truth*; whose memory was enriched from the wisdom of Boethius and the Bible; who was moved by the beauty of the hymns and the service of the Church, and who turned at will

B

to the sublimest cantos of the *Purgatorio* and the *Paradiso*—that poet was not deficient in seriousness, high or deep. He had, to be sure, no 'message'. But his sanity ('He is,' said Dryden, 'a perpetual fountain of good sense'), his soundness, his freedom from sentimentality, his balance of humorous detachment and directness of vision, and above all his large humanity —those are the qualities which 'give us', to apply Arnold's own criterion, 'what we can rest upon'. And we should be hard put to it to name another poet with clearer title to rank with those who, in Philip Sidney's words, 'teach by a divine delightfulness'.

Geoffrey Chaucer 1934

Spenser

Among the Elizabethan poets there were many who wrote almost as well as Spenser, and almost as much. But for some reason he alone emerges into critical history as a separate figure; the rest are lost in a bright mist of general admiration as far as the common reader is concerned, only becoming distinct for the purposes of the scholar. I think they enjoy the singular good fortune to be read rather than criticized.

The main problem of Spenserian criticism has been furnished by the discrepancy between Spenser's intentions and his readers' inclinations. He intended to write a poem on the grand scale; they wish to sample it in small pieces; he intended it to expound an important moral and intellectual system; they wish to read it rather as children read Gulliver, *just for the story and the poetry.*

During the period of classical criticism this conflict took the form mainly of discussing whether the Faerie Queene *could be said to possess unity of structure or not. But no sooner was this question settled, on the whole in its favour, than the Romantic critics began to feel difficulties over his moral and his allegory. He was compared unfavourably in this respect with Bunyan, and it was widely concluded that he should be read as a very otherworldly kind of poet, just for his verbal music and his elfish imagination. Apart from rare protests (one from Ruskin) this has become orthodoxy, and perhaps accounts (as Professor Lewis suggests) for the present neglect of Spenser.*

It is possible, too, that Spenser suffers a good deal from the habits of reading engendered by our present admiration for Donne. For the problem before Spenser was to find some way of expressing in poetry a body of beliefs which grew from real intellectual work. And he did not completely solve it. His poetry is generally at too great a distance from its intellectual basis. Donne, on the other hand, appears to have solved this problem completely ; his poetry is apparently very close to its intellectual basis. In fact, of course, Donne's success is only superficial, because his poetry has no intellectual basis. Thinking—orderly, coherent thinking—was foreign to his temperament. Thoughts, on the other hand, isolated and uprooted from their true soil, excited him profoundly, and entered into firm fusion with his feelings. It is very probable that intellectual confusion of this sort provides the best background for poetry. But readers who have acquired a taste for intellectual confusion for Donne's sake find it hard to grapple with intellectual clarity only for the sake of Spenser.

However that may be, the history of Spenserian criticism gives reason for believing that a revaluation of his work is both possible and probable in the near future.

E. K.

But I dout not, so soone as his name shall come into the knowledg of men, and his worthines be sounded in the tromp of fame, but that he shall be not onely kiste, but also beloved of all, embraced of the most, and wondred at of the best. No lesse I thinke, deserveth his wittinesse in devising, his pithinesse in uttering, his complaints of love so lovely, his discourses of pleasure so pleasantly, his pastorall rudenesse, his morall wisenesse, his dewe observing of Decorum everye where, in personages, in seasons, in matter, in speach, and generally in al seemely simplycitie of handeling his matter, and framing his words: the which of many thinges which in him be straunge, I know will seeme the straungest, the words them selves being so auncient, the knitting of them so short and intricate, and the whole Periode and compasse of speache so delightsome for the roundnesse, and so grave for the straungenesse. And firste of the wordes to speake, I graunt they be something hard, and of most men unused, yet both

English, and also used of most excellent Authors and most
famous Poetes. In whom whenas this our Poet hath bene much
traveiled and throughly redd, how could it be, (as that worthy
Oratour sayde) but that walking in the sonne although for
other cause he walked, yet needes he mought be sunburnt;
and having the sound of those auncient Poetes still ringing in
his eares, he moight needes in singing hit out some of theyr
tunes. But whether he useth them by such casualtye and
custome, or of set purpose and choyse, as thinking them fittest
for such rusticall rudenesse of shepheards, eyther for that theyr
rough sounde would make his rymes more ragged and rustical,
or else because such olde and obsolete wordes are most used
of country folke, sure I think, and I think not amisse, that
they bring great grace, and, as one would say, auctoritie to
the verse.

Now for the knitting of sentences, whych they call the
ioynts and members thereof, and for al the compasse of the
speach, it is round without roughnesse, and learned wythout
hardnes, such indeede as may be perceived of the leaste, under-
stoode of the moste, but judged onely of the learned. For what
in most English wryters useth to be loose, and as it were
ungyrt, in this Author is well grounded, finely framed, and
strongly trussed up together.

Epistle prefaced to The Shepheardes Calendar 1579

SPENSER

Sir knowing how doubtfully all Allegories may be construed, and this booke of mine, which I have entituled the
Faery Queene, being a continued Allegory, or darke conceit,
I have thought good as well for avoyding of gealous opinions
and misconstructions, as also for your better light in reading
thereof (being so by you commanded), to discover unto you
the general intention and meaning, which in the whole course
thereof I have fashioned, without expressing of any particular
purposes or by-accidents therein occasioned. The generall end
therefore of all the booke is to fashion a gentleman or noble
person in vertuous and gentle discipline: Which for that I

conceived should be most plausible and pleasing, being coloured with an historicall fiction, the which the most part of men delight to read, rather for variety of matter, then for profite of the ensample: I chose the historye of king Arthure, as most fitte for the excellency of his person, being made famous by many men's former workes, and also furthest from the daunger of envy, and suspition of present time. In which I have followed all the antique Poets historicall. . . .

But because the beginning of the whole worke seemeth abrupte and as depending upon other antecedents, it needs that ye know the occasion of these three knights severall adventures. For the Methode of a Poet historical is not such, as of an Historiographer. For an Historiographer discourseth of affayres orderly as they were donne, accounting as well the times as the actions, but a Poet thrusteth into the middest, even where it most concerneth him, and there recoursing to the thinges forepaste, and divining of things to come, maketh a pleasing Analysis of all. . . .

But by occasion thereof, many other adventures are intermeddled, but rather as Accidents, then intendments. As the love of Britomart, the overthrow of Marinell, the misery of Florimell, the vertuousnes of Belphoebe, the lasciviousnes of Hellenora, and many the like.

Thus much Sir, I have briefly overronne to direct your understanding to the wel-head of the History, that from thence gathering the whole intention of the conceit, ye may as in a handfull gripe al the discourse, which otherwise may happily seeme tedious and confused.

Letter to Sir Walter Raleigh expounding his Whole Intention in the course of this worke 1596

BEN JONSON

Spencer, in affecting the Ancients, writ no language: Yet I would have him read for his matter, but as Virgil read Ennius.

Timber, or Discoveries 1620–35?

Spenser's stanzaes pleased him not, nor his matter; the meaning of which Allegorie he had delivered in papers to Sir Walter Raughlie. . . .

He hath by heart some verses of Spenser's Calendar about wyne, between Coline and Percye.

> *Conversations of Ben Jonson and William*
> *Drummond of Hawthornden*   1619

DRAYTON

Grave morrall *Spencer* after these came on,
Than whom I am perswaded there was none
Since the blind *Bard* his *Iliads* up did make,
Fitter a taske like that to undertake,
To set downe boldly, bravely to invent,
In all high knowledge surely excellent.

> *Epistle to Reynolds*   1627

REYNOLDS

Next, I must approve the learned *Spencer*, in the rest of his Poems no lesse than his *Fairy Queene*, an exact body of the *Ethicke* doctrine; though some good judgments have wisht, and perhaps not without cause, that he had therein beene a little freer of his fiction, and not so close rivetted to his Morrall.

> *Mythomystes*   1633?

SIR KENELM DIGBY

His learned workes confirme me in the beliefe that our Northern climate may give life to as well tempered a brain, and to as rich a mind as where the sunne shineth fairest. When I read him methinks our country needeth not envy either Greece Rome or Tuscany; for if affection deceive me not very much, their Poets excel in nothing but he is admirable in the same: and in this he is the more admirable that what perfections they have severally, you may find all in him alone; as though nature had strived to show in him that when she pleaseth to make a Masterpiece, she can give in one subiect all those excellencies that to be in height would seeme to require every one of them a different temper and complexion. And if at any time he plucketh a flower out of their gardens, he transplanteth it soe happily into his owne, that it groweth there fairer and sweeter than it did where it first sprang up. His works are such, were their true worth knowne abroad, I am persuaded the best witts and most learned men of other parts, would study our long neglected language, to be capable of his rich conceptions and smooth delivery of them. For certainly weight of matter was never better ioyned with propriety of language and with maiesty and sweetness of verse, than by him. And if any should except against his reviving some obsolete words, and using some ancient formes of speech, in my opinion he blameth that which deserveth much praise; for Spencer doth not that out of affectation (although his assiduity in Chawcer might make his language familier to him) but only then when they serve to expresse more lively and more concisely what he would say: and whensoever he useth them, he doth so polish their native rudeness, as retaining the maiesty of antiquity they want no thing of the elegancy of our sweetest speech. I hope that what he hath written will be a meanes that the english tongue will receive no more alterations and changes, but will remaine & continue settled in that frame it now hath; for excellent authours doe drawe unto them the study of posterity, and whosoever is delighted with what he readeth in an other feeleth in himselfe a desire to expresse like thinges in a like manner: and the more resemblance his elocutions have to his authours the nearer he perswadeth himselfe he arriveth to perfection: and thus, much conversation and study in what he would imitate, begetteth a habit of doing the like. This is the cause that after the great lights of learning among the Graecians their language received no further alterations & that the Latine hath ever since re- mained in the same state whereunto it was reduced by Cicero, Virgil, and the other great men of that time; and the Tuscane toungue is at this day the same as it was left about 300 years agoe by Dante, Petracke and Boccace. It is true that the vicissitudes of things (change being a necessary and inseparable condition of all sublunary creatures) and the inundations of barbarous nations, may overgrow and overrun the vulgar practise of the perfectest languages, as we see of the forementioned Greeks & Latine, yet the use of those toungues will flourish among learned men as long as those excellent authours remaine in the world. Which maketh me consider that noe fate nor length of time will bury Spencers workes and memory, nor indeed alter that language that out of his schoole we now use untill some generall innovation happen that may shake as well the foundations of our nation as of our speech: from which hard law of step-mother nature what Empire or Kingdome hath ever yet bin free? And herein Spencer hath bin very happy that he hath had one immediately succeeding him of partes and power to make what he planted, take deepe rootes. . . . [Here follows a critique of Ben Jonson]

Spencer in what he saith hath a way of expression peculiar to him selfe; he bringeth downe the highest and deepest misteries that are contained in human learning, to an easy and gentle forme of delivery: which sheweth he is Master of what he treateth of; he can wield it as he pleaseth; And this he hath done soe cunningly, that if one heed him not with great attention, rare and wonderfull conceptions will unperceived slide by him that readeth his workes, & he will thinke he hath mett with nothing but familiar and easy discourses. But let one dwell a while upon them and he shall feele a strange fulnesse and roundnesse in all he saith. The most generous wines tickle the palate least, but they are noe sooner in the stomach but by their warmth and strength there, they discover what they are: And those streames that steale away with least noyse are usually deepest, and most dangerous to passe over.

His knowledge in profound learning both divine and humane appeareth to me without controversie the greatest that any Poet before him ever had, excepting Virgil: whom I dare not meddle withall, otherwise than (as witty Scaliger did) erecting an altar to him; And this his knowledge was not such as many Poets are contented with all; which is but a meere sprinkling of generall sciences of which they have some

generall and superficiall notions to beautify their Poems with:
But he had a solide & deepe insight in Theologie, Philosophy
(especially the Platonicke) and the Mathematicall sciences, and
in what others depend of these three (and indeed all others doe).
He was a Master in every one of them; and where he maketh
use of any of them, it is not by gathering a posie out of other
mens workes, but by spending of his owne stocke.

And lastly where he treateth Morall or Politicall learning,
he giveth evidence of himselfe that he had a most excellently
composed head to observe and governe mens actions; & might
have bin eminent in the active part that way, if his owne choice
or fortune had given him employment in the Common wealth.

A Discourse concerning Edmund Spencer (*British
Museum, Ms. Harl.* 4153)   1638?

DAVENANT

. . . the unlucky choice of his stanza hath by repetition of
rhyme brought him to the necessity of many exploded words.

If we proceed from his language to his argument, we must
observe with others, that his noble and most artful hands
deserved to be employed upon matters of a more natural and
therefore of a more useful kind: his allegorical story, by many
held defective in the connection, resembling methinks, a
continuance of extraordinary dreams, such as excellent poets
and painters, by being over-studious, may have in the beginning
of fevers: and those moral visions are just of so much use to
human application as painted history, when with the cousenage
of lights it is represented in scenes, by which we are much less
informed than by actions on the stage.

Preface to Gondibert   1650

RYMER

Spencer, I think, may be reckon'd the first of our *Heroick
Poets*; he had a large spirit, a sharp judgment, and a *Genius*
for *Heroick Poesie*, perhaps above any that ever writ since

Virgil. But our misfortune is, he wanted a tru *Idea*, and lost himself by following an unfaithful guide. Though besides *Homer* and *Virgil* he had read *Tasso*, yet he rather suffer'd himself to be misled by *Ariosto*; with whom blindly rambling on marvellous Adventures, he makes no Conscience of *Probability*. All is fanciful and chimerical, without uniformity, without any foundation in truth; his Poem is perfect *Fairy-land*.

Preface to Rapin 1674

DRYDEN

The English have only to boast of Spenser and Milton, who neither of them wanted either genius or learning to have been perfect poets, and yet both of them are liable to many censures. For there is no uniformity in the design of Spenser: he aims at the accomplishment of no one action; he raises up a hero for every one of his adventures; and endows each of them with some particular moral virtue, which renders them all equal, without subordination, or preference. Every one is most valiant in his own legend: only we must do him that justice to observe, that magnanimity, which is the character of Prince Arthur, shines throughout the whole poem; and succours the rest, when they are in distress. The original of every knight was then living in the court of Queen Elizabeth; and he attributed to each of them that virtue, which he thought was most conspicuous in them; an ingenious piece of flattery, though it turned not much to his account. Had he lived to finish his poem, in the six remaining legends, it had certainly been more of a piece; but could not have been perfect, because the model was not true. But Prince Arthur, or his chief patron Sir Philip Sidney, whom he intended to make happy by the marriage of his Gloriana, dying before him, deprived the poet both of means and spirit to accomplish his design: for the rest, his obsolete language, and the ill choice of his stanza, are faults but of the second magnitude; for, notwithstanding the first, he is still intelligible, at least after a little practice; and for the last, he is the more to be admired, that, labouring under such a difficulty, his verses are so numerous, so various, and so harmonious, that only Virgil, whom he profestly imitated, has surpassed him among the Romans; and only Mr. Waller among the English. . . .

A Discourse Concerning the Original and Progress of
                                        Satire 1693

HUGHES

The chief Merit of this Poem [the *Faerie Queene*] consists in that surprizing Vein of fabulous Invention, which runs thro it, and enriches it every where with Imagery and Descriptions more than we meet with in any other modern Poem. The Author seems to be possess'd of a kind of Poetical Magic; and the Figures he calls up to our View rise so thick upon us, that we are at once pleased and distracted by the exhaustless Variety of them; so that his Faults may in a manner be imputed to his Excellencies: his Abundance betrays him into Excess, and his Judgement is overborne by the Torrent of his Imagination.

That which seems the most liable to Exception in this Work, is the Model of it, and the Choice the Author has made of so romantick a Story. The several Books appear rather like so many several Poems, than one entire Fable: Each of them has its peculiar Knight and is independent of the rest; and tho some of the Persons make their Appearance in different Books yet this has very little Effect in connecting them. Prince *Arthur* is indeed the principal Person, and has therefore a share given him in every Legend; but his Part is not considerable enough in any one of them: He appears and vanishes again like a Spirit; and we lose sight of him too soon to consider him as the Hero of the Poem.

These are the most obvious Defects in the Fable of the *Fairy Queen*. The want of Unity in the Story makes it difficult for the Reader to carry it in his Mind, and distracts too much his Attention to the several Parts of it; and indeed the whole Frame of it wou'd appear monstrous, if it were to be examin'd by the Rules of Epick Poetry, as they have been drawn from the Practice of *Homer* and *Virgil*. But as it is plain the Author never design'd it by those Rules, I think it ought rather to be consider'd as a Poem of a particular kind, describing in a Series of Allegorical Adventures or Episodes the most noted Virtues and Vices: to compare it therefore with the Models of Antiquity, wou'd be like drawing a Parallel between the *Roman* and the *Gothick* Architecture. In the first there is doubtless a more natural Grandeur and Simplicity: in the latter, we find great Mixtures of Beauty and Barbarism, yet assisted by the Invention of a Variety of inferior Ornaments; and tho the former is more majestick in the whole, the latter may be very surprizing and agreeable in its Parts. . . .

I have not yet said any thing concerning Spenser's versification, in which, though he is not always equal to himself, it may be affirmed that he is superior to all his contemporaries, and even to those that followed him for some time. . . .

As to the stanza in which the *Faerie Queene* is written, though the author cannot be commended for his choice of it, yet it is much more harmonious in its kind than the heroick verse of that age: it is almost the same with what the Italians call their Ottave Rime, which is used both by Ariosto and Tasso, but improved by Spenser, with the addition of a line more in the close, of the length of our Alexandrines. The defect of it in long or narrative poems is apparent: the same measure, closed always by a full stop, in the same place, by which every stanza is made as it were a distinct paragraph, grows tiresome by continual repetition, and frequently breaks the sense, when it ought to be carried on without interruption. With this exception the reader will, however, find it harmonious, full of well-sounding epithets, and of such elegant turns of the thought and words, that Dryden himself owns he learned these graces of style chiefly from our author. . . .

Introduction to his edition 1715

POPE

After my reading a canto of Spenser two or three days ago to an old lady between 70 and 80, she said that I had been showing her a collection of pictures. She said very right; and

I know not how it is, but there is something in Spenser that
pleases one as strongly in one's old age as it did in one's youth.
I read the *Faery Queene* when I was about 12, with a vast deal
of delight; and I think it gave me as much when I read it over
about a year or two ago.

Spence's Anecdotes 1744

SPENCE

Had Spenser formed his allegories on the plan of the ancient
poets and artists, as much as he did from Ariosto and the
Italian allegorists, he might have followed nature more closely;
and would not have wandered so often into such strange and
inconsistent imaginations. I am apt to believe, that he considered the *Orlando Furioso*, in particular, as a poem wholly
serious; though the author of it certainly wrote it partly in jest.
There are several lines and passages in it, that must have been
intended for burlesque; and they surely consider that poem in
the truest light, who consider it as a work of a mixed nature;
as something between the professed gravity of Tasso, and the
broad laugh of Berni and his followers. Perhaps Spenser's
taking some things to be said seriously, which Ariosto meant
for ridicule, may have led him now and then to say things that
are ridiculous, where he meant to be serious.

Dissertation on the Defects of Spenser's Allegory
(From *Polymetis*) 1747

T. WARTON

. . . Though the *Faerie Queene* does not exhibit that economy of plan, and exact arrangement of parts which Epic
severity requires, yet we scarcely regret the loss of these, while
their place is so amply supplied, by something which more
powerfully attracts us, as it engages the affection of the heart,
rather than the applause of the head; and if there be any poem
whose graces please, because they are situated beyond the
reach of art, and where the faculties of creative imagination
delight us, because they are unassisted and unrestrained by

those of deliberate judgment, it is in this of which we are now speaking. To sum up all in a few words; though in the *Faerie Queene* we are not satisfied as critics, yet we are transported as readers. . . .

Spenser, in choosing this stanza, did not sufficiently consider the genius of the English language, which does not easily fall into a frequent repetition of the same termination. . . .

This constraint led our author into many absurdities; the most striking and obvious of which seem to be the following.

I. It obliged him to dilate the thing to be expressed, however unimportant, with trifling and tedious circumlocutions, viz. *F.Q.* ii. ii. 44.

> 'Now hath fair Phoebe with her silver face
> Thrice seene the shadowes of this neather world,
> Sith last I left that honourable place,
> In which her roiall presence is enrold.'

That is, It is three months since I left her palace.

II. It necessitated him, when matter failed towards the close of a stanza, to run into a ridiculous redundancy and repetition of words, as in *F.Q.* ii. ix. 33.

> 'In which was nothing *pourtrahed nor wrought,*
> *Nor wrought nor pourtrahed,* but easie to be thought.'

III. It forced him, that he might make out his complement of rhymes, to introduce a puerile or impertinent idea, as in *F.Q.* ii. ix. 45.

> 'Nor that proud towre of Troy, though richly GUILT.'

Being here laid under the compulsion of producing a consonant word to *spilt* and *built,* which are preceding rhymes, he has mechanically given us an image at once little and improper.

To the difficulty of a stanza so injudiciously chosen, I think we may properly impute the great number of his ellipses; and it may be easily conceived, how that constraint, which occasioned superfluity, should at the same time be the cause of omission.

Notwithstanding these inconveniences flow from Spenser's measure, it must yet be owned, that some advantages arise from it; and we may venture to affirm, that the fullness and significancy of Spenser's descriptions, is often owing to the prolixity of his stanza, and the multitude of his rhymes. . . .

It is indeed surprising upon the whole, that Spenser should execute a poem of uncommon length, with so much spirit and ease, laden as he is with so many shackles, and embarrassed with so complicated a Bondage of Rhyming. . . .

Notwithstanding our author's frequent and affected usage of obsolete words and phrases, yet it may be affirmed, that his style, in general, has great perspicuity and facility. It is also remarkable, that his lines are seldom broken by transpositions, antitheses, or parentheses. His sense and sound are equally flowing and uninterrupted. . . .

In reading the works of a poet who lived in a remote age, it is necessary that we should look back upon the customs and manners which prevailed in that age. We should endeavour to place ourselves in the writer's situation and circumstances. Hence we shall become better enabled to discover, how his turn of thinking, and manner of composing, were influenced by familiar appearances and established objects, which are utterly different from those with which we are at present surrounded. For want of this caution, too many readers view the knights and damsels, the tournaments and enchantments, of Spenser, with modern eyes; never considering that the encounters of chivalry subsisted in our author's age; that romances were then most eagerly and universally studied; and that consequently Spenser, from the fashion of the times, was induced to undertake a recital of chivalrous achievements, and to become, in short, a *romantic* poet.

Nor is it sufficiently considered, that a popular practice of Spenser's age contributed, in a considerable degree, to make him an *allegorical* poet. We should remember, that, in this age, allegory was applied as the subject and foundation of public shows and spectacles, which were exhibited with a magnificence superior to that of former times. The virtues and vices, distinguished by their respective emblematical types, were frequently personified, and represented by living actors. . . .

In the mean time, I do not deny that Spenser was, in great measure, tempted by the *Orlando Furioso*, to write an allegorical poem. Yet it must still be acknowledged, that Spenser's peculiar mode of allegorizing seems to have been dictated by those spectacles, rather than by the fictions of Ariosto.

Observations on the Faerie Queene of Spenser 1754

UPTON

In every poem there ought to be simplicity and unity; and in the epic poem the unity of the action should never be violated by introducing any ill-joined or heterogeneous parts. This essential rule Spenser seems to me strictly to have followed: for what story can well be shorter, or more simple, than the subject of his poem? A British Prince sees in a vision the Fairy Queen; he falls in love, and goes in search after this unknown fair; and at length finds her. This fable has a beginning, a middle, and an end. The beginning is, the British Prince saw in a vision the Fairy Queen, and fell in love with her: the middle, his search after her, with the adventures that he underwent: the end his finding whom he sought.

Preface to his edition 1758

HURD

When an architect examines a Gothic structure by Grecian rules, he finds nothing but deformity. But the Gothic architecture has its own rules, by which when it comes to be examined, it is seen to have its merit, as well as the Grecian. The question is not, which of the two is conducted in the simplest or truest taste: but, whether there be not sense and design in both, when scrutinized by the laws on which each is projected.

The same observation holds of the two sorts of poetry. Judge of the *Faery Queen* by the classic models, and you are shocked with its disorder: consider it with an eye to its Gothic original, and you find it regular. The unity and simplicity of the former are more complete: but the latter has that sort of unity and simplicity, which results from its nature.

The *Faery Queen* then, as a Gothic poem, derives its *Method*, as well as the other characters of its composition, from the established modes and ideas of chivalry.

It was usual, in the days of knight-errantry, at the holding of any great feast, for Knights to appear before the Prince, who presided at it, and claim the privilege of being sent on any adventure, to which the solemnity might give occasion. For it was supposed that, when such a *throng of knights and barons bold*, as Milton speaks of, were got together, the distressed would flock in from all quarters, as to a place where they knew they might find and claim redress for all their grievances.

That feast was held for *twelve* days: and each day was distinguished by the claim and allowance of some adventure.

Now laying down this practice, as a foundation for the poet's design, you will see how properly the *Faery Queen* is conducted. . . .

If you ask then, what is this *Unity* of Spenser's Poem? I say, It consists in the relation of its several adventures to one common *original*, the appointment of the Faery Queen; and to one common *end*, the completion of the Faery Queen's injunctions. . . .

This, it is true, is not the classic Unity, which consists in the representation of one entire action: but it is an Unity of another sort, an unity resulting from the respect which a number of related actions have to one common purpose. In other words, it is an unity of *design*, and not of action. . . .

Thus far he drew from Gothic ideas, and these ideas, I think, would lead him no farther. But, as Spenser knew what belonged to classic composition, he was tempted to tie his subject still closer together by *one* expedient of his own, and by *another* taken from his classic models.

His *own* was to interrupt the proper story of each book, by dispersing it into several; involving by this means, and as it were intertwisting the several actions together, in order to give something like the appearance of one action to his twelve adventures. And for this conduct, absurd as it seems, he had some great examples in the Italian poets, tho' I believe, they were led into it by different motives.

The *other* expedient, which he borrowed from the classics, was by adopting one superior character, which should be seen throughout. Prince Arthur, who had a separate adventure of his own, was to have his part in each of the others; and thus several actions were to be embodied by the interest which one principal Hero had in them all. It is even observable, that Spenser gives this adventure of Prince Arthur, in quest of Gloriana, as the proper subject of his poem. . . . The truth was, the violence of classic prejudices forced the poet to affect the appearance of unity, tho' in contradiction to his *Gothic* system. And, as far as we can judge of the whole work from the finished half of it, the adventure of Prince Arthur, whatever the author pretended . . . was but an after-thought; and at least with regard to the *historical fable*, which we are now considering, was only one of the expedients by which he would conceal the disorder of his Gothic plan.

And if this was his design, I will venture to say that both his expedients were injudicious. Their purpose was to ally two things in nature incompatible, the Gothic, and the classic unity; the effect of which misalliance was to discover and expose the nakedness of the Gothic. . . .

But how faulty soever this conduct be in the literal story, it is perfectly right in the *moral*: and that for an obvious reason, tho' his critics seem not to have been aware of it. His chief hero was not to have the twelve virtues in the *degree* in which the knights had, each of them, their own; (such a character would be a monster) but he was to have so much of each as was requisite to form his superior character. Each virtue, in its perfection, is exemplified in its own knight: they are all, in a due degree, concenter'd in Prince Arthur.

This was the poet's *moral*: And what way of expressing this moral in the *history*, but by making Prince Arthur appear in each adventure, and in a manner subordinate to its proper hero? Thus, tho' inferior to each in his own specific virtue, he is superior to all by uniting the whole circle of their virtues in himself: And thus he arrives, at length, at the possession of that bright form of *Glory*, whose ravishing beauty, as seen in a dream or vision, had led him out into these miraculous adventures in the land of Faery.

The conclusion is, that, as an *allegorical* poem, the method of the *Faery Queen* is governed by the justness of the *moral*: As a *narrative* poem, it is conducted on the ideas and usages of *chivalry*. In either view, if taken by itself, the plan is defensible. But from the union of the two designs there arises a perplexity and confusion, which is the proper, and only considerable, defect of this extraordinary poem.

Letters on Chivalry and Romance   1762

CAMPBELL

His command of imagery is wide, easy, and luxuriant. He threw the soul of harmony into our verse, and made it more warmly, tenderly, and magnificently descriptive, than it ever was before, or, with a few exceptions, than it has ever been since. It must certainly be owned that in description he exhibits nothing of the brief strokes and robust power, which characterise the very greatest poets; but we shall nowhere find more airy and expansive images of visionary things, a sweeter tone of sentiment, or a finer flush in the colours of language, than in this Rubens of English poetry. His fancy teems exuberantly in minuteness of circumstance, like a fertile soil sending bloom and verdure through the utmost extremities of the foliage which it nourishes. On a comprehensive view of the whole work, we certainly miss the charm of strength, symmetry, and rapid or interesting progress; for, though the plan which the poet designed is not completed, it is easy to see that no additional cantos could have rendered it less perplexed. But still there is a richness in his materials, even where their coherence is loose, and their disposition confused. The clouds of his allegory may seem to spread into shapeless forms, but they are still the clouds of a glowing atmosphere. Though his story grows desultory, the sweetness and grace of his manner still abide by him. . . .

Allegorical fable *may* be made entertaining. With every disadvantage of dress and language, the humble John Bunyan has made this species of writing very amusing.

The reader may possibly smile at the names of Spenser and Bunyan being brought forward for a moment in comparison; but it is chiefly because the humbler allegorist is so poor in language, that his power of interesting the curiosity is entitled to admiration. We are told by critics that the passions may be allegorized, but that Holiness, Justice, and other such thin abstractions of the mind, are too unsubstantial machinery for a poet—yet we all know how well the author of the *Pilgrim's Progress* (and he was a poet though he wrote in prose) has managed such abstractions as Mercy and Fortitude. In his artless hands, those attributes cease to be abstractions, and become our most intimate friends. Had Spenser, with all the wealth and graces of his fancy, given his story a more implicit and animated form, I cannot believe that there was anything in the nature of his machinery to set bounds to his power of enchantment. Yet, delicious as his poetry is, his story, considered as a romance, is obscure, intricate, and monotonous. . . . Hurd and others, who forbid us to judge of the *Fairy Queen* by the test of classical unity, and who compare it to a gothic church, or a gothic garden, tell us what is little to the purpose. They cannot persuade us that the story is not too intricate and too diffuse. . . .

Essay on English Poetry 1819

HAZLITT

The love of beauty, however, and not of truth, is the moving principle of his mind; and he is guided in his fantastic delineations by no rule but the impulse of an inexhaustible imagination. He luxuriates equally in scenes of Eastern magnificence; or the still solitude of a hermit's cell—in the extremes of sensuality or refinement. . . .

But some people will say that all this may be very fine, but that they cannot understand it on account of the allegory. They are afraid of the allegory, as if they thought it would bite them; they look at it as a child looks at a painted dragon, and they think it will strangle them in its shining folds. This is very idle. If they do not meddle with the allegory, the allegory will not meddle with them. Without minding it at all, the whole is as plain as a pikestaff. . . .

His versification is, at once, the most smooth and the most sounding in the language. It is a labyrinth of sweet sounds, 'in many a winding bout of linked sweetness long drawn out'— that would cloy by their very sweetness, but that the ear is constantly relieved and enchanted by their continued variety of modulation—dwelling on the pauses of the action, or flowing on in a fuller tide of harmony with the movement of the senti- ment. It has not the bold dramatic transitions of Shakespeare's blank verse, nor the high-raised tone of Milton's; but it is the perfection of melting harmony, dissolving the soul in pleasure, or holding it captive in the chains of suspense. Spenser was the poet of our waking dreams; and he has invented not only a language, but a music of his own for them. The undulations are infinite, like those of the waves of the sea: but the effect is still the same, lulling the senses into a deep oblivion of the jarring noises of the world, from which we have no wish to be ever recalled.

Lectures on the English Poets 1818

COLERIDGE

There is this difference, among many others, between Shakspeare and Spenser: Shakspeare is never coloured by the customs of his age. . . . In Spenser the spirit of chivalry is entirely predominant, although with a much greater infusion of the poet's own individual self into it than is found in any other writer. He has the wit of the southern with the deeper inwardness of the northern genius. . . .

As characteristic of Spenser, I would call your particular attention in the first place to the indescribable sweetness and fluent projection of his verse, very clearly distinguishable from the deeper and more inwoven harmonies of Shakspeare and Milton. . . .

2. Combined with this sweetness and fluency, the scientific construction of the metre of the *Faery Queene* is very noticeable. One of Spenser's arts is that of alliteration, and he uses it with great effect in doubling the impression of an image:

> In *w*ilderness and *w*astful deserts,—
>
> Through *w*oods and *w*astness wide,— . . .

He is particularly given to an alternate alliteration, which is, perhaps, when well used, a great secret in melody:

> A *r*amping lyon *r*ushed suddenly,—
>
> And *s*ad to *s*ee her *s*orrowful constraint,—
>
> And on the grasse her *d*aintie *l*imbs *d*id *l*ay,—&c.

You cannot read a page of the *Faery Queene*, if you read for that purpose, without perceiving the intentional alliterativeness of the words; and yet so skilfully is this managed, that it never strikes any unwarned ear as artificial, or other than the result of the necessary movement of the verse.

3. Spenser displays great skill in harmonizing his descriptions of external nature and actual incidents with the allegorical character and epic activity of the poem. . . .

Observe also the exceeding vividness of Spenser's descriptions. They are not, in the true sense of the word, picturesque; but are composed of a wondrous series of images, as in our dreams. . . .

4. You will take especial note of the marvellous independence and true imaginative absence of all particular space or time in the *Faery Queene*. It is in the domains neither of history or geography; it is ignorant of all artificial boundary, all material obstacles; it is truly in land of Faery, that is, of mental space. The poet has placed you in a dream, a charmed sleep, and you neither wish, nor have the power, to inquire where you are, or how you got there. . . .

5. You should note the quintessential character of Christian chivalry in all his characters, but more especially in his women.

The Greeks, except, perhaps, in Homer, seem to have had no way of making their women interesting, but by unsexing them, as in the instances of the tragic Medea, Electra, &c. Contrast such characters with Spenser's Una, who exhibits no prominent feature, has no particularization, but produces the same feeling that a statue does, when contemplated at a distance. . . .

6. In Spenser we see the brightest and purest form of that nationality which was so common a characteristic of our elder poets. . . .

Lastly, the great and prevailing character of Spenser's mind is fancy under the conditions of imagination, as an ever present but not always active power. He has an imaginative fancy, but he has not imagination, in kind or degree, as Shakspeare and Milton have; the boldest effort of his powers in this way is the character of Talus. Add to this a feminine tenderness and almost maidenly purity of feeling, and above all, a deep moral earnestness which produces a believing sympathy and acquiescence in the reader, and you have a tolerably adequate view of Spenser's intellectual being.

Lectures   1818

Spenser's *Epithalamion* is truly sublime; and pray mark the swanlike movement of his exquisite *Prothalamion*. His attention to metre and rhythm is sometimes so extremely minute as to be painful to my ear, and you know how highly I prize good versification.

Table Talk   1827

LEIGH HUNT

Spenser's great characteristic is poetic luxury. If you go to him for a story, you will be disappointed; if for a style, classical or concise, the point against him is conceded; if for pathos, you must weep for personages half-real and too beautiful; if for mirth, you must laugh out of good breeding, and because it pleaseth the great, sequestered man, to be facetious. But if you love poetry well enough to enjoy it for its own sake, let no evil reports of his 'allegory' deter you from his acquaintance, for great will be your loss. His allegory itself is but one part allegory and nine parts beauty and enjoyment; sometimes an excess of flesh and blood. His forced rhymes, and his sentences written to fill up, which in a less poet would be intolerable, are accompanied with such endless grace and dreaming pleasure. . . .

Spenser is the farthest removed from the ordinary cares and haunts of the world of all the poets that ever wrote, except perhaps Ovid; and this, which is the reason why mere men of business and the world do not like him, constitutes his most bewitching charm with the poetical. He is not so great a poet as Shakspeare or Dante—he has less imagination, though more fancy, than Milton. He does not see things so purely in their elements as Dante; neither can he combine their elements like Shakspeare, nor bring such frequent intensities of words, or of wholesale imaginative sympathy, to bear upon his subject as any one of them; though he has given noble diffuser instances of the latter in his Una, and his Mammon, and his accounts of Jealousy and Despair. . . .

Take him in short for what he is, whether greater or less than his fellows, the poetical faculty is so abundantly and beautifully predominant in him above every other, though he had passion, and thought, and plenty of ethics, and was as learned a man as Ben Jonson, perhaps as Milton himself, that he has always been felt by his countrymen to be what Charles Lamb called him, the 'poets' poet'. He has had more idolatry and imitation from his brethren than all the rest put together.

Imagination and Fancy 1844

RUSKIN

The *Faerie Queen*, like Dante's *Paradise*, is only half estimated, because few persons take the pains to think out its meaning. I have put a brief analysis of the first book in Appendix 2, Vol. III; which may perhaps induce the reader to follow out the subject for himself. No time devoted to profane literature will be better rewarded than that spent *earnestly* on Spenser.

The Stones of Venice 1853

GILFILLAN

Diffusion is at once the power and the weakness of Spenser's style. His riches consist of gold-leaf, not of guineas nor of bullion; but then the gold-leaf he possesses is immense in quantity, and is always spread out in graceful forms. From this diffusion, however, there springs an occasional languor of style and heaviness of general effect. His flowers of speech often droop their heads, and slumber under the still, sultry fervour of his tropical imagination. In reading Shakespeare, you can never sleep for a moment—in reading Spenser, you often feel drowsy; but it is the sleep of fulness, not of starvation—it is the slumber of the Enchanted Garden, and it is always starred with dreams. . . .

. . . the coarseness of Spenser is as remarkable as his delicacy and refinement. As if to prove himself no mere dreaming child, but a stalwart man, he becomes naked, and is not ashamed. His descriptions are sometimes gross and grotesque in the extreme. He luxuriates downwards as well as upwards; and while the topmost branches of the tree are towering to heaven, the lower are mixed in the mire of the ways, and covered with incrustations of the veriest mud. Yet his coarseness never becomes corruption, and the imaginations of his readers are filled, without being contaminated, by his sensuous pictures. Parts of the *Faerie Queene* may be condemned by the purists, but the general effect and purpose of the poem is purity. Even as the face of Una

> Made a sunshine in the shady place,

so the darkest depths of sin, which are here and there sounded, seem sanctified by the pervading spirit of the holy song. And yet Spenser's great power lies in his command over the beautiful. Truly has it been said that 'the love of beauty, not of truth, is the moving spring and guiding principle of his mind and imagination'. His poem, indeed, has a high moral purpose, but it is not very steadily pursued: he diverges from it in every direction where the picturesque opens up a path, or beauty sheds a bewitching and bewildering smile. His passion for form, colour, the new, the fair, the pictorial, amounts almost to a disease. . . . Perhaps a portion of the fatigue felt by many of Spenser's readers springs from this. The poet describes all things with such fulness and minute detail, and gives them such form and pressure, that you by and by stagger under his stanzas as under a burden. . . .

To complete the sum of qualifications befitting the author of such a poem, not only imagination, picturesque power, learning, and language were requisite, but also the music of a rich and peculiar versification. And this element, too, was not wanting to our all-accomplished poet. He chose a stanza which, on the whole, was best adapted to his purpose, and which has produced miracles of melody, being at once soft and sounding, simple yet elaborate, varied in pause and voluminous in general effect; and which, while never swift in its course, rolls on with a lingering, long-drawn out, luxurious swell of music, producing the effect of enchantment, and reminding you of the melody heard sometimes in morning dreams. . . . On the whole, there seems a pre-established harmony between Spenser's soul and subject and his verse., Indeed, his stanza is a very Proteus. When he means to be weighty and powerful, it is strong—when he becomes sentimental and love-sick, it languishes in sympathy—when he darkens into sublimity, it can give back frown for frown—when he trembles into pathos, it can wail in concert—when he assumes an elephantine gaiety, it can 'wreathe its lithe proboscis', and lead its heavy dance—when he gets coarse, it too trails in, and gathers a thick coating from the mire—and when he is ethereal in spirit and elevated in joy, it shoots out airy branches,

> And seems to dance for jollity,
> Like to an almond tree, ymounted high
> On top of green Selinus, all alone,
> With blossoms brave bedecked daintily,
> Whose tender locks do tremble every one,
> At every little breath that under heaven is blown.

Gallop, indeed, his verse can hardly do, but he seldom, if ever, requires it for that end—his steps are always measured and majestical, and those of his stanza are in constant keeping; even in its 'motion there is rest', and its very dance of rapture is subdued, like that of a painted Bacchante. . . .

The great defect in the *Faerie Queene* is one incident to its plan—the absence of human interest. Shakespeare, in his most imaginative plays, never altogether forgets, or allows us to forget, the ongoings of the everyday world. Trinculo and Stephano mingle with Ariel and Caliban in the *Tempest*; and Bottom and Quince relieve the supernaturalism of the *Midsummer Night's Dream*. But in Spenser the earth and all its doings are shut out or transformed, and although we hear of sun, moon, and stars, it is in reality the glory of 'The Faerie Queene's' countenance, in which for a season we walk and bask and have our being. . . .

Bunyan and Spenser resemble each other, not only in the blended ingenuity and imperfections of their allegory, but in the intense realising power of their imagination. They are both for the time the dupes of their own fancies. Their personifications, as well as their persons, are to them living, moving, and speaking beings. . . .

The main differences between Spenser and Bunyan are partly to the advantage of the first, and partly to that of the second of these great poets. Spenser had more learning, more power of passion, more sensuousness of spirit, and more luxuriance of fancy, as well as a vastly more musical tone of mind; phrenologically speaking, he had more tune, colour, wit, amativeness, and perhaps ideality. Hence the incomparably richer writing and more complicated structure of the *Faerie Queene*, the greater breadth and brilliance of its pictures, and the loftier expansion of its poetic wings. But Bunyan, on the other hand, with inventiveness hardly inferior, had a simpler, more Dante-like power of mind, a directer purpose, a clearer eye, a more earnest and unearthly spirit, less of dilution of fancy, and more of the concentrated essence of imagination; his style is generally bare, few golden images sparkle on his page; but his figures are forms, his images are characters, he does not decorate but create, and though seeming, like that prophet of old, to stand in a valley of dry bones, he soon causes them to live and move, an exceeding great army, fresh with colour, strong in sinew, and prepared for the battle. Hence, we venture to assert that now and then he has reached bald and awful crags of imaginative composition—pinnacles of Dantesque power and simplicity, which Spenser has seldom if ever attained.

The Genius and Poetry of Spenser 1859

RUSSELL LOWELL

That, when the personal allusions have lost their meaning and the allegory has become a burden, the book should continue to be read with delight, is proof enough, were any wanting, how full of life and light and the other-worldliness of poetry it must be. As a narrative it has, I think, every fault of which that kind of writing is capable. The characters are vague, and, even were they not, they drop out of the story so often and remain out of it so long, that we have forgotten who they are when we meet with them again; the episodes hinder the advance of the action instead of relieving it with variety of incident or novelty of situation; the plot, if plot it may be called,

That shape has none
Distinguishable in member, joint, or limb,

recalls drearily our ancient enemy, the Metrical Romance; while the fighting, which in those old poems was tediously sincere, is between shadow and shadow, where we know that neither can harm the other, though we are tempted to wish he might. Hazlitt bids us not mind the allegory, and says that it won't bite us nor meddle with us if we do not meddle with it. But how if it bore us, which after all is the fatal question? The truth is that it is too often forced upon us against our will, as people were formerly driven to church till they began to look on a day of rest as a penal institution. . . .

The vast superiority of Bunyan over Spenser lies in the fact that we help make his allegory out of our own experience. Instead of striving to embody abstract passions and temptations, he has given us his own in all their pathetic simplicity. He is the Ulysses of his own prose-epic. This is the secret of his power and his charm, that, while the representation of what *may* happen to all men comes home to none of us in particular, the story of any man's real experience finds its startling parallel in that of every one of us. The very homeliness of Bunyan's names and the everydayness of his scenery too, put us off our guard, and we soon find ourselves on as easy a footing with his allegorical beings as we might be with Adam or Socrates in a dream. The long nights of Bedford jail had so intensified his imagination, and made the figures with which it peopled his solitude so real to him, that the creatures of his mind become *things*, as clear to the memory as if we had seen them. But Spenser's are too often mere names, with no bodies to back them, entered on the Muses's muster-roll by the specious trick of personification. . . .

Charles Lamb made the most pithy criticism of Spenser when he called him the 'poets' poet'. We can fairly leave the allegory on one side, for perhaps, after all, he adopted it only for the reasons that it was in fashion, and put it on as he did his ruff, not because it was becoming, but because it was the only wear. The true use of him is a gallery of pictures which we visit as the mood takes us, and where we spend an hour or two at a time, long enough to sweeten our perceptions, not so long as to cloy them. . . .

His natural tendency is to shun whatever is sharp and abrupt. He loves to prolong emotion, and lingers in his honeyed sensations like a bee in the translucent cup of a lily. So entirely are beauty and delight in it the native element of Spenser, that, whenever in the *Faery Queen* you come suddenly on the moral, it gives you a shock of unpleasant surprise, a kind of grit, as when one's teeth close on a bit of gravel in a dish of strawberries and cream. He is the most fluent of our poets. Sensation passing through emotion into revery is a prime quality of his manner. And to read him puts one in the condition of revery, a state of mind in which our thoughts and feelings float motionless, as one sees fish do in a gentle stream, with just enough vibration of their fins to keep themselves from going down with the current, while their bodies yield indolently to all its soothing curves. He chooses his language for its rich canorousness rather than for intensity of meaning. To characterize his style in a single word, I should call it *costly*. None but the daintiest and nicest phrases will serve him, and he allures us from one to the other with such cunning baits of alliteration, and such sweet lapses of verse, that never any word seems more eminent than the rest, nor detains the feeling to eddy around it, but you must go on to the end before you have time to stop and muse over the wealth that has been lavished on you. . . .

Despite Spenser's instinctive tendency to idealize, and his habit of distilling out of the actual and ethereal essence in which very little of the possible seems left, yet his mind, as is generally true of great poets, was founded on a solid basis of good-sense. I do not know where to look for a more cogent and at the same time picturesque confutation of Socialism than in the Second Canto of the Fifth Book. If I apprehend rightly his words and images, there is not only subtle but profound thinking here. The French Revolution is prefigured in the well-meaning but too theoretic giant, and Rousseau's fallacies exposed two centuries in advance. Spenser was a conscious Englishman to his utmost fibre, and did not lack the sound judgement in politics which belongs to his race.

Spenser 1875

C. S. LEWIS

Misconceptions about the real merit and limitation of Spenser's genius have led to his present neglect. The very phrase 'poets' poet', I believe, has done incalculable damage. The genitive of *poets'* is taken to have an intensive force and the phrase is interpreted on the analogy of *Holy of Holies*. Readers trained on such a conception open their Spenser expecting to find some quintessential 'poeticalness' in the lowest and most obvious sense of that word—something more mellifluous than Shakespeare's sonnets, more airy than Shelley, more swooningly sensuous than Keats, more dreamlike than William Morris: and then, as likely as not, what first meets their eye is something of this sort:

> But I with better reason him aviz'd,
> And shew'd him how, through error and misthought
> Of our like persons, each to be disguiz'd,
> Or his exchange or freedom might be wrought.
> Whereto full loth was he, ne would for ought
> Consent that I, who stood all fearlesse free,
> Should wilfully be into thraldome brought,
> Till fortune did perforce it so decree:
> Yet, over-ruld at last, he did to me agree.

Such a reader, at this point, excusably throws the book away. Now you may say that I have selected a specimen of Spenser at his worst; and so I have. But this 'worst' would not matter unless Spenser had a false reputation for sheer 'poeticalness'. The reader, unless he were a fool, would be prepared for flats in a long poem: he would not be put off by one such experience from making the acquaintance of Wordsworth or Chaucer. The real trouble is that he cannot be prepared for such a flat as this is in a poem such as *The Faerie Queene* is commonly supposed to be: he has been taught not to look for vigorous thought or serious issues or even coherence and sanity in his Spenser— taught that the man's only merit is voluptuousness and day dream. And if Spenser can, in any passage, do so badly the only thing he is supposed to be able to do at all, he is naturally rejected. We tolerate bad manners in a learned, or a funny, or a good man; but how if the man admittedly has no claim on us except his reputed good breeding, and then turns out to be deficient even in that? In order to avoid such false judgements we must revise the popular opinion of Spenser. So far from being a poet whose excellent and sustained mastery of language is his only merit, he is a poet whose chief fault is the uncertainty of his style. He can be as prosaic as Wordsworth:

he can be clumsy, unmusical, and flat. On this side, and on this side only, his work requires historical extenuation. . . .

From this discussion I hope it has now become plain in what sense Spenser is the 'poets' poet'. He is so called in virtue of the historical fact that most of the poets have liked him very much. And with this conclusion comes the important corollary that perhaps poets, when they read poetry, do not demand that it should be specially 'poetical'—perhaps, indeed, this demand is one of the marks of the prosaic reader who secretly suspects that poetry is at bottom nonsensical and, if he is in for a penny, would fain be in for a pound. In the same way, those who have least real sympathy for childhood become most laboriously childish when they talk to children; and no one has such high-flown notions of refinement as the temporarily converted boor. But these are generalities. For the study of Spenser himself, I think the most useful thing we can do as a preparative ('Laughing to teach the truth, what hinders?') is to draw up two lists of epithets after the manner of Rabelais. The first would run something like this:

Elfin Spenser: Renaissance Spenser: voluptuous Spenser: courtly Spenser: Italianate Spenser: decorative Spenser.

For the second I propose:

English Spenser: Protestant Spenser: rustic Spenser: manly Spenser: churchwardenly Spenser: domestic Spenser: thrifty Spenser: honest Spenser.

All that I have hitherto said has been directed to persuading the reader that the second of these lists is quite as fully justi-fied as the first—that Spenser is the master of Milton in a far deeper sense than we had supposed. It is the measure of his greatness that he deserves the epithets of both lists.

The Allegory of Love 1936

C

TILLYARD

Whatever the exceptions, it is safe to say that now and for
many years past English readers consider that in the larger
literary forms the normal method of conveying states of mind
is through dramatic action and descriptions of nature which
are not evidently symbolic. They derive their norm from classical narrative and drama, from parts of Chaucer, from Shakespeare, from parts of Milton, and from some nineteenth-century
nature-poetry. They are also convinced that the general state
of mind is more naturally conveyed through the particular
detail. The general state of mind which the author is interested
in and which he wishes to convey is broken down and parcelled
out into a number of easily assimilable details, to be reassem-
bled as a generalization in the minds of the readers. And the
details are most easily assimilable if they consist of human
action or natural objects. Wordsworth, wanting to convey a
certain kind of awe, translates it into a description of a wild
landscape on the Simplon Pass; and the English reader thinks
this is a very natural and proper method. That he is able to
include in his own response to Wordsworth's poetry his own
recollections of similar scenes is for him a legitimate advantage.
Shakespeare, wanting to convey a general sentiment concerning duty, breaks it into a number of pieces and embodies them
in the characters that transact the rejection of Falstaff in the
closing scenes of *Henry IV*, *Part 2*. But though this is the popular (and not on that account inferior) method it is not the only
one, and it was not Spenser's. Janet Spens describes another
method, Spenser's, as follows:

> Spenser, though he loved the world of sense, thought
> it almost accidental. The true life of man lies not in this
> temporal and material realm of mutability, but in the
> invisible world of mind. The soul's dealings with abstrac-
> tions and values is the measure of its true character: the
> real tissue even of our secular existence is not the visible

world but our reactions to it . . . it is this inner life that is Spenser's Land of Faerie.

That is how Spenser, according to Miss Spens, saw his material. In another passage she indicates how he shaped it:

> He never deals so much with the sensual fact as with the mental translation of the fact—with the use which the soul's faculty makes of the impact and stir of the physical sensation; and he is more excited by the infinitely various web which man has woven to adorn and clothe the physical universe than by the simple physical facts themselves. He cared more for the artificial than for nature, because in the artefact the sensuous element is more visibly held in solution by the concept.

When Spenser, then, is most himself, he translates his general feelings about life not into the forms of men and nature that remind us of the real world but into dehumanised or monstrous figures and into physical objects that correspond but vaguely to the objects we see and touch. If this method succeeds, it should have the advantage of great directness. There is no translating the feeling into and back from the world of men and of tangible objects. But, in compensation, the dead and artificial conceptions into which the poet translates his feelings so directly must be very apt and striking to do their work; and the risk of signifying nothing is greater than in the more naturalistic method.

I will illustrate from an episode from the Pastorella incident in Book Six of the *Faerie Queene*. While Calidore, the book's hero, was living the life of a shepherd and courting Pastorella, he wandered off one day alone and came on 'a place, whose pleasaunce did appere to passe all others on the earth'. This was a hill, set in the open country girt with high trees, and crowned with a spacious plot of flat ground, a perfect dancing-place. Hearing the sound of a pipe and yet fearing to appear in

the open, he kept within the covert of the wood and looked to
see what was going on. What he saw was the dance of 'an
hundred naked Maidens lilly white' in a ring, three other
ladies within this ring, and in the very centre a single girl. All
these are dancing to the music of Colin Clout. It is a rapturous
description, and the vision ends thus:

> Much wondred Calidore at this straunge sight,
> Whose like before his eye had never seene;
> And standing long astonished in spright,
> And rapt with pleasaunce wist not what to weene;
> Whether it were the traine of Beauties Queene,
> Or Nymphes, or Faeries, or enchaunted show,
> With which his eyes mote have deluded beene.
> Therefore, resolving what it was to know,
> Out of the wood he rose, and toward them did go.

> But, soone as he appeared to their vew,
> They vanisht all away out of his sight,
> And cleane were gone, which way he never knew;
> All save the Shepherd, who, for fell despight
> Of that displeasure, broke his bag-pipe quight,
> Aud made great mone for that unhappy tune:
> But Calidore, though no lesse sory wight
> For that mishap, yet seeing him to mourne,
> Drew neare, that he the truth of all by him mote learne.

In the conversation that follows we learn that the maidens
were Graces, the three dancers the three chief Graces, and the
single girl Colin Clout's betrothed. We know already that
Colin Clout is Spenser himself. The general feeling the poet
seeks to convey is the rapture and the elusiveness of poetic
inspiration. The episode itself is intensely alive but is concerned
neither with living characters nor with events that could occur
in actual life. Nor is it primarily allegorical. It is the vision and
its disappearance that matter, not the identification of the
dancers with the Graces. And the vision is a wonderfully suc-

cessful and direct agent of a general feeling, a feeling that has to do with the act of writing poetry. How successful we may better realize if we meditate on what some recent writers, even respectable ones, have made of their objectifications of the artistic temperament.

The English Epic and its Background 1954

Donne and the Metaphysicals

Of all the critical histories presented in this book, this is certainly the most curious and the most confused.

The source of the confusion would seem to be the fact that in this group of poets the greatest was overshadowed at first by one of the lesser. Donne's individual pre-eminence was temporarily lost sight of because Cowley stood more in the main current of literary development. And poor Cowley is the outstanding example of a poet whose historical importance in the development of poetry was vastly greater than his intrinsic worth as a poet. When fashion turned against Cowley, it turned against Donne as well, and for a long time he was criticized for faults which were much more those of Cowley. So that the history of Donne criticism must include a good deal about Cowley as well.

Towards the end of the seventeenth-century, Donne became the stock example of a man whose wit (whatever that meant from one time to another) was greater than his poetry, and whose versification was lamentable. This belief proved very durable, and only disappeared recently.

By the end of the eighteenth century, however, the confusion over Cowley was less important, since Cowley was no longer read, and the Romantics were able to 'discover' Donne for themselves, giving him real admiration without making him the centre of their whole view of poetry. And from that time onwards his reputation has steadily increased. Browning laid him firmly before the late Victorian critics; Mr Eliot has brought him even more emphatically before modern critics. Donne is sitting pretty.

I should take this opportunity of retracting a passage ascribed to Pope in the first edition. Whoever wrote it, Pope did not. My only excuse is that the work was being done in the midst of the late war. I am grateful to Mr F. W. Bateson, not only for drawing

my attention to this gaffe, but for the gentleness with which he
performed the office.

CHAPMAN

But that Poesy should be as pervial as oratory, and plain-
ness her special ornament, were the plain way to barbarism,
and to make the ass run proud of his ears, to take away strength
from lions, and give camels horns.

That *Energia*, or clearness of representation, required in
absolute poems, is not the perspicuous delivery of a low invention; but high and hearty invention expressed in most
significant and unaffected phrase. It serves not a skilful
painter's turn to draw the figure of a face only to make known
who it represents; but he must limn, give lustre, shadow, and
heightening; which though ignorants will deem spiced, and
too curious, yet such as have the judicial perspective will see it
hath motion, spirit, and life.

There is no confection made to last, but it is admitted
more cost and skill than presently-to-be-used simples; and in
my opinion, that which being with a little endeavour searched,
adds a kind of majesty to Poesy, is better than that which every
cobbler may sing to his patch.

Obscurity in affection of words and indigested conceits, is
pedantical and childish; but where it shroudeth itself in the
heart of his subject, uttered with fitness of figure and expressive
epithets, with that darkness will I still labour to be shadowed.
Rich minerals are digged out of the bowels of the earth, not
found in the superficies and dust of it; charms made of unlearned characters are not consecrate by the Muses, which are
divine artists, but by Euippe's daughters, that challenged them
with mere nature, whose breasts I doubt not had been well worthy
commendation, if their comparison had not turned them into pyes.

Prefatory letter to Matthew Roydon, before Ovid's
Banquet of Sense 1595

[Though not strictly one of the Metaphysical poets, Chapman has many things in common with them, and this letter

expresses very well a tendency of taste and critical theory by which Donne may have been affected, even unconsciously. At all events, it does describe pretty nearly the actual practice of the Metaphysicals]

DONNE

Come live with mee, and bee my love,
And wee will some new pleasures prove
Of golden sands, and christall brookes,
With silken lines, and silver hookes.

The Baite   1600?

[The point of these lines is that they echo Marlowe's:

Come live with mee, and be my love,
And we will all the pleasures prove,
That Vallies, groves, hills and fields,
Woods, or steepie mountaine yeeldes.

The poem which these lines open, *The passionate Shepheard to his love*, seems to have been regarded by contemporaries as the most typical exposition of the pastoral conventions. Thus Raleigh took it as the text of his famous criticism of idyllic joys:

If all the world and love were young,
And truth in every Sheepheards tongue,
These pretty pleasures might me move,
To live with thee, and be thy love.

Donne's poem should also be regarded as criticism of the pastoral convention, though from a different point of view. Raleigh rejects the pastoral because he is a realist. Donne rejects it because he is tired of its conventions, and would like some new ones. So where Marlowe had written 'all the pleasures', because he had the traditional catalogue at his fingers' ends, and could be sure of putting them all down,

Donne wrote 'some new pleasures', and went on to give some pastoral images quite as artificial in their own way as the older ones, but much more astonishing.

It won't do, of course, to read a great deal into a single phrase like this. But in view of the fact that Marlowe's poem seems to have been taken as the typical pastoral lyric, we may be allowed to infer that Donne was not only departing from the older conventions; he was also departing from them in a quite conscious search for novelty]

JONSON

... That Done's Anniversarie was profane and full of blasphemies; that he told Mr Done, if it had been written of the Virgin Marie it had been something; to which he answered that he described the Idea of a Woman, and not as she was. That Done, for not keeping of accent, deserved hanging. ...

He esteemeth John Done the first poet in the world in some things: his verses of the Lost Chaine he hath by heart, and that passage of the Calme, *That dust and feathers doe not stir, all was so quiet.* Affirmeth Done to have written all his best pieces ere he was 25 years old. ...

That Done said to him, he wrote that Epitaph on Prince Henry, *Look to me, Faith,* to match Sir Ed. Herbert in obscurenesse ...

That Done himself, for not being understood, would perish.

Conversations with William Drummond of Hawthornden
1619

DRUMMOND OF HAWTHORNDEN

Donne, among the Anacreontick Lyricks, is Second to none, and far from all Second. But as *Anacreon* doth not approach *Callimachus,* tho' he excels in his own kind, nor *Horace* to *Virgil,* no more can I be brought to think him to excel either *Alexander's* or *Sidney's* Verses. They can hardly be compared together, treading diverse Paths—the one flying swift but low, the other, like the Eagle, surpassing the

Clouds. I think, if he would, he might easily be the best Epigrammatist we have found in *English*, of which I have not yet seen any come near the Ancients.

Conversations 1619

CAREW

The Muses garden with Pedantique weedes
O'rspred, was purg'd by thee; The lazie seeds
Of servile imitation throwne away;
And fresh invention planted, Thou didst pay
The debts of our penurious bankrupt age;
Licentious thefts, that make poetique rage
A Mimique fury, when our soules must bee
Possest, or with Anacreons Extasie,
Or Pindars, not their owne; The subtle cheat
Of slie Exchanges, and the jugling feat
Of two-edg'd words, or whatsoever wrong
By ours was done the Greeke, or Latine tongue,
Thou hast redeem'd, and open'd Us a Mine
Of rich and pregnant phansie, drawne a line
Of masculine expression. . . .

Thou shalt yield no precedence, but of time,
And the blinde fate of language, whose tun'd chime
More charmes the outward sense; Yet thou maist claime
From so great disadvantage greater fame,
Since to the awe of thy imperious wit
Our stubborne language bends, made only fit
With her tough-thick-rib'd hoopes to gird about
Thy Giant phansie, which had prov'd too stout
For their soft melting Phrases. . . .

But thou art gone, and thy strict lawes will be
Too hard for Libertines in Poetrie.
They will repeale the goodly exil'd traine
Of gods and goddesses, which in thy just raigne
Were banish'd nobler Poems, now, with these
The silenc'd tales o' the' Metamorphoses

Shall stuffe their lines, and swell the windy Page,
Till Verse refin'd by thee, in this last Age,
Turne ballad rime, Or those old Idolls bee
Ador'd againe, with new apostasie. . . .

Here lies a King, that rul'd as hee thought fit
The universall Monarchy of wit ;
Here lie two Flamens, and both those, the best,
Apollo's first, at last, the true God's Priest.

An Elegie upon the death of the Deane of Pauls,
Dr Iohn Donne 1633

CORBET

Hee that would write an Epitaph for thee,
And do it well, must first beginne to be
Such as thou wert; for, none can truly know
Thy worth, thy life, but he that hath liv'd so;
He must have wit to spare and to hurle downe:
Enough, to keepe the gallants of the towne.
He must have learning plenty; both the Lawes,
Civill, and Common, to judge any cause;
Divinity great store, above the rest;
Not of the last Edition, but the best.
He must have language, travaile, all the Arts;
Judgement to use; or else he wants thy parts.

On Doctor Donne 1632?

IZAAK WALTON

Is *Donne*, great *Donne* deceas'd? then England say
Thou hast lost a man where language chose to stay
And shew it's graceful power. I would not praise
That and his vast wit (which in these vaine dayes
Make many proud) but as they serv'd to unlock
That Cabinet, his minde: where such a stock

Of knowledge was repos'd, as all lament
(Or should) this generall cause of discontent.

An Elegie upon Dr Donne 1633

MAYNE

For, who hath read thee, and discernes thy worth,
That will not say, thy carelesse houres brought forth
Fancies beyond our studies, and thy play
Was happier, then our serious time of day?
So learned was thy chance; thy haste had wit,
And matter from thy pen flow'd rashly fit,
What was thy recreation turnes our braine,
Our rack and palenesse, is thy weakest straine.
And when we most come neere thee, 'tis our blisse
To imitate thee, where thou dost amisse.

On Dr Donne's death 1633

DRYDEN

. . . we cannot read a verse of Cleveland's without making
a face at it, as if every word were a pill to swallow: he gives us
many times a hard nut to break our teeth, without a kernel for
our pains. So that there is this difference betwixt his *Satires*
and doctor Donne's; that the one gives us deep thoughts in
common language, though rough cadence; the other gives us
common thoughts in abstruse words. . . .

An Essay of Dramatic Poesy 1668

Would not Donne's *Satires*, which abound with so much
wit, appear more charming, if he had taken care of his words,
and of his numbers? . . .
He affects the metaphysics, not only in his satires, but in
his amorous verses, where nature only should reign; and
perplexes the minds of the fair sex with nice speculations of

philosophy, when he should engage their hearts, and entertain
them with the softnesses of love. In this (if I may be pardoned
for so bold a truth) Mr Cowley has copied him to a fault;
so great a one, in my opinion, that it throws his *Mistress*
infinitely below his *Pindarics* and his latter compositions, which
are undoubtedly the best of his poems, and the most correct.

A Discourse concerning the Original and Progress of
Satire 1693

PHILLIPS

John Donne . . . accomplished himself with the politer kind
of Learning . . . and frequented good company, to which the
sharpness of his wit, and gaiety of fancy, rendered him not a
little grateful: in which state of life he composed his more
brisk and youthful poems, which are rather commended for
the height of fancy and acuteness of the conceit, than for the
smoothness of the verse . . .

Theatrum Poetarum Anglicanorum 1675

THEOBALD

Now, the Age in which Shakespeare liv'd, having, above all
others, a wonderful Affection to appear Learned, They declined
vulgar Images, such as are immediately fetch'd from Nature,
and rang'd thro' the Circle of the Sciences to fetch their Ideas
from thence. But as the Resemblances of such Ideas to the
subject must necessarily lie very much out of the common
Way, and every Piece of Wit appear a Riddle to the Vulgar;
This, that should have taught them the forced, quaint, unnatural Tract they were in (and induce them to follow a more
natural One), was the very Thing that kept them attach'd to it.
The ostentatious Affectation of abstruse Learning, peculiar to
that time, the Love that Men naturally have to every Thing
that looks like Mystery, fixed them down to this Habit of
Obscurity. Thus became the Poetry of Donne (tho' the

wittiest Man of that Age,) nothing but a continued Heap of
Riddles.

Shakespeare 1733

POPE

Why should we not ask too, when we read the writings of
Lucilius, whether the grimness that keeps his verses under-
wrought and ungentle lies in himself or in his subject?

*Translation of the epigraph from Horace placed by Pope
before his versification of Donne's Satires* 1735

Herbert is lower than Crashaw; Sir John Beaumont higher;
and Donne a good deal so.... Donne had no imagination, but
as much wit, I think, as any writer can possibly have....
... William D'Avenant a better poet than Donne. ...

Sir William D'Avenant's *Gondibert* is not a good poem,
if you take it on the whole; but there are a great many good
things in it. He is a scholar of Donne's, and took his sententious-
ness and metaphysics from him.

Spence's Anecdotes 1744

JOHNSON

Wit, like all other things subject by their nature to the
choice of man, has its changes and fashions, and at different
times takes different forms. About the beginning of the
seventeenth century, appeared a race of writers that may be
termed the metaphysical poets, of whom in a criticism of the
works of Cowley, it is not improper to give some account.

The metaphysical poets were men of learning, and to show
their learning was their whole endeavour: but, unluckily
resolving to show it in rhyme, instead of writing poetry they
only wrote verses, and very often such verses as stood the
trial of the finger better than of the ear; for the modulation was
so imperfect that they were only found to be verses by counting
the syllables.

If the father of criticism has rightly denominated poetry τέχνη μιμητική, *an imitative art*, these writers will without great wrong lose their right to the name of poet, for they cannot be said to have imitated any thing: they neither copied nature nor life; neither painted the forms of matter nor represented the operations of intellect.

Those however who deny them to be poets allow them to be wits. Dryden confesses of himself and his contemporaries that they fall below Donne in wit, but maintains that they surpass him in poetry.

If Wit be well described by Pope as being 'that which has been often thought, but was never before so well expressed', they certainly never attained, nor ever sought it, for they endeavoured to be singular in their thoughts, and were careless of their diction. But Pope's account of wit is undoubtedly erroneous; he depresses it below its natural dignity, and reduces it from strength of thought to happiness of language.

If by a more noble and more adequate conception that be considered as Wit which is at once natural and new, that which though not obvious is, upon its first production, acknowledged to be just; if it be that, which he that never found it, wonders how he missed; to wit of this kind the metaphysical poets have seldom risen. Their thoughts are often new, but seldom natural; they are not obvious, but neither are they just; and the reader, far from wondering that he missed them, wonders more frequently by what perverseness of industry they were ever found.

But Wit, abstracted from its effects upon the hearer, may be more rigorously and philosophically considered as a kind of *discordia concors*; a combination of dissimilar images, or discovery of occult resemblances in things apparently unlike. Of wit, thus defined, they have more than enough. The most heterogeneous ideas are yoked by violence together; nature and art are ransacked for illustrations, comparisons, and allusions; their learning instructs, and their subtilty surprises; but the reader commonly thinks his improvement dearly bought, and, though he sometimes admires, is seldom pleased.

From this account of their compositions it will be readily

inferred that they were not successful in representing or moving the affections. As they were wholly employed on something unexpected and surprising they had no regard to that uniformity of sentiment which enables us to conceive and excite the pains and the pleasure of other minds: they never enquired what on any occasion they should have said or done, but wrote rather as beholders than as partakers of human nature; as beings looking upon good and evil, impassive and at leisure; as Epicurean deities making remarks on the actions of men and the vicissitudes of life, without interest and without emotion. Their courtship was void of fondness and their lamentation of sorrow. Their wish was only to say what they hoped had been never said before.

Nor was the sublime more within their reach than the pathetick; for they never attempted that comprehension and expanse of thought which at once fills the whole mind, and of which the first effect is sudden astonishment, and the second rational admiration. Sublimity is produced by aggregation, and littleness by dispersion. Great thoughts are always general, and consist in positions not limited by exceptions, and in descriptions not descending to minuteness. It is with great propriety that subtlety, which in its original import means exility of particles, is taken in its metaphorical meaning for nicety of distinction. Those writers who lay on the watch for novelty could have little hope of greatness; for great things cannot have escaped former observation. Their attempts were always analytick; they broke every image into fragments, and could no more represent by their slender conceits and laboured particularities the prospects of nature or the scenes of life, than he who dissects a sun-beam with a prism can exhibit the wide effulgence of a summer noon.

Yet great labour, directed by great abilities, is never wholly lost: if they frequently threw away their wit upon false conceits, they likewise sometimes struck out unexpected truth: if their conceits were far-fetched, they were often worth the carriage. To write on their plan it was at least necessary to read and think. No man could be born a metaphysical poet, nor assume the dignity of a writer by descriptions copied from descriptions, by imitations borrowed from imitations, by traditional imagery and hereditary similes, by readiness of rhyme, and volubility of syllables.

In perusing the works of this race of authors the mind is exercised either by recollection or inquiry; either something already learned is to be retrieved, or something new is to be examined.

This kind of writing, which was, I believe, borrowed from Marino and his followers, had been recommended by the example of Donne, a man of very extensive and various knowledge, and by Jonson, whose manner resembled that of Donne more in the ruggedness of his lines than in the cast of his sentiments.

Life of Cowley 1778

ANDERSON

Donne is better known as a poet than as a divine . . . All his contemporaries are lavish in his praise. Prejudiced, perhaps, by the style of writing which was then fashionable, they seem to have rated his performances beyond their just value. To the praise of wit and sublimity his title is unquestionable. In all his pieces he displays a prodigious richness of fancy, and an elaborate minuteness of description; but his thoughts are seldom natural, obvious, or just, and much debased by the carelessness of his versification.

In his edition of Donne's Poems 1793

HAZLITT

Of Donne I know nothing but some beautiful verses to his wife, dissuading her from accompanying him on his travels abroad, and some quaint riddles in verse, which the Sphinx could not unravel.

Lectures on the English Poets 1818

COLERIDGE

The wit of Donne, the wit of Butler, the wit of Pope, the wit of Congreve, the wit of Sheridan—how many disparate things are here expressed by one and the same word, Wit!—Wonder-exciting vigour, intenseness and peculiarity of thought, using at will the almost boundless stores of a capacious memory, and exercised on subjects where we have no right to expect it—this is the wit of Donne! . . .

To read Dryden, Pope, &c., you need only count syllables; but to read Donne you must measure *time*, and discover the time of each word by the sense of passion. I would ask no surer test of a Scotchman's *substratum* (for the turf-cover of pretension they all have) than to make him read Donne's satires aloud. If he made manly metre of them and yet strict metre, then—why, then he wasn't a Scotchman, or his soul was geographically slandered by his body's first appearing there.

Doubtless all the copies I have ever seen of Donne's poems are grievously misprinted. Wonderful that they are not more so, considering that not one in a thousand of his readers has any notion how his lines are to be read—to the many, five out of six appear anti-metrical. How greatly this aided the compositor's negligence or ignorance, and prevented the corrector's remedy, any man may ascertain by examining the earliest editions of blank verse plays, Massinger, Beaumont, and Fletcher, &c. Now, Donne's rhythm was as inexplicable to the many as blank verse, spite of his rhymes—*ergo*, as blank verse, misprinted. I am convinced that where no mode of rational declamation by pause, hurrying of voice, or apt and sometimes double emphasis, can at once make the verse metrical and bring out the sense of passion more prominently, that there we are entitled to alter the text, when it can be done by simple omission or addition of *that*, *which*, *and*, and such 'small deer'; or by mere new placing of the same words—I would venture nothing beyond. . . .

Woman's Constancy

After all, there is but one Donne! and now tell me yet, wherein, in *his own kind*, he differs from the similar power in Shakespeare? Shakespeare was all men, potentially, except Milton; and they differ from him by negation, or privation, or both. This power of dissolving orient pearls worth a kingdom, in a health to a whore!—this absolute right of dominion over all thoughts, that dukes are bid to clean his shoes, and are yet honoured by it! But, I say, in this lordliness of opulence, in which *the* positive of Donne agrees with *a* positive of Shakespeare, what is it that makes them *homoi*ousian, indeed: yet not homoousian?

Canonization

One of my favourite poems. As late as ten years ago, I used to seek and find out grand lines and fine stanzas; but my delight has been far greater since it has consisted more in tracing the leading thought thro'out the whole. The former is too much like coveting your neighbour's goods; in the latter you merge yourself in the author, you *become He*.

Lectures 1818

One great distinction I appeared to myself to see plainly, between even the characteristic faults of our elder poets and the false beauties of the moderns. In the former, from Donne to Cowley, we find the most fantastic out-of-the-way thoughts, but in the most pure and genuine mother English; in the latter, the most obvious thoughts, in language the most fantastic and arbitrary. Our faulty elder poets sacrificed the passion, and passionate flow of poetry to the subtleties of intellect and to the starts of wit; the moderns to the glare and glitter of a perpetual yet broken and heterogeneous imagery, or rather to an amphibious something, made up, half of image and half of abstract meaning. The one sacrificed the heart to the head, the other both heart and head to point and drapery.

Biographia Literaria

CAMPBELL

Donne was the 'best good-natured man, with the worst-natured Muse'. A romantic and uxorious lover, he addresses the object of his real tenderness with ideas that outrage decorum. He begins his own epithalamium with a most indelicate invocation to his bride. His ruggedness and whim are almost proverbially known. Yet there is a beauty of thought which at intervals rises from his chaotic imagination, like the form of Venus smiling on the waters.

Essay on English Poetry 1819

DE QUINCEY

. . . the first very eminent rhetorician in the English Literature is Donne. Dr Johnson inconsiderately classes him in company with Cowley, &c., under the title of *Metaphysical* Poets: metaphysical they were not: *Rhetorical* would have been a more accurate designation. In saying *that*, however, we must remind our readers that we revert to the original use of the word *Rhetoric*, as laying the principal stress upon the management of the thoughts, and only a secondary one upon the ornaments of style. Few writers have shown a more extraordinary compass of powers than Donne; for he combined—what no other man has done—the last sublimation of dialectical subtlety and address with the most impassioned majesty. Massy diamonds compose the very substance of his poem on the Metempsychosis, thoughts and descriptions which have the fervent and gloomy sublimity of Ezekiel or Aeschylus, whilst a diamond dust of rhetorical brilliancies is strewed over the whole of his occasional verses and his prose. No criticism was ever more unhappy than that of Dr Johnson's which denounces all this artificial display as so much perversion of taste. There cannot be a falser thought than this; for upon that principle a whole class of compositions might be vicious by conforming to its own ideal. The artifice and machinery of rhetoric furnishes in its degree as legitimate a basis for intellectual pleasure as any other; that the pleasure is of an inferior order, can no more attaint the idea or model of the composition than it can impeach the excellence of an epigram that is not a tragedy. Every species of composition is to be tried by its own laws. . . . It may be very true that the age of Donne gave too much encouragement to his particular vein of composition. That, however, argues no depravity of taste, but a taste erring only in being too limited and exclusive.

Rhetoric 1828

I have heard it said, by the way, that Donne's intolerable defect of ear grew out of his own baptismal name, when harnessed to his own surname—John Donne. No man, it was said, who had listened to this hideous jingle from childish years could fail to have his genius for discord, and the abominable in sound improved to the utmost.

The Lake Poets: William Wordsworth and
Robert Southey 1839

WORDSWORTH

The tenth sonnet of Donne, beginning 'Death, be not proud' is so eminently characteristic of his manner, and at the same time so weighty in the thought, and vigorous in the expression, that I would entreat you to insert it, though to modern taste it may be repulsive, quaint, and laboured.

Letter to Dyce 1833

LEIGH HUNT

Hence the conceits that astonish us in the gravest, and even subtlest thinkers, whose taste is not proportionate to their mental perceptions; men like Donne, for instance; who, apart from accidental personal impressions, seem to look at nothing as it really is, but only as to what may be thought of it.

Fancy and Imagination 1844

HALLAM

Donne is the most inharmonious of our versifiers, if he can be said to have deserved such a name by lines too rugged to seem metre. Of his earlier poems many are very licentious; the latter are chiefly devout. Few are good for much; the conceits have not even the merit of being intelligible; it would perhaps be difficult to select three passages that we should care to read again.

The Literature of Europe 1839

SWINBURNE

That chance is the ruler of the world I should be sorry to believe and reluctant to affirm; but it would be difficult for any competent and careful student to maintain that chance is not the ruler of the world of letters. Gray's odes are still, I suppose, familiar to thousands who know nothing of Donne's *Anniversaries.* . . . And yet it is certain that in fervour of inspiration, in depth and force and glow of thought and emotion and expression, Donne's verses are . . . far above Gray's. . . .

Study of Ben Jonson 1889

DOWDEN

There is indeed a large expense of spirit in the poems of Donne, an expense of spirit not always judicious or profitable, and the reader who comes with reasonable expectations will get a sufficient reward. When prospecting for gold the miner considers himself fortunate if he can reckon on finding some twenty-five pennyweights of the precious metal in a ton of quartz and wash-dirt. The prospector in the lesser poetry of any former age must be content to crush a good deal of quartz and wash a good deal of sand in the expectation of an ounce of pure gold. But by vigour and perseverance in the pursuit large fortunes may be amassed.

Donne as a poet is certainly difficult of access. How shall we approach him, how effect an entrance? With different authors we need different methods of approach, different kinds of cunning to become free of their domain. Some must be taken by storm, some must be entreated, caressed, wheedled into acquiescence. There are poets who in a single lyric give us, as it were, a key which admits us to the mastery of all their wealth. Towards others we must make an indirect advance, we must reach them through the age which they represent, or the school in which they have been teachers or pupils. It is as the founder of a school of English poetry that Donne is ordinarily set before us. We are told that in the decline of the greater poetry of the Elizabethan period a 'metaphysical school' arose, and that Donne was the founder or the first eminent member of this school. I do not believe in the existence of this so-called 'metaphysical school'. Much of the most characteristic poetry of Donne belongs to the floodtide hour of Elizabethan literature; to the time when Spenser was at work on the later books of the *Faerie Queene* and Shakespeare was producing his early histories and comedies. The delight in subtleties of thought, in over-ingenious fantasies, in far-fetched imagery, in curiosity, and not always felicitous curiosity, of expression was common to almost all the writers of the period. The dramatists were to some extent preserved from the abuse of fantastic ingenuity by the fact that they wrote for a popular audience, and must have failed unless they were at once intelligible. But authors of prose as well as authors in verse were fascinated by subtleties of the fancy; the theologian and the philosopher, as well as the poet, swung in the centre of a spider's web of fantasies

'All the waving mesh
Laughing with lucid dew-drops rainbow-edged.'

There was no special coterie or school of 'metaphysical poets', but this writer or that yielded with more *abandon* than the rest to a tendency of the time.

It is not then by studying Donne as the leader of a school that we shall come to understand him. We get access to his writings, I believe, most readily through his life, and through an interest in his character as an individual.

The Poetry of John Donne   1890

SAINTSBURY

He was 'of the first order of poets'; but he was not of the first amongst the first. . . . It is seldom that even for a few lines, seldomer that for a few stanzas, the power of the furnace is equal to the volumes of ore and fuel that are thrust into it. But the fire is always there—over-tasked, over-mastered for a time, but never choked or extinguished; and ever and anon from gaps in the smouldering mass there breaks forth such a sudden flow of pure molten metal, such a flower of incandescence, as not even in the very greatest poets of all can be ever surpassed or often rivalled. . . .

But for those who have experienced, or at least understand, the ups-and-downs, the ins-and-outs of human temperament, the alternations not merely of passion and satiety, but of passion and laughter, of passion and melancholy reflection, of passion earthly enough and spiritual rapture almost heavenly there is no poet and hardly any writer like Donne. They may even be tempted to see in the strangely mixed and flawed character of his style, an index and reflection of the variety and rapid changes of his thought and feeling. To the praise of the highest poetical art he cannot indeed lay claim. He is of course entitled to the benefit of the pleas that it is uncertain whether he ever prepared definitely for the press a single poetical work of his; that it is certain that his age regarded his youth with too much disapproval to bestow any critical care on his youthful poems. But it may be retorted that no one with the finest sense of poetry as an art, could have left things so formless as he has left, that it would have been intolerable pain and grief to any such till he had got them, even in MS., into shape. The retort is valid. But if Donne cannot receive the praise due to the accomplished poetical artist, he has that not perhaps higher but certainly rarer, of the inspired poetical creator. No study could have bettered—I hardly know whether any study could have produced—such touches as the best of those which have been quoted, and as many which perforce have been left out. And no study could have given him the idiosyncrasy which he has. *Nos passions*, says Bossuet, *ont quelque chose d'infini*. To express infinity no doubt is a contradiction in terms. But no poet has gone nearer to the hinting and adumbration of this infinite quality of passion, and of the relapses and reactions from passion, than the author of *The Second Anniversary* and *The Ecstasy*.

Introduction to Donne's Poems 1896

GOSSE

We read Donne, however, to little purpose if we do not perceive that he was above all things sincere. His writings, like his actions, were faulty, violent, a little morbid even, and abnormal. He was not, and did not attempt to be, an average man. But actions and writings alike, in their strangeness and aloofness, were unadulterated by a tinge of affectation. . . .

The modern appreciation of Donne seems to begin with Robert Browning, who met with his poems when he was still a boy (about 1827), and was greatly influenced by them. He put the Mandrake song to music. He quoted and praised the Dean so constantly in later years that Miss Barrett noticed it early in their acquaintance; 'your Donne', she says on several occasions. The stamp of the Dean's peculiar intensity of feeling can be traced in any of Browning's lyrics; his famous 'obscurity' is closely analogous to Donne's. Of subsequent instances of the influence of Donne on English poetry this is hardly the place to speak . . .

. . . the remarkably wide and deep, though almost entirely malign, influence of Donne upon the poetry of this country. . . .

The Life and Letters of John Donne 1899

RALEIGH

When Milton does fall into a vein of conceit, it is generally both trivial and obvious, with none of the saving quality of Donne's remoter extravagances. In Donne they are hardly extravagances; the vast overshadowing canopy of his imagination seems to bring the most wildly dissimilar things together with ease. To his unfettered and questioning thought the real seems unreal, the unreal real; he moves in a world of shadows, cast by the lurid light of his own emotions; they take grotesque shapes and beckon to him, or terrify him. All realities are immaterial and insubstantial; they shift their expressions, and lurk in many forms, leaping forth from the most unlikely disguises, and vanishing as suddenly as they came.

Milton 1900

GRIERSON

Alike in his poetry and in his soberest prose, treatise or sermon, Donne's mind seems to want the high seriousness which comes from a conviction that truth is, and is to be found. A spirit of scepticism and paradox plays through and disturbs almost everything he wrote, except at moments when an intense mood of feeling, whether love or devotion, begets faith, and silences the sceptical and destructive wit by the power of vision rather than of intellectual conviction. Poles apart as the two poets seem at first glance to lie in feeling and in art, there is yet something of Tennyson in the conflict which wages perpetually in Donne's poetry between feeling and intellect.

But short of the highest gifts of serene imagination or serene wisdom Donne's mind has every power it well could, wit, insight, imagination; and these move in such a strange medium of feeling and learning, mediaeval, renaissance and modern, that every imprint becomes of interest. . . .

But it is not true either that the thought and the imagery of love-poetry must be of the simple, obvious kind which Steel supposes, that any display of dialectical subtlety, any scintillation of wit, must be fatal to the impression of sincerity and feeling, or on the other hand that love is always a beautiful emotion naturally expressing itself in delicate and beautiful language. To some natures love comes as above all things a force quickening the mind, intensifying its purely intellectual energy, opening new vistas of thought abstract and subtle, making the soul 'intensely, wondrously alive'. Of such were Donne and Browning. . . .

Donne's love poetry is a very complex phenomenon, but the two dominant strains in it are just these: the strain of dialectic, subtle play of argument and wit, erudite and fantastic; and the strain of vivid realism, the record of a passion, which is not ideal or conventional, neither recollected in tranquillity nor a pure product of literary fashion, but love as an actual immediate experience in all its moods, gay and angry, scornful and rapturous with joy, touched with tenderness and darkened with sorrow—though these last two moods, the commonest in love-poetry, are with Donne the rarest. . . .

The Poems of John Donne 1912

KER

The conceits of Donne are utterly different in effect from the conceits of Cowley. Donne is a poet who can use the simplest language with tremendous effect. He takes us sometimes as Wordsworth does, and forces us to look at something undisguised, as it is, until we feel some strange purport in it. In his *Calm at Sea*, for example, the poem praised by Ben Jonson to Drummond of Hawthornden, the overpowering effect of a calm at sea in hot weather, of the same sort as is described in the *Ancient Mariner*, is brought out simply by forcing the reader to think of it. This intensity of vision and feeling, bending the mind upon the subject, has a counterpart in the search for comparisons. Now the conceited things in Donne which seem to resemble those of Cowley are found often to be brought in, not from love of fancy-work, but from inability to get direct expression. That is the meaning of the well-known comparison of the two separated lovers, the husband in one place, the wife in another, to the two legs of a pair of compasses. Where the mind is intent on a subject, it often finds expression in something indirect, removed from the subject, as in the imagery of the Hebrew prophets. Donne besides is a comic or humorous poet, fond of grotesque work, not generally for its own sake, but as the expression of a deep and ironical mind, not always in a pleasant mood and working through contradictions.

Form and Style in Poetry   1914–15

ELIOT

If so shrewd and sensitive (though so limited) a critic as Johnson failed to define metaphysical poetry by its faults, it is worth while to inquire whether we may not have more success by adopting the opposite method: by assuming that the poets of the seventeenth century (up to the Revolution) were the direct and normal development of the precedent age; and, without prejudicing their case by the adjective 'metaphysical', consider whether their virtue was not something permanently valuable, which subsequently disappeared, but ought not to have disappeared. Johnson has hit, perhaps by accident, on one of their peculiarities, when he observes that 'their attempts were always analytic'; he would not agree that, after the dissociation, they put the material together again in a new unity.

It is certain that the dramatic verse of the later Elizabethan and early Jacobean poets expresses a degree of development of sensibility which is not found in any of the prose, good as it often is. If we except Marlowe, a man of prodigious intelligence, these dramatists were directly or indirectly (it is at least a tenable theory) affected by Montaigne. Even if we except also Jonson and Chapman, these two were notably erudite, and were notably men who incorporated their erudition into their sensibility: their mode of feeling was directly and freshly altered by their reading and thought. In Chapman especially there is a direct sensuous apprehension of thought, or a recreation of thought into feeling, which is exactly what we find in Donne:

> . . . in this one thing, all the discipline
> Of manners and of manhood is contained;
> A man to join himself with th' Universe
> In his main sway, and make in all things fit
> One with that All, and go on, round as it;
> Not plucking from the whole his wretched part,
> And into straits, or into nought revert,
> Wishing the complete Universe might be
> Subject to such a rag of it, as he;
> But to consider great Necessity.

We compare this with some modern passage:

> No, when the fight begins within himself,
> A man's worth something. God stoops o'er his head,
> Satan looks up between his feet—both tug—
> He's left, i' the middle; the soul wakes
> And grows. Prolong that battle through his life!

. . . The difference is not a simple difference of degree between poets. It is something which had happened to the mind of England between the time of Donne or Lord Herbert of Cherbury and the time of Tennyson and Browning; it is the difference between the intellectual poet and the reflective poet. Tennyson and Browning are poets, and they think; but they do not feel their thought as immediately as the odour of a rose. A thought to Donne was an experience; it modified his sensibility. When a poet's mind is perfectly equipped for its work, it is constantly amalgamating disparate experience; the ordinary man's experience is chaotic, irregular, fragmentary. The latter falls in love, or reads Spinoza, and these two experiences have nothing to do with each other, or with the noise of the typewriter or the smell of cooking; in the mind of the poet these experiences are always forming new wholes.

We may express the difference by the following theory: The poets of the seventeenth century, the successors of the dramatists of the sixteenth, possessed a mechanism of sensibility which could devour any kind of experience. They are simple, artificial, difficult, or fantastic, as their predecessors were; no less nor more than Dante, Guido Cavalcanti, Guinicelli, or Cino. In the seventeenth century a dissociation of sensibility set in, from which we have never recovered; and this dissociation, as is natural, was aggravated by the influence of the two most powerful poets of the century, Milton and Dryden. Each of these men performed certain poetic functions so magnificently well that the magnitude of the effect concealed the absence of others. The language went on and in some respects improved; the best verse of Collins, Gray, Johnson, and even Goldsmith satisfies some of our fastidious demands better than that of Donne or Marvell or King. But while the language became more refined, the feeling became more crude. The feeling, the sensibility, expressed in the *Country Churchyard* (to say nothing of Tennyson and Browning) is cruder than that in the *Coy Mistress*.

The second effect of the influence of Milton and Dryden followed from the first, and was therefore slow in manifestation. The sentimental age began early in the eighteenth century, and continued. The poets revolted against the ratiocinative, the descriptive; they reflected. In one or two passages of Shelley's *Triumph of Life*, in the second *Hyperion*, there are traces of a struggle toward unification of sensibility. But Keats and Shelley died, and Tennyson and Browning ruminated.

After this brief exposition of a theory—too brief, perhaps, to carry conviction—we may ask, what would have been the fate of the 'metaphysical' had the current of poetry descended in a direct line from them, as it descended in a direct line to them? They would not, certainly, be classified as metaphysical. The possible interests of a poet are unlimited; the more intelligent he is the better; the more intelligent he is the more likely that he will have interests: our only condition is that he turn them into poetry, and not merely meditate on them poetically. A philosophical theory which has entered into poetry is established, for its truth or falsity in one sense ceases to matter, and its truth in another sense is proved. The poets in question have, like other poets, various faults. But they were, at best, engaged in the task of trying to find the verbal equivalent for states of mind and feeling. And this means both that they are more mature, and that they wear better, than later poets of certainly not less literary ability. . . .

Those who object to the 'artificiality' of Milton or Dryden sometimes tell us to 'look into our hearts and write'. But that is not looking deep enough; Racine or Donne looked into a good deal more than the heart. One must look into the cerebral cortex, the nervous system, and the digestive tracts.

May we not conclude, then, that Donne, Crashaw, Vaughan, Herbert and Lord Herbert, Marvell, King, Cowley at his best, are in the direct current of English poetry, and that their faults should be reprimanded by this standard rather than coddled by antiquarian affections? They have been enough praised in terms which are implicit limitations because they are 'metaphysical' or 'witty', 'quaint' or 'obscure', though at their best they have not these attributes more than other serious poets.

The Metaphysical Poets 1921

. . . as I believe, Donne's poetry is a concern of the present and the recent past, rather than of the future.

I by no means wish to affirm that the importance of a particular poet, or of a particular type of poetry, is merely a matter of capricious fashion. I wish simply to distinguish between the absolute and the relative in popularity, and to recognise in the relative (both when a poet is unduly preferred and when he is unduly ignored) an element of the reasonable, the just and the significant. . . .

And detaching Donne from his relation to a particular generation, our own, a relation which may never be repeated at any subsequent time, this I think we can say at least. Donne will remain permanently in a higher place than he has occupied before. For he was a great reformer of the English language, of English verse. We may continue always to find him more of a poet, of deeper knowledge and more intense and moving expression, than Dryden; but here we can compare him favourably to Dryden in the very matter in which Dryden deserves our warmest gratitude and admiration. The verse of Dryden was once

thought artificial, pedestrian and prosaic; just as in a previous
century the verse of Donne was thought to be artificial, pedestrian and prosaic, as well as uncouth. But in truth Dryden and
Donne are both highly natural; and the merit of both is to have
established a natural conversational diction instead of a conventional one. Each effected a revolution of the kind which
has to occur from time to time, which will have to occur again
in nearly measurable time, if the English language is to retain
its vigour.

The revolutionary activity of Donne is not so immediately
apparent as that of Dryden, because it began before the
previous revolution, that of dramatic blank verse was exhausted. For the age of Shakespeare, blank verse was the perfect
vehicle for impassioned thought, and indeed Shakespeare himself succeeded in getting more thought expressed in great verse
than any English poet before or after him. But lyric verse, under
these conditions, remained subordinate to the musical instrument and to the dramatic setting. . . .

It is hardly too much to say that Donne enlarged the pos-
sibilities of lyric verse as no other English poet has done. M.
Legouis has pointed out very pertinently how largely his lyrics
are dramatic, in monologue and dialogue. . . .

But Donne effected not only a development, but a reform,
of the language, just as Dryden, in his turn, reformed the language from the excesses of the minor followers of Donne.
The minor Elizabethan dramatists sometimes tormented the
language; where the content is often quite simple, the expression is perverse. In the verse of Donne the thought is sometimes
over-ingenious and perverse, but the language is always pure
and simple. The conceit itself is primarily an eccentricity of
imagery, the far-fetched association of the dissimilar, or the
over-elaboration of one metaphor or simile; only with such
writers as Cleveland or Benlowes it tends to corrupt the
language itself—because with them, the content of thought and
feeling is seldom subtle enough to justify such obscure expression. Donne introduced the natural or conversational style,
which the Elizabethans at their best had excelled in producing
in a highly sophisticated metric of blank verse, into the lyric;

he first made it possible to think in lyric verse, and in a variety of rhythms and stanza schemes which forms an inexhaustible subject of study; and at the same time retained a quality of song and the suggestion of the instrumental accompaniment of the earlier lyric. No poet has excelled him in this peculiar combination of qualitities. . . .

Such, I believe, are some of the conclusions of praise which another generation, not enjoying the fulness of satisfaction in Donne that we have felt, will be able to confer on him. . . . For one age or another his personality may be no more interesting than has been, for the last seventy-five years or so (I am not at the moment careful to answer in respect of that reputation) the personality of Byron. But at any time Donne ought always to be recognized as one of the few great reformers and preservers of the English tongue.

Donne in our Time (*A Garland for John Donne*)
1931

D

Milton

Miltonic criticism is vast but unadventurous. After a certain initial neglect, due largely to political reasons, and in any case not so great as Johnson thought, Paradise Lost *made its way rapidly to the head of English poetry. And there, until the present century, it stayed. The classical critics, of course, found it more amenable to their discipline than any other great work, since it was conceived on the lines of the classical epic. They compared it with Homer and Virgil, and often favourably. The Romantics, too, accepted Milton—it is one of the few points in which they did not demand a revision of classical tastes. The Victorian critics continued to admire, and Milton occupied a very important place in Arnold's Rugbeian classicism. Only in the last few years has Milton's reputation sunk a little, Mr Eliot being the first critic who has dared (perhaps excepting Lord Chester-field) to treat the subject with flippancy.*

It is just possible, I think, to trace a steady and gradual decline in the quality of Miltonic criticism over its whole period. Here, and here only, the classical critics are the best, because they are thoroughly at home in the framework and atmosphere of the classical epic; they liked Milton for the reasons which were important to Milton. The Romantics have already moved a little further away from Milton himself, and begin to like him for qualities which were only incidental to his design—for his style and diction. They appreciate his classicism less, and are further from his doctrine.

The modern reader is further away still. He is not born and bred in the classical atmosphere, and Milton's religious doctrine is generally foreign to him, even repugnant. One or the other

*of these difficulties might not matter; both together, they are
formidable, and there can be no doubt that the position of*
Paradise Lost *is precarious.*

The minor poems, of course, are in a different case.

MILTON

. . . although a Poet, soaring in the high region of his
fancies, with his garland and singing robes about him, might
without apology speak more of himself then I mean to do,
yet for me sitting here below in the cool element of prose, a
mortall thing among many readers of the Empyreall conceit,
to venture and divulge unusual things of my selfe, I shall
petition to the gentler sort, if it may not be envy to me. I must
say therefore that after I had from my first yeeres by the
ceaselesse diligence and care of my father, whom God recom-
pence, bin exercis'd to the tongues, and some sciences, as my
age would suffer, by sundry masters and teachers both at home
and at the schools, it was found that whether ought was
impos'd me by them that had the overlooking, or betak'n to
of mine own choice, in English or other tongue, prosing or
versing, but chiefly this latter, the stile, by certain vital signes
it had, was likely to live. But much latelier in the privat
Academies of *Italy*, whither I was favor'd to resort, perceiving
that some trifles which I had in memory, compos'd at under
twenty or thereabout (for the manner is that every one must
give some proof of his wit and reading there) met with accep-
tance above what was lookt for, and other things which I had
shifted in scarsity of books and conveniences to patch up
amongst them were receiv'd with written Encomiums, which
the Italian is not forward to bestow on men of this side the
Alps, I began thus farre to assent both to them and divers of
my friends here at home, and not lesse to an inward prompting
which now grew daily upon me, that by labour and intent
study (which I take to be my portion in this life) joyn'd with the
strong propensity of nature, I might perhaps leave something
so written to aftertimes as they would not willingly let it die.
These thoughts at once possest me, and these other: That if I

were certain to write as men buy Leases, for three lives and downward, there ought no regard be sooner had then to God's glory by the honour and instruction of my country. For which cause, and not only for that I knew it would be hard to arrive at the second rank among the Latines, I apply'd my selfe to that resolution which *Ariosto* follow'd against the perswasions of *Bembo*, to fix all the industry and art I could unite to the adorning of my native tongue: not to make verbal curiosities the end (that were a toylsom vanity), but to be an interpreter & relater of the best and sagest things among mine own Citizens throughout this Iland in the mother dialect. . . .

The Reason of Church Government   1641

MARVELL

That majesty which through thy work doth reign,
Draws the devout, deterring the profane.
And things divine thou treat'st of in such state
As them preserves, and thee, inviolate.
At once delight and horror on us seize,
Thou sing'st with so much gravity and ease;
And above human flight dost·soar aloft
With plume so strong, so equal, and so soft.
The bird nam'd from that Paradise you sing
So never flags, but always keeps on wing.

    Where couldst thou words of such a compass find?
Whence furnish such a vast expense of mind?
Just Heav'n thee like Tiresias to requite
Rewards with prophecy thy loss of sight.

    Well might'st thou scorn thy readers to allure
With tinkling rhime, of thy own sense secure;
While the Town-Bays writes all the while and spells,
And like a pack-horse tires without his bells.
Their fancies like our bushy-points appear,
The poets tag them; we for fashion wear.
I too transported by the mode offend,
And while I meant to Praise thee must Commend.

Thy verse created like thy theme sublime,
In number, weight, and measure, needs not rhime.

Commendatory Verses prefixed to Paradise Lost   1667

WALLER and ST. EVREMOND

Waller

There is one *John Milton*, an old commonwealth's man,
who hath in the latter part of his life, written a poem entituled
Paradise Lost; and to say the truth, it is not without some
fancy and bold invention. But I am much better pleased with
some smaller productions of his in the scenical and pastoral
way; one of which called *Lycidas* I shall forthwith send you. . . .

St. Evremond

The poem called *Lycidas*, which you say is written by Mr.
Milton, has given me much pleasure. It has in it what I conceive
to be the true spirit of pastoral poetry, the old Arcadian enthusiasm. . . . What pleases me in *John Milton's* poem, besides
the true pastoral enthusiasm and the scenical merit, is the
various and easy flow of its numbers. Those measures are well
adapted to the tender kind of imagery though they are not
expressive of the first strong impressions of grief.

*Letters supposed to have passed between M. de St.
Evremond & Mr Waller*   1673?

DRYDEN

As for Mr. Milton, whom we all admire with so much
justice . . . his thoughts are elevated, his words sounding, and
no man has so happily copied the manner of Homer, or so
copiously translated his Grecisms, and the Latin elegancies
of Virgil. 'Tis true, he runs into a flat of thought, sometimes for
a hundred lines together, but it is when he is got into a track
of Scripture. His antiquated words were his choice, not his
necessity; for therein he imitated Spenser, as Spenser did
Chaucer. And though, perhaps, the love of their masters may
have transported both too far, in the frequent use of them, yet,

in my opinion, obsolete words may then be laudably revived, when either they are more sounding, or more significant, than those in practice; and when their obscurity is taken away, by joining other words to them, which clear the sense; according to the rule of Horace, for the admission of new words. But in both cases moderation is to be observed in the use of them: for unnecessary coinage, as well as unnecessary revival, runs into affectation; a fault to be avoided on either hand. Neither will I justify Milton for his blank verse, though I may excuse him, by the example of Hannibal Caro, and other Italians who have used it; for whatever causes he alleges for the abolishing of rhyme (which I have not the leisure to examine), his own particular reason is plainly this, that rhyme was not his talent; he had neither the ease of doing it, nor the graces of it; which is manifest in his *Juvenilia*, or verses written in his youth, where his rhyme is always constrained and forced, and comes hardly from him, at an age when the soul is most pliant, and the passion of love makes almost every man a rhymer, though not a poet.

A Discourse concerning the Original and Progress of
Satire 1693

In the meantime, I may be bold to draw this corollary from what has been already said, that the file of heroic poets is very short; all are not such who have assumed that lofty title in ancient or modern ages, or have been so esteemed by their partial and ignorant admirers. . . .

Spenser had a better plea for his Fairy Queen, had his action been finished, or had been one. And Milton, if the Devil had not been his hero, instead of Adam; if the giant had not foiled the knight, and driven him out of his stronghold, to wander through the world with his lady errant; and if there had not been more machining persons than human in his poem.

Dedication of the Aeneis 1697

Spenser and Fairfax both flourished in the reign of Queen Elizabeth; great masters in our language, and who saw much further into the beauties of our numbers than those who immediately followed them. Milton was the poetical son of Spenser, and Mr. Waller of Fairfax; for we have our lineal descents as well as other families. Spenser more than once insinuates, that the soul of Chaucer was transfused into his body; and that he was begotten by him two hundred years after his decease. Milton has acknowledged to me, that Spenser was his original. . . .

Preface to Fables   1700

SHAFTESBURY

. . . our most approv'd *heroick Poem* [*Paradise Lost*] has neither the Softness of Language, nor the fashionable Turn of Wit; but merely solid Thought, strong Reasoning, noble Passion, and a continued Thred of moral Doctrine, Piety, and Virtue to recommend it. . . .

Characteristicks   1711

ADDISON

Among great geniuses, those few draw the admiration of all the world upon them, and stand up as the prodigies of mankind, who by the mere strength of natural parts, and without any assistance of art or learning, have produced works that were the delight of their own times, and the wonder of posterity. . . .

There is another kind of great geniuses which I shall place in a second class, not as I think them inferior to the first, but only for distinction's sake, as they are of a different kind. This second class of great geniuses are those that have formed themselves by rules, and submitted the greatness of their natural talents to the corrections and restraints of art. Such among the Greeks were Plato and Aristotle; among the Romans, Virgil and Tully; among the English, Milton and Sir Francis Bacon.

Spectator No. 160   1711

Milton's characters, most of them, lie out of nature, and were to be formed purely by his own invention. It shows a greater genius in Shakespeare to have drawn his Caliban, than his Hotspur or Julius Caesar: the one was to be supplied out of his own imagination, whereas the other might have been formed upon tradition, history, and observation. It was much easier, therefore, for Homer to find proper sentiments for an assembly of Grecian generals, than for Milton to diversify his infernal council with proper characters, and inspire them with a variety of sentiments. The loves of Dido and Aeneas are only copies of what has passed between other persons. Adam and Eve, before the fall, are a different species from that of man-kind who are descended from them; and none but a poet of the most unbounded invention, and the most exquisite judg-ment, could have filled their conversation and behaviour with so many circumstances during their state of innocence.

Nor is it sufficient for an epic poem to be filled with such thoughts as are natural, unless it abound also with such as are sublime. . . .

Milton's chief talent, and, indeed, his distinguishing excellence, lies in the sublimity of his thoughts. There are others of the moderns who rival him in every other part of poetry; but in the greatness of his sentiments he triumphs over all the poets both modern and ancient, Homer only excepted . . . the metaphors are very bold, but just; I must, however, observe, that the metaphors are not too thick-sown in Milton, which always savours too much of wit; that they never clash with one another, which, as Aristotle observes, turns a sentence into a kind of enigma or riddle; and that he seldom has re-course to them where the proper and natural words will do as well. . . .

Milton, by the above-mentioned helps, and by the choice of the noblest words and phrases which our tongue would afford him, has carried our language to a greater height than any of the English poets have ever done before or after him, and made the sublimity of his style equal to that of his senti-ments. . . .

There is another objection against Milton's fable, . . . that

the hero in the *Paradise Lost* is unsuccessful, and by no means
a match for his enemies. This gave occasion to Mr. Dryden's
reflection, that the devil was in reality Milton's hero. I think
I have obviated this objection in my first paper. The *Paradise
Lost* is an epic, or a narrative poem, and he that looks for an
hero in it, searches for that which Milton never intended; but
if he will needs fix the name of an hero upon any person in it,
it is certainly the Messiah, who is the hero, both in the principal
action, and in the chief episodes. . . .

I must in the next place observe, that Milton has interwoven
in the texture of his fable some particulars which do not seem to
have probability enough for an epic poem, particularly in the
actions which he ascribes to Sin and Death, and the picture
which he draws of the Limbo of Vanity, with other passages
in the second book. Such allegories rather savour of the spirit
of Spenser and Ariosto, than of Homer and Virgil.

In the structure of his poem, he has likewise admitted of
too many digressions . . . though I must confess there is so
great a beauty in these very digressions, that I would not wish
them out of his poem . . .

If we look into his sentiments, I think they are sometimes
defective under the following heads; first, as there are several
of them too much pointed, and some that degenerate even
into puns. Of this last kind, I am afraid, is that in the first book,
where speaking of the pigmies, he calls them

—The small infantry
Warr'd on by cranes—

Another blemish that appears in some of his thoughts, is
his frequent allusion to heathen fables, which are not certainly
of a piece with the divine subject of which he treats. I do not
find fault with these allusions, where the poet himself represents
them as fabulous, as he does in some places, but where he
mentions them as truths and matters of fact. . . .

A third fault in his sentiments, is an unnecessary ostentation of learning, which likewise occurs very frequently. It is
certain that both Homer and Virgil were masters of all the

learning of their times, but it shows itself after an indirect and concealed manner. Milton seems ambitious of letting us know, by his excursions on free-will and predestination, and his many glances upon history, astronomy, geography, and the like, as well as by the terms and phrases he sometimes makes use of, that he was acquainted with the whole circle of arts and sciences.

If, in the last place, we consider the language of this great poet, we must allow what I have hinted in a former paper, that it is often too much laboured, and sometimes obscured by old words, transpositions, and foreign idioms. . . . Milton's sentiments and ideas were so wonderfully sublime, that it would have been impossible for him to have represented them in their full strength and beauty, without having recourse to these foreign assistances. Our language sunk under him, and was unequal to that greatness of soul which furnished him with such glorious conceptions. . . .

I have now finished my observations on a work which does an honour to the English nation. . . .

Spectator Nos. 267 to 369   1712

THOMAS ELLWOOD (QUAKER)

After some common discourses had passed between us, he called for a manuscript of his: which being brought, he delivered to me; bidding me, 'Take it home with me, and read it at my leisure; and, when I had so done, return it to him, with my judgment thereupon!'

When I came home, and had set myself to read it; I found it was that excellent poem, which he entitled, *Paradise Lost*.

After I had, with the best attention, read it through: I made him another visit, and returned him his book; with due acknowledgement of the favour he had done me, in communicating it to me.

He asked me, 'How I liked it? And what I thought of it?' Which I, modestly but freely, told him.

And, after some further discourse about it, I pleasantly said to him, 'Thou hast said much, here, of *Paradise lost*: but what hast thou to say of *Paradise found*?'

He made me no answer; but sat some time in a muse: then brake off that discourse, and fell upon another subject. . . .

And when, afterwards, I went to wait on him there (which I seldom failed of doing, whenever my occasions drew me to London), he showed me his second poem, called *Paradise Regained*: and in a pleasant tone, said to me, 'This is owing to you! For you put it into my head, by the question you put to me at Chalfont! which, before, I had not thought of.'

History of Himself 1713

BENTLEY

But I wonder not so much at the Poem it self, though worthy of all Wonder; as that the Author could so abstract his Thoughts from his own Troubles, as to be able to make it; that confin'd in a narrow and to Him a dark Chamber, surrounded with Cares and Fears, he could spatiate at large through the Compass of the whole Universe, and through all Heaven beyond it; could survey all Periods of Time from before the Creation to the Consummation of all Things. This Theory, no doubt, was a great Solace to him in his Affliction; but it shews in him a greater Strength of Spirit, that made him capable of such a Solace.

Preface to his Edition 1732

[Bentley's emendations to the text of *Paradise Lost* are, after all, one species, and one of the most remarkable species, of Miltonic criticism. And so an example of them may properly be included here. He assumed that the text, unrevised by Milton himself, had fallen into the hands of some villainous editor, and that it needed much radical correction. This correction he was willing to supply, using the formidable technique which he had developed in the editing of classical texts]

On XII. 648

If I might presume, says an ingenious and celebrated Writer, *to offer at the smallest Alteration in this Divine Work*. If to make

one small Alteration appear'd to be so *Presumptuous*; what
Censure must I expect to incur, who have presum'd to make
so many? But *Jacta est Alea*; and *Non iniussa cecini*: . . . The
Gentleman would eject these last two lines of the Book, and
close it with the Verse before. He seems to have been induc'd
to this, by a Mistake of the Printer, THEY *hand in hand*;
which Reading does indeed make the last Distich seem loose,
unconnected, and abscinded from the rest. But the Author
gave it, THEN *hand in hand*: which continues the prior Sentence:

> *Some natural tears they drop'd, but wip'd them soon:*
> Then *hand in hand.*

Nor can these two Verses possibly be spar'd from the Work;
for without them *Adam* and *Eve* would be left in the Territory
and Suburbane of Paradise, in the very view of the *dreadful
faces.*

> *Apparent dirae facies, inimicaque Trojae*
> *Numina magna Deum:*

They must therefore be dismiss'd out of *Eden*, to live thence-
forward in some other Part of the World. And yet this Distich,
as the Gentleman well judges, *falls very much below the Passage
foregoing.* It contradicts the Poet's own Scheme; nor is the
Diction unexceptionable. He tells us before, that *Adam*, upon
hearing Michael's Predictions, was even *surcharg'd with Joy,*
v. 372; was *replete with Joy and Wonder,* 468; was in doubt,
whether he should *repent of,* or *rejoice in his Fall,* 475; was
in great Peace of Thought, 558: and Eve herself *not sad,* but
full of Consolation, 620. Why then does this Distich dismiss
our first Parents in Anguish, and the Reader in Melancholy?
And how can the Expression be justified, *with wand'ring Steps
and slow?* Why *wand'ring?* Erratic Steps? Very improper; when
in the Line before, they were *guided by Providence.* And why
Slow? when even *Eve* profess'd her Readiness and Alacrity
for the Journey, 614: *But now lead on:*

> In Me is no delay.

And why *their solitary Way*? All words to represent a sorrow-ful Parting? When even their former Walks in Paradise were as solitary, as their Way now: there being no Body besides Them Two, both here and there. Shall I therefore, after so many prior Presumptions, presume at last to offer a Distich, as close as may be to the Author's Words, and entirely agree-able to his Scheme?

> THEN *hand in hand with* SOCIAL *steps their Way*
> *Through* Eden *took*, WITH HEA'NLY COMFORT
> CHEER'D.

Notes to the Edition

RICHARDSON

As his Mind was Rich in Ideas, and in Words of various Languages to Cloathe them with, and as he had a Vast Fire, Vigour and Zeal of Imagination, his Style must Necessarily Distinguish it Self; it Did So; and even in his Younger days, his Juvenile Poems, English, Latin, and Italian, have a Brilliant not Easily found Elsewhere; Nor is it not seen in his Con-troversial Prose Works; *Paradise Lost* wants it not, in which there are Specimens of All his Kinds of Styles, the Tender, the Fierce, the Narrative, the Reasoning, the Lofty, &c. So Early as when he Wrote for Divorce, though he Conceal'd his Name his Hand was known—*My Name I did not Publish* (says He) *as not willing it should Sway the Reader either For me or Against me, but when I was told that the Style, which what it Ails to be so soon distinguishable, I cannot tell, was known by most Men*—There is Somthing in Every Man's whereby he is Known, as by his Voice, Face, Gait &c. in *Milton* there is a certain Vigour, whether *Versing or Prosing*, which will Awaken Attention be She never so Drowsy, and then Persuade her to be Thankful though She was Disturb'd.

A Reader of *Milton* must be Always upon Duty; he is Surrounded with Sense, it rises in every Line, every Word is to the Purpose; There are no Lazy Intervals, All has been Consider'd, and Demands, and Merits Observation. Even in

the Best Writers you Somtimes find Words and Sentences
which hang on so Loosely you may Blow 'em off; *Milton's*
are all Substance and Weight; Fewer would not have Serv'd
the Turn, and More would have been Superfluous.

His Silence has the Same Effect, not only that he leaves
Work for the Imagination when he has Entertain'd it, and
Furnish'd it with Noble Materials; but he Expresses himself
So Concisely, Employs Words So Sparingly, that whoever
will Possess His Ideas must Dig for them, and Oftentimes
pretty far below the Surface.

Explanatory Notes and Remarks on Milton's
Paradise Lost 1734

POPE

Milton's strong pinion now not Heaven can bound,
Now serpent-like, in prose he sweeps the ground;
In quibbles, angel and archangel join,
And God the Father turns a school-divine.
Not that I'd lop the beauties from his book,
Like slashing Bentley with his desperate hook. . . .

Imitations of Horace: To Augustus 1737

Milton's style in his *Paradise Lost* is not natural; it is an
exotic style. As his subject lies a good deal out of our world,
it has a particular propriety in those parts of the poem; and
when he is on earth, whenever he is describing our parents in
Paradise, you see he uses a more easy and natural way of
writing. Though his forced style may fit the higher parts of
his own poem, it does very ill for others who write on natural
and pastoral subjects.

Spence's Anecdotes 1744

LORD CHESTERFIELD

But what will you say, when I tell you truly, that I cannot
possibly read our countryman Milton through. I acknowledge

him to have some most sublime passages, some prodigious flashes of light; but then you must acknowledge, that light is often followed by *darkness visible*, to use his own expression. Besides, not having the honour to be acquainted with any of the parties in his Poem, except the Man and Woman, the characters and the speeches of a dozen or two of Angels, and of as many Devils, are as much above my reach as my entertainment. Keep this secret for me; for if it should be known, I should be abused by every tasteless Pedant, and every solid Divine in England.

Letter to his Son   1752

JOHNSON

The English poems, though they make no promises of *Paradise Lost*, have this evidence of genius, that they have a cast original and unborrowed. But their peculiarity is not excellence: if they differ from the verse of others, they differ for the worse. . . .

One of the poems on which much praise has been bestowed is *Lycidas*; of which the diction is harsh, the rhymes uncertain, and the numbers unpleasing. What beauty there is we must therefore seek in the sentiments and images. It is not to be considered as the effusion of real passion; for passion runs not after remote allusions and obscure opinions. Passion plucks no berries from the myrtle and ivy, nor calls upon Arethuse and Mincius, nor tells of rough *satyrs* and *fawns with cloven heel*. Where there is leisure for fiction, there is little grief.

In this poem there is no nature, for there is no truth; there is no art, for there is nothing new. Its form is that of a pastoral, easy, vulgar, and therefore disgusting: whatever images it can supply are long ago exhausted; and its inherent improbability always forces dissatisfaction on the mind. When Cowley tells of Hervey, that they studied together, it is easy to suppose how much he must miss the companion of his labours, and the partner of his discoveries; but what images of tenderness can be excited by these lines!

We drove a field, and both together heard,
What time the grey fly winds her sultry horn,
Battening our flocks with the fresh dews of night.

We know that they never drove a field, and that they had no
flocks to batten; and though it be allowed that the representation may be allegorical, the true meaning is so uncertain and
remote that it is never sought, because it cannot be known
when it is found.

Among the flocks and copses and flowers appear the heathen
deities, Jove and Phoebus, Neptune and Aeolus, with a long
train of mythological imagery, such as a College easily supplies.
Nothing can less display knowledge or less exercise invention
than to tell how a shepherd has lost his companion and must
now feed his flocks alone, without any judge of his skill in
piping; and how one god asks another god what is become of
Lycidas, and how neither god can tell. He who thus grieves will
excite no sympathy; he who thus praises will confer no honour.

This poem has yet a grosser fault. With the trifling fictions
are mingled the most awful and sacred truths, such as ought
never to be polluted with such irreverent combinations. The
shepherd likewise is now a feeder of sheep, and afterwards an
ecclesiastical pastor, a superintendent of a Christian flock.
Such equivocations are always unskilful; but here they are
indecent, and at least approach to impiety, of which, however,
I believe the writer not to have been conscious.

Such is the power of reputation justly acquired that its
blaze drives away the eye from nice examination. Surely no
man could have fancied that he read *Lycidas* with pleasure had
he not known the author. . . .

The characteristick quality of his poem [*Paradise Lost*] is
sublimity. He sometimes descends to the elegant, but his
element is the great. He can occasionally invest himself with
grace; but his natural port is gigantick loftiness. He can please
when pleasure is required; but it is his peculiar power to
astonish.

He seems to have been well acquainted with his own
genius, and to know what it was that Nature had bestowed

upon him more bountifully than upon others; the power of displaying the vast, illuminating the splendid, enforcing the awful, darkening the gloomy, and aggravating the dreadful: he therefore chose a subject on which too much could not be said, on which he might tire his fancy without the censure of extravagance.

The appearances of nature and the occurrences of life did not satiate his appetite of greatness. To paint things as they are requires a minute attention, and employs the memory rather than the fancy. Milton's delight was to sport in the wide regions of possibility; reality was a scene too narrow for his mind. He sent his faculties out upon discovery, into worlds where only imagination can travel, and delighted to form new modes of existence, and furnish sentiment and action to superior beings, to trace the counsels of Hell, or accompany the choirs of heaven.

In Milton every line breathes sanctity of thought and purity of manners, except when the train of the narration requires the introduction of the rebellious spirits; and even they are compelled to acknowledge their subjection to God in such a manner as excites reverence and confirms piety . . .

The defects and faults of *Paradise Lost*, for faults and defects every work of man must have, it is the business of impartial criticism to discover. . . .

Here is a full display of the united force of study and genius; of a great accumulation of materials, with judgement to digest and fancy to combine them: Milton was able to select from nature or from story, from ancient fable or from modern science, whatever could illustrate or adorn his thoughts. An accumulation of knowledge impregnated his mind fermented by study and exalted by imagination.

It has been therefore said without an indecent hyperbole by one of his encomiasts, that in reading *Paradise Lost* we read a book of universal knowledge.

But original deficiency cannot be supplied. The want of human interest is always felt. *Paradise Lost* is one of the books which the reader admires and lays down, and forgets to take up again. None ever wished it longer than it is. Its perusal is a duty rather than a pleasure. We read Milton for instruction, retire harassed and overburdened, and look elsewhere for recreation; we desert our master, and seek for companions. . . .

Through all his greater works there prevails an uniform peculiarity of *Diction*, a mode and cast of expression which bears little resemblance to that of any former writer, and which is so far removed from common use that an unlearned reader when he first opens his book finds himself surprised by a new language.

This novelty has been, by those who can find nothing wrong in Milton, imputed to his laborious endeavours after words suitable to the grandeur of his ideas. *Our language*, says Addison, *sunk under him*. But the truth is, that both in prose and verse, he had formed his style by a perverse and pedantick principle. He was desirous to use English words with a foreign idiom. This in all his prose is discovered and condemned, for there judgement operates freely, neither softened by the beauty nor awed by the dignity of his thoughts; but such is the power of his poetry that his call is obeyed without resistance, the reader feels himself in captivity to a higher and a nobler mind, and criticism sinks in admiration.

Milton's style was not modified by his subject: what is shown with greater extent in *Paradise Lost* may be found in *Comus*. One source of his peculiarity was his familiarity with the Tuscan poets: the disposition of his words is, I think, frequently Italian; perhaps sometimes combined with other tongues. Of him, at last, may be said what Jonson says of Spenser, that *he wrote no language*, but has formed what Butler calls a *Babylonish Dialect*, in itself harsh and barbarous but made by exalted genius and extensive learning the vehicle of so much instruction and so much pleasure that, like other lovers, we find grace in its deformity.

Whatever be the faults of his diction he cannot want the praise of copiousness and variety; he was master of his language in its full extent and has selected the melodious words with such diligence, that from his book alone the Art of English poetry might be learned.

Life of Milton 1779

COPLESTON

L'Allegro. A Poem
By John Milton
No Printer's Name

It has become a practice of late with a certain description of people, who have no visible means of subsistence, to string together a few trite images of rural scenery, interspersed with vulgarisms in dialect, and traits of vulgar manners; to dress up these materials in a Sing-Song jingle; and to offer them for sale as a Poem. According to the most approved recipes, something about the heathen gods and goddesses; and the schoolboy topics of Styx and Cerberus, and Elysium; are occasionally thrown in, and the composition is complete. The stock in trade of these Adventurers is in general scanty enough; and their Art therefore consists in disposing it to the best advantage. But if such be the aim of the Writer, it is the Critic's business to detect and defeat the imposture; to warn the public against the purchase of shop-worn goods and tinsel wares; to protect the fair trader, by exposing the tricks of needy Quacks and Mountebanks; and to chastise that forward and noisy importunity with which they present themselves to the public notice.

How far Mr. Milton is amenable to this discipline, will best appear from a brief analysis of the Poem before us.

In the very opening he assumes a tone of authority which might better suit some veteran Bard than a raw candidate for the Delphic bays: for, before he proceeds to the regular process of Invocation, he clears the way, by driving from his presence (with sundry hard names; and bitter reproaches on her father, mother, and all the family) a venerable Personage, whose age at least and staid matronlike appearance, might have entitled her to more civil language.

> Hence loathed Melancholy!
> Of *Cerberus* and blackest Midnight born,
> In Stygian cave forlorn, &c.

There is no giving rules, however, in these matters, without a knowledge of the case. Perhaps the old lady had been frequently warned off before; and provoked this violence by still continuing to lurk about the Poet's dwelling. And, to say the truth, the Reader will have but too good reason to remark, before he gets through the Poem, that it is one thing to tell the Spirit of Dulness to depart; and another to get rid of her in reality. Like *Glendower's* Spirits, any one may order them away; 'but will they go, when you do order them?'

But let us suppose for a moment that the Parnassian decree is obeyed; and, according to the letter of the *Order* (which is as precise and wordy as if Justice *Shallow* himself had drawn it) that the obnoxious female is sent back to the place of her birth,

> 'Mongst horrid shapes, shrieks, sights, &c.

At which we beg our fair readers not to be alarmed; for we can assure them they are only words of course in all poetical Instruments of this nature, and mean no more than the 'force of arms' and 'instigation of the Devil' in a common Instrument.

This nuisance then being abated; we are left at liberty to contemplate a character of a different complexion, 'buxom, blithe, and debonair': one who, although evidently a great favourite of the Poet's, and therefore to be received with all due courtesy, is notwithstanding introduced under the suspicious description of an *alias*.

> In heaven, ycleped *Euphrosyne*;
> And by men, heart-easing Mirth.

Judging indeed from the light and easy deportment of this gay Nymph; one might guess there were good reasons for a change of name as she changed her residence. . . .

But how are we to understand the stage directions?

> *Come*, and trip it as you *go*.

Are the words used synonymously? Or is it meant that this airy gentry shall come in a Minuet step, and go off in a Jig?

The phenomenon of a *tripping crank* is indeed novel, and would doubtless attract numerous spectators.

But it is difficult to guess to whom, among this jolly company, the Poet addresses himself: for immediately after the Plural appellative *you*, he proceeds:

> And in *thy* right hand lead with *thee*
> The mountain Nymph, sweet Liberty.

No sooner is this fair damsel introduced; but Mr M., with most unbecoming levity, falls in love with her: and makes a request of her companion which is rather greedy, that he may live with both of them.

> To live with her, and live with thee.

Even the gay libertine who sang 'How happy could I be with either!' did not go so far as this. But we have already had occasion to remark on the laxity of Mr M.'s amatory notions.

The Poet, intoxicated with the charms of his Mistress, now rapidly runs over the pleasures which he proposes to himself in the enjoyment of her society. But though he has the advantage of being his own caterer, either his palate is of a peculiar structure, or he has not made the most judicious selection.

> To begin the day well, he will have the *sky-lark*
> to come in *spite of sorrow*
> And at his window bid 'Good Morrow!'

The sky-lark, if we know anything of the nature of that bird, must come 'in spite' of something else as well as 'of sorrow', to the performance of this office.

In the next image, the Natural History is better preserved; and, as the thoughts are appropriate to the time of day, we will venture to transcribe the passage, as a favourable specimen of the Author's manner:

> While the Cock, with lively din,
> Scatters the rear of darkness thin,
> And to the stack, or the barn door,
> Stoutly struts his dames before;
> Oft listening how the hounds and horn
> Cheerly rouse the slumbering morn,
> From the side of some hoar hill,
> Through the high wood echoing still.

Is it not lamentable that, after all, whether it is the Cock, or the Poet, that listens, should be left entirely to the Reader's conjectures? Perhaps also his embarrassment may be increased by a slight resemblance of character in these two illustrious Personages, at least as far as relates to the extent and numbers of their seraglio. . . .

Upon the whole, Mr *Milton* appears to be possessed of some fancy and talent for rhyming; two most dangerous endowments which often unfit men for acting a useful part in life without qualifying them for that which is great and brilliant. If it be true, as we have heard, that he has declined advantageous prospects in business, for the sake of indulging his poetical humour; we hope it is not yet too late to prevail upon him to retract his resolution. With the help of *Cocker* and common industry, he may become a respectable Scrivener: but it is not all the *Zephyrs*, and *Auroras*, and *Corydons*, and *Thyrsis's*; aye, nor his 'junketing Queen *Mab*' and 'drudging Goblins', that will ever make him a Poet.

> *Advice to a Young Reviewer, with a Specimen of the*
> *Art* 1807

[This excellent piece of parody does not, perhaps, bear much relation to Milton. But it seemed to deserve a place somewhere, because it shows that reviewers in the early nineteenth century were forming a definite manner for unfavourable reviews—in some ways rather a good one. Copleston was probably writing with an eye on the critiques in the *British Critic*, a periodical founded in 1793, and very influential

between that time and about 1812. It was not until later that
the Edinburgh critics adopted the same manner. But it is well
worth remembering that this parody was written ten years
before the famous review of Keats which it so closely resem-
bles—even in the cruel injunction to adopt some more useful
way of earning a living. Surely Keats was well able to perceive
that what was there said of himself was rather part of a literary
convention than a personal attack—at any rate, this weighs
a little on the side of the view that he did not die of that review,
but of Koch's bacillus. And it is a good thing to read this
parody before you attempt to assess the real effect and *tone*
of the reviews in the *Edinburgh* and *Blackwood's*]

COLERIDGE

Although it was and is my intention to defer the consideration of Milton's own character to the conclusion of this
Lecture, yet I could not prevail on myself to approach the
Paradise Lost without impressing on your minds the conditions under which such a work was in fact producible at all,
the original genius having been assumed as the immediate
agent and efficient cause; and these conditions I find in the
character of the times and in his own character. The age in
which the foundations of his mind were laid, was congenial
to it as one golden aera of profound erudition and individual
genius—that in which the superstructure was carried up was
no less favourable to it by a sternness of discipline and a show
of self-control, highly flattering to the imaginative dignity of
an heir of fame, and which won Milton over from the dear-
loved delights of academic groves and cathedral aisles to the
anti-prelatic party. It acted on him, too, no doubt, and modified his studies by a characteristic controversial spirit (his pre-
sentation of God is tinted with it)—a spirit not less busy indeed
in political than in theological and ecclesiastical dispute, but
carrying on the former almost always, more or less, in the
guise of the latter. And so far as Pope's censure of our poet—
that he makes God the Father a school divine—is just, we must
attribute it to the character of his age, from which the men of

genius, who escaped, escaped by a worse disease, the licentious indifference of a Frenchified court.

Such was the *nidus* or soil, which constituted, in the strict sense of the word, the circumstances of Milton's mind. In his mind itself there were purity and piety absolute; an imagination to which neither the past nor the present were interesting, except as far as they called forth and enlivened the great ideal, in which and for which he lived; a keen love of truth, which, after many weary pursuits, found a harbour in a sublime listening to the still voice in his own spirit, and as keen a love of his country, which, after a disappointment still more depressive, expanded and soared into a love of man as a probationer of immortality. These were, these alone could be, the conditions under which such a work as the *Paradise Lost* could be conceived and accomplished. . . .

The character of Satan is pride and sensual indulgence, finding in self the sole motive of action. It is the character so often seen *in little* on the political stage. It exhibits all the restlessness, temerity, and cunning which have marked the mighty hunters of mankind from Nimrod to Napoleon. The common fascination of men is, that these great men, as they are called, must act from some great motive. Milton has carefully marked in his Satan the intense selfishness, the alcohol of egotism, which would rather reign in hell than serve in heaven. To place this lust of self in opposition to denial of self or duty, and to show what exertions it would make, and what pains endure to accomplish its end, is Milton's particular object in the character of Satan. But around this character he has thrown a singularity of daring, a grandeur of sufferance, and a ruined splendour, which constitute the very height of poetic sublimity.

Lastly, as to the execution:

The language and versification of the *Paradise Lost* are peculiar in being so much more necessarily correspondent to each than those in any other poem or poet. The connexion of the sentences and the position of the words are exquisitely artificial; but the position is rather according to the logic of passion or universal logic, than to the logic of grammar. Milton attempted to make the English language obey the logic of passion as perfectly as the Greek and Latin. Hence the occasional harshness in the construction.

Sublimity is the pre-eminent characteristic of the *Paradise Lost*. It is not an arithmetical sublime like Klopstock's, whose rule always is to treat what we might think large as contemptibly small. Klopstock mistakes bigness for greatness. There is a greatness arising from images of effort and daring, and also from those of moral endurance; in Milton both are united. The fallen angels are human passions, invested with a dramatic reality.

In the description of Paradise itself you have Milton's sunny side as a man; here his descriptive powers are exercised to the utmost, and he draws deep upon his Italian resources. In the description of Eve, and throughout this part of the poem, the poet is predominant over the theologian. Dress is the symbol of the Fall, but the mark of intellect; and the metaphysics of dress are, the hiding what is not symbolic and displaying by discrimination what is. The love of Adam and Eve in Paradise is of the highest merit—not phantomatic, and yet removed from everything degrading. It is the sentiment of one rational being towards another made tender by a specific difference in that which is essentially the same in both; it is a union of opposites, a giving and receiving mutually of the permanent in either, a completion of each in the other.

Milton is not a picturesque, but a musical poet; although he has this merit that the object chosen by him for any particular foreground always remains prominent to the end, enriched, but not incumbered, by the opulence of descriptive details furnished by an exhaustless imagination. I wish the *Paradise Lost* were more carefully read and studied than I can see any ground for believing it is, especially those parts which from the habit of always looking for a story in poetry, are scarcely read at all—as for example, Adam's vision of future events in the 11th and 12th books. No one can rise from the perusal of this immortal poem without a deep sense of the grandeur and the purity of Milton's soul, or without feeling how susceptible of domestic enjoyments he really was, notwithstanding the discomforts which actually resulted from an apparently unhappy choice in marriage. He was, as every truly great poet has ever been, a good man; but finding it impossible to realize his own aspirations, either in religion, or politics, or society, he gave up his heart to the living spirit and light within him, and avenged himself on the world by enriching it with this record of his own transcendent ideal.

Lectures of 1818

The reader of Milton must be always on his duty: he is surrounded with sense; it rises in every line; every word is to the purpose. There are no lazy intervals: all has been considered and demands and merits observation. If this be obscurity, let it be remembered 'tis such a one as is complaisant to the reader: not that vicious obscurity, which proceeds from a muddled head.

From a commonplace book   1796?
(cf. Richardson on p. 109)

HAZLITT

Milton, therefore, did not write from casual impulse, but after a severe examination of his own strength, and with a resolution to leave nothing undone which it was in his power to do. He always labours, and almost always succeeds. He strives hard to say the finest things in the world, and he does say them. He adorns and dignifies his subject to the utmost: he surrounds it with every possible association of beauty or grandeur, whether moral, intellectual, or physical. He refines on his descriptions of beauty; loading sweets on sweets, till the sense aches at them; and raises his images of terror to a gigantic elevation, that 'makes Ossa like a wart'. In Milton, there is always an appearance of effort: in Shakespeare, scarcely any.

Milton has borrowed more than any other writer, and exhausted every source of imitation, sacred or profane; yet he is perfectly distinct from every other writer. He is a writer of centos, and yet in originality scarcely inferior to Homer. The power of his mind is stamped on every line. The fervour of his imagination melts down and renders malleable, as in a furnace, the most contradictory materials. In reading his works, we feel ourselves under the influence of a mighty intellect, that the nearer it approaches to others, becomes more distinct from them. The quantity of art in him shews the strength of his genius: the weight of his intellectual obligations would have oppressed any other writer. Milton's learning has the effect of intuition. He describes objects, of which he could only have read in books, with the vividness of actual observation. His imagination has the force of nature. He makes words tell as pictures.

> Him followed Rimmon, whose delightful seat
> Was fair Damascus, on the fertile banks
> Of Abbana and Pharpar, lucid streams.

The word *lucid* here gives to the idea all the sparkling effect of the most perfect landscape. . . .

We might be tempted to suppose that the vividness with which he describes visible objects, was owing to their having acquired an unusual degree of strength in his mind, after the privation of his sight; but we find the same palpableness and truth in the descriptions which occur in his early poems. In *Lycidas* he speaks of 'the great vision of the guarded mount', with that preternatural weight of impression with which it would present itself suddenly to 'the pilot of some small night-foundered skiff': and the lines in the *Penseroso*, describing 'the wandering moon':

> Riding near her highest noon,
> Like one that had been led astray
> Through the heaven's wide pathless way,

are as if he had gazed himself blind in looking at her. There is also the same depth of impression in his descriptions of the objects of all the different senses, whether colours, or sounds, or smells—the same absorption of his mind in whatever engaged his attention at the time. It has been indeed objected to Milton, by a common perversity of criticism, that his ideas were musical rather than picturesque, as if because they were in the highest degree musical, they must be (to keep the sage critical balance even, and to allow no one man to possess two qualities at the same time) proportionately deficient in other respects. But Milton's poetry is not cast in any such narrow, commonplace mould; it is not so barren of resources. His worship of the Muse was not so simple or confined. A sound arises 'like a steam of rich distilled perfumes'; we hear the pealing organ, but the incense on the altars is also there, and the statues of the gods are ranged around! The ear indeed predominates over the eye, because it is more immediately affected, and because the language of music blends more immediately with, and forms a more natural accompaniment to, the variable and indefinite associations of ideas conveyed by words. But where the associations of the imagination are not the principal thing, the individual object is given by Milton with equal force and beauty. . . .

Force of style is one of Milton's greatest excellences. Hence, perhaps, he stimulates us more in the reading, and less afterwards. The way to defend Milton against all impugners, is to take down the book and read it.

Milton's blank verse is the only blank verse in the language (except Shakspeare's) that deserves the name of verse. . . .

Of Adam and Eve it has been said, that the ordinary reader can feel little interest in them, because they have none of the passions, pursuits, or even relations of human life, except that of man and wife, the least interesting of all others, if not to the parties concerned, at least to by-standers. . . . It is true, there is little action in this part of Milton's poem; but there is much repose, and more enjoyment. . . .

On Shakspeare and Milton 1818

KEATS

Here I must think Wordsworth is deeper than Milton, though I think it has depended more upon the general and gregarious advance of intellect, than individual greatness of Mind. From the *Paradise Lost* and the other works of Milton,

I hope it is not too presuming, even between ourselves, to say that his Philosophy, human and divine, may be tolerably understood by one not much advanced in years. In his time englishmen were just emancipated from a great superstition, and Men had got hold of certain points and resting places in reasoning which were too newly born to be doubted, and too much opposed by the Mass of Europe not to be thought etherial and authentically divine—who could gainsay his ideas on virtue, vice, and Chastity in *Comus* just at the time of the dismissal of Cod-pieces and a hundred other disgraces? who would not rest satisfied with his hintings at good and evil in the *Paradise Lost*, when just free from the inquisition and burning in Smithfield? The Reformation produced such immediate and great benefits, that Protestantism was considered under the immediate eye of heaven, and its own remaining Dogmas and superstitions, then, as it were, regenerated, constituted those resting places and seeming sure points of Reasoning—from that I have mentioned, Milton, whatever he may have thought in the sequel, appears to have been content with these by his writings. He did not think into the human heart, as Wordsworth has done. Yet Milton as a Philosopher, had sure as great powers as Wordsworth. What is then to be inferr'd? O many things. It proves there is really a grand march of intellect. It proves that a mighty providence subdues the mightiest Minds to the service of the time being, whether it be in human Knowledge or Religion.

Letter 1818

The *Paradise Lost* though so fine in itself is a corruption of our Language—it should be kept as it is unique—a curiosity —a beautiful and grand Curiosity. The most remarkable Production of the world. A northern dialect accommodating itself to greek and latin inversions and intonations. The purest english I think—or what ought to be the purest—is Chatterton's. The Language had existed long enough to be entirely uncorrupted of Chaucer's gallicisms, and still the old words are used. Chatterton's language is entirely northern. I prefer the native music of it to Milton's cut by feet. I have but lately stood on my guard against Milton. Life to him would be death to me. Miltonic verse cannot be written but is the verse of art. I wish to devote myself to another sensation.

Letter 1819

SHELLEY

Milton's poem contains within itself a philosophical refutation of that system, of which, by a strange and natural antithesis, it has been a chief popular support. Nothing can exceed the energy and magnificence of the character of Satan as expressed in *Paradise Lost*. It is a mistake to suppose that he could ever have been intended for the popular personification of evil. Implacable hate, patient cunning, and a sleepless refinement of device to inflict the extremest anguish on an enemy, these things are evil; and, although venial in a slave, are not to be forgiven in a tyrant; although redeemed by much that ennobles his defeat in one subdued, are marked by all that dishonours his conquest in the victor. Milton's Devil as a moral being is as far superior to his God, as one who perseveres in some purpose which he has conceived to be excellent in spite of adversity and torture, is to one who in the cold security of undoubted triumph inflicts the most horrible revenge upon his enemy, not from any mistaken notion of inducing him to repent of a perseverance in enmity, but with the alleged design of exasperating him to deserve new torments. Milton has so far violated the popular creed (if it shall be judged to be a violation) as to have alleged no superiority of moral virtue to his God over his Devil. And his bold neglect of a moral purpose is the most decisive proof of the supremacy of Milton's genius.

A Defence of Poetry 1821

MACAULAY

It is by his poetry that Milton is best known; and it is of his poetry that we wish first to speak. By the general suffrage of the civilised world, his place has been assigned among the greatest masters of the art. . . .

The most striking characteristic of the poetry of Milton is the extreme remoteness of the associations by means of which it acts on the reader. Its effect is produced, not so much by what it expresses, as by what it suggests; not so much by the ideas which it directly conveys, as by other ideas which are connected with them. He electrifies the mind through conductors. The most unimaginative man must understand the Iliad. Homer gives him no choice, and requires from him no exertion, but takes the whole upon himself, and sets the images in so clear a light, that it is impossible to be blind to them. The works of Milton cannot be comprehended or enjoyed, unless the mind of the reader co-operate with that of the writer. He does not paint a finished picture, or play for a mere passive listener. He sketches, and leaves others to fill up the outline. He strikes a key-note, and expects his hearer to make out the melody.

We often hear of the magical influence of poetry. The expression in general means nothing; but, applied to Milton, it is most appropriate. His poetry acts like an incantation. Its merit lies less in its obvious meaning than in its occult power. There would seem, at first sight, to be no more in his words than in other words. But they are words of enchantment. No sooner are they pronounced than the past is present and the distant near. New forms of beauty start at once into existence, and all the burial-places of the memory give up their dead. Change the structure of the sentence; substitute one synonyme for another, and the whole effect is destroyed. The spell loses its power; and he who should then hope to conjure with it would find himself as much mistaken as Cassim in the Arabian tale, when he stood crying, 'Open Wheat', 'Open Barley', to the door which obeyed no sound but 'open Sesame'. The miserable failure of Dryden in his attempt to translate into his own diction some parts of the *Paradise Lost*, is a remarkable instance of this.

In support of these observations we may remark, that scarcely any passages in the poems of Milton are more generally known or more frequently repeated than those which are little more than muster-rolls of names. They are not always more appropriate or more melodious than other names. But they are charmed names. Every one of them is the first link in a long chain of associated ideas. Like the dwelling-place of our infancy revisited in man-hood, like the song of our country heard in a strange land, they produce upon us an effect wholly independent of their intrinsic value. One transports us back to a remote period of history. Another places us among the novel scenes and manners of a distant region. A third evokes all the dear classical recollections of childhood, the school-room, the dog-eared Virgil, the holiday, and the prize. A fourth brings before us the splendid phantoms of chivalrous romance, the trophied lists, the embroidered housings, the quaint devices, the haunted forests, the enchanted gardens, the achievements of enamoured knights, and the smiles of rescued princesses.

The poetry of Milton differs from that of Dante as the hieroglyphics of Egypt differed from the picture-writing of Mexico. The images which Dante employs speak for themselves; they stand simply for what they are. Those of Milton have a signification which is often discernible only to the initiated. Their value depends less on what they directly represent than on what they remotely suggest. However strange, however grotesque, may be the appearance which Dante undertakes to describe, he never shrinks from describing it. He gives us the shape, the colour, the sound, the smell, the taste; he counts the numbers; he measures the size. His similes are the illustrations of a traveller. Unlike those of other poets, and especially of Milton, they are introduced in a plain, business-like manner; not for the sake of any beauty in the objects from which they are drawn; not for the sake of any ornament which they may impart to the poem; but simply in order to make the meaning of the writer as clear to the reader as it is to himself. The ruins of the precipice which led from the sixth to the seventh circle of hell were like those of the rock which fell into the Adige on the south of Trent. The cataract of Phlegethon was like that of Aqua Cheta at the monastery of St. Benedict. The place where the heretics were confined in burning tombs resembled the vast cemetery of Arles.

Now let us compare with the exact details of Dante the

dim intimations of Milton. We will cite a few examples. The English poet has never thought of taking the measure of Satan. He gives us merely a vague idea of vast bulk. In one passage the fiend lies stretched out huge in length, floating many a rood, equal in size to the earth-born enemies of Jove, or to the sea-monster which the mariner mistakes for an island. When he addresses himself to battle against the guardian angels, he stands like Teneriffe or Atlas: his stature reaches the sky. Contrast with these descriptions the lines in which Dante has described the gigantic spectre of Nimrod. 'His face seemed to me as long and as broad as the ball of St. Peter's at Rome; and his other limbs were in proportion; so that the bank, which concealed him from the waist downwards, nevertheless showed so much of him, that three tall Germans would in vain have attempted to reach to his hair. . . .'

Once more, compare the lazar-house in the eleventh book of the *Paradise Lost* with the last ward of Malebolge in Dante. Milton avoids the loathsome details, and takes refuge in indistinct but solemn and tremendous imagery. Despair hurrying from couch to couch to mock the wretches with his attendance. Death shaking his dart over them, but, in spite of supplications, delaying to strike. What says Dante? 'There was such a moan there as there would be if all the sick who, between July and September, are in the hospitals of Valdichiana, and of the Tuscan swamps, and of Sardinia, were in one pit together; and such a stench was issuing forth as is wont to issue from decayed limbs. . . .'

Poetry which relates to the beings of another world ought to be at once mysterious and picturesque. That of Milton is so. . . .

The spirits of Milton are unlike those of almost all other writers, his fiends, in particular, are wonderful creations. They are not metaphysical abstractions. They are not wicked men. They are not ugly beasts. They have no horns, no tails, none of the fee-faw-fum of Tasso and Klopstock. They have just enough in common with human nature to be intelligible to human beings. . . .

Milton 1825

E

BLAKE

The reason Milton wrote in fetters when he wrote of Angels & God, and at liberty when of Devils and Hell, is because he was a true Poet and of the Devils party without knowing it.

The Marriage of Heaven and Hell 1827

DE QUINCEY

I, if abruptly called upon in that summary fashion to convey a *commensurate* idea of Milton, one which might at once correspond to his pretensions, and yet be readily intelligible to the savage, should answer perhaps thus: Milton is not an author amongst authors, not a poet amongst poets, but a power amongst powers; and the *Paradise Lost* is not a book amongst books, not a poem amongst poems, but a central force amongst forces. . . .

If the man had failed, the power would have failed. In that mode of power which he wielded, the function was exhausted in the man—the species was identified with the individual—the poetry was incarnated in the poet.

Let it be remembered, that, of all powers which act upon man through his intellectual nature, the very rarest is that which we moderns call the *sublime*. . . .

Laying this one insulated case apart [the *Prometheus* of Aeschylus], and considering that the Hebrew poetry of Isaiah and Ezekiel, as having the benefit of inspiration, does not lie within the just limits of competition, we may affirm that there is no human composition which can be challenged as constitutionally sublime—sublime equally by its conception and by its execution, or as uniformly sublime from first to last, excepting the *Paradise Lost*. In Milton only does this great agency blaze and glow as a furnace kept up to a white heat—without suspicion of collapse. . . .

The first of these two charges respects a supposed pedantry, or too ambitious display of erudition. It is surprising to us that such an objection should have occurred to any man: both

because, after all, the quantity of learning cannot be great for
which any poem can find an opening; and because, in any poem
burning with concentrated fire, like the Miltonic, the passion
becomes a law to itself, and will not receive into connection
with itself any parts so deficient in harmony as a cold ostentation of learned illustrations must always have been found.
Still, it is alleged that such words as *frieze, architrave, cornice,
zenith,* &c., are words of art, out of place amongst the primitive
simplicities of Paradise, and at war with Milton's purpose of
exhibiting the paradisiacal state.

Now, here is displayed broadly the very perfection of
ignorance, as measured against the very perfection of what
may be called poetic science. We will lay open the true purpose
of Milton by a single illustration. In describing impressive
scenery as occurring in a hilly or a woody country, everybody
must have noticed the habit which young ladies have of using
the word *amphitheatre*: 'amphitheatre of woods', 'amphitheatre of hills'—these are their constant expressions. Why?
Is it because the word *amphitheatre* is a Grecian word? We
question if one young lady in twenty knows that it is; and very
certain we are that no word would recommend itself to her use
by that origin, if she happened to be aware of it. The reason
lurks here: In the word *theatre* is contained an evanescent
image of a great audience, of a populous multitude. Now, this
image—half-withdrawn, half-flashed upon the eye, and combined with the word *hills* or *forests*—is thrown into powerful
collision with the silence of hills, with the solitude of forests;
each image, from reciprocal contradiction, brightens and
vivifies the other. The two images act, and react, by strong
repulsion and antagonism.

This principle I might exemplify and explain at great
length; but I impose a law of severe brevity upon myself.
And I have said enough. Out of this one principle of subtle
and lurking antagonism may be explained everything which
has been denounced under the idea of pedantry in Milton.
It is the key to all that lavish pomp of art and knowledge
which is sometimes put forward by Milton in situations of
intense solitude, and in the bosom of primitive nature—as, for

example, in the Eden of his great poem, and in the Wilderness of his *Paradise Regained*. The shadowy exhibition of a regal banquet in the desert draws out and stimulates the sense of its utter solitude and remotion from men or cities. The images of architectural splendour suddenly raised in the very centre of Paradise, as vanishing shows by the wand of a magician, bring into powerful relief the depth of silence and the unpopulous solitude which possess this sanctuary of man whilst yet happy and innocent. Paradise could not in any other way, or by any artifice less profound, have been made to give up its essential and differential characteristics in a form palpable to the imagination. As a place of rest, it was necessary that it should be placed in close collision with the unresting strife of cities; as a place of solitude, with the image of tumultuous crowds; as the centre of mere natural beauty in its gorgeous prime, with the images of elaborate architecture and of human workmanship; as a place of perfect innocence in seclusion, that it should be exhibited as the antagonist pole to the sin and misery of social man.

Such is the covert philosophy which governs Milton's practice and which might be illustrated by many scores of passages from both the *Paradise Lost* and the *Paradise Regained*.

For instance, this is the key to that image in the *Paradise Regained* where Satan, on first emerging into sight, is compared to an old man gathering sticks, 'to warm him on a winter's day.' This image, at first sight, seems little in harmony with the wild and awful character of the supreme fiend. No; it is *not* in harmony, nor is it meant to be in harmony. On the contrary, it is meant to be in antagonism and intense repulsion. The household image of old age, of human infirmity, and of domestic hearths, are all meant as a machinery for provoking and soliciting the fearful idea to which they are placed in collision, and as so many repelling poles.

On Milton 1839

Milton was not an extensive or discursive thinker, as Shakespeare was; for the motions of his mind were slow—

solemn—sequacious, like those of the planets; not agile and assimilative; not attracting all things within its own sphere; not multiform; repulsion was the law of his intellect; he moved in solitary grandeur. Yet merely from this quality of grandeur —unapproachable grandeur—his intellect demanded a large infusion of Latinity into his diction. For the same reason (and without such aids, he would have had no proper element in which to move his wings), he enriched his diction with Hellenisms and with Hebraisms; but never, as could be easy to show, without a full justification in the result. Two things may be asserted of all his exotic idioms—first, that they express what could not have been expressed by any native idiom; second, that they harmonize with the English language, and give a colouring of the antique, but not any sense of strangeness to the diction. Thus, in the double negative—'nor did they not perceive', &c., which is classed as a Hebraism—if any man fancy that it expresses no more than the simple affirmative, he shows that he does not understand its force; and, at the same time, it is a form of thought so natural and universal, that I have heard English people, under corresponding circumstances, spontaneously fall into it. In short, whether a man differs from others by greater profundity or by greater sublimity, and whether he write as a poet or as a philosopher, in any case, he feels, in due proportion to the necessities of his intellect, an increasing dependence upon the Latin section of the English language.

Autobiography of an English Opium-Eater 1835

LEIGH HUNT

Milton was a very great poet second only (if second) to the very greatest, such as Dante and Shakspeare; and, like all great poets, equal to them in particular instances. He had no pretensions to Shakspeare's universality; his wit is dreary; and (in general) he had not the faith in things that Homer and Dante had, apart from the intervention of words. He could not let them speak for themselves without helping them with his learning. In all he did, after a certain period of youth (not to speak it irreverently), something of the schoolmaster is visible; and a gloomy religious creed removes him still farther from the universal gratitude and delight of mankind. He is understood, however, as I have just intimated, to have given this up before he died. He had then run the circle of his knowledge, and probably come round to the wiser, more cheerful, and more poetical beliefs of his childhood. . . .

. . . upon the same principle on which nature herself loves joy better than grief, health than disease, and a general amount of welfare than the reverse (urging men towards it where it does not prevail, and making many a form of discontent itself but a mode of pleasure and self-esteem), so Milton's great poem never has been, and never can be popular (sectarianism apart) compared with his minor ones; nor does it, in the very highest sense of popularity, deserve to be. It does not work out the very piety it proposes; and the piety which it does propose wants the highest piety of an intelligible charity and reliance. Hence a secret preference for his minor poems, among the truest and selectest admirers of *Paradise Lost*—perhaps with all who do not admire power in any shape above truth in the best; hence Warton's fond edition of them, delightful for its luxurious heap of notes and parallel passages; and hence the pleasure of being able to extract the finest of them, without misgiving, into a volume like the present.

Imagination and Fancy   1844

Dr Johnson would have us believe, that *Lycidas* is 'not the effusion of real passion'.—'Passion', says he, in his usual conclusive tone (as if the force of critic could no further go), 'plucks no berries from the myrtle and ivy; nor calls upon Arethuse and Mincius, nor tells of rough Satyrs and Fauns with cloven heel. Where there is leisure for fiction, there is little grief.' This is only a more genteel common-place, brought in to put down a vulgar one. Dr Johnson, like most critics, had no imagination; and because he found nothing natural to his own impulses in the associations of poetry, and saw them so often abused by the practice of versifiers inferior to himself, he was willing to conclude, that on natural occasions they were always improper. But a poet's world is as real to him as the more palpable one to people in general. He spends his time in it as truly as Dr Johnson did his in Fleet-street or at the club. Milton felt that the happiest hours he had passed with his friend had been passed in the regions of poetry. He had been accustomed to be transported with him 'beyond the visible diurnal sphere' of his fire-side and supper-table, things which he could record nevertheless with a due relish. (See the *Epitaphium Damonis*) The next step was to fancy himself again among them, missing the dear companion of his walks; and then it is that the rivers murmur complainingly, and the flowers hang their heads—which to a truly poetical habit of mind, though to no other, they may literally be said to do, because such is the aspect which they present to an afflicted imagination. 'I see nothing in the world but melancholy,' is the common phrase with persons who are suffering under a great loss. With ordinary minds in this condition, the phrase implies a vague feeling, but still an actual one. The poet, as in other instances, gives it a life and particularity. The practice has doubtless been abused; so much so, that even some imaginative minds may find it difficult at first to fall in with it, however beautifully managed. But the very abuse shows that it is founded on a principle in nature. And a great deal depends upon the character of the poet. What is mere frigidity and affectation in common magazine rhymers, or men of wit and fashion about town, becomes another thing in minds accustomed to live in the sphere I spoke of. It was as unreasonable in Dr. Johnson to sneer at Milton's grief in *Lycidas*, as it was reasonable in him to laugh at Prior and Congreve for comparing Chloe to Venus and Diana, and *pastoralizing* about Queen Mary. Neither the turn of their genius, nor their habits of life, included this sort of ground. We feel that Prior should have stuck to his tuckers and boddices, and Congreve appeared in his proper Court-mourning.

From *The Examiner*, 1822 (Attributed to Leigh Hunt)

LANDOR

Southey. . . . In the *Paradise Lost* no principal character seems to have been intended. There is neither truth nor wit however in saying that Satan is hero of the piece, unless, as is usually the case in human life, he is the greatest hero who gives the widest sway to the worst passions. It is Adam who acts and suffers most, and on whom the consequences have most influence. This constitutes him the main character; although Eve is the most interesting, Satan the more energetic, and on whom the greater force of poetry is displayed. The Creator and his angels are quite secondary.

Landor. Must we not confess that every epic hitherto has been defective in plan; and even that each, until the time of Tasso, was more so than its predecessors? Such stupendous genius, so much fancy, so much eloquence, so much vigor of intellect, never were united as in *Paradise Lost*. Yet it is neither so correct nor so varied as the *Iliad*, nor, however important the action, so interesting. The moral itself is the reason why it wearies even those who insist on the necessity of it. Founded on an event believed by nearly all nations, certainly by all who read the poem, it lays down a principle which concerns every man's welfare, and a fact which every man's experience confirms: that great and irremediable misery may arise from apparently small offences. But will any one say that, in a poetical view, our certainty of moral truth in this position is an equivalent for the uncertainty *which* of the agents is what critics call the hero of the piece?

Imaginary Conversation between Southey and Landor 1846

BAGEHOT

These are the two contrasts which puzzle us at first in Milton, and which distinguish him from other poets in our remembrance afterwards. We have a superficial complexity in illustration, and imagery, and metaphor: and in contrast with it we observe a latent simplicity of idea, an almost rude strength of conception. The underlying thoughts are few, though the flowers on the surface are so many. We have like-wise the perpetual contrast of the soft poetry of the memory, and the firm, as it were fused, and glowing poetry of the imagination. His words, we may half fancifully say, are like his character. There is the same austerity in the real essence, the same exquisiteness of sense, the same delicacy of form which we know that he had, the same music which we imagine there was in his voice. In both his character and his poetry there was an ascetic nature in a sheath of beauty. . . .

. . . the great error which pervades *Paradise Lost*. Satan is made *interesting*. . . . The interest of Satan's character is at its height in the first two books. Coleridge justly compared it to that of Napoleon. There is the same pride, the same Satanic ability, the same will, the same egotism. . . . Few Englishmen feel a profound reverence for Napoleon I. There was no French alliance in *his* time; we have most of us some tradition of antipathy to him. Yet hardly any Englishman can read the account of the campaign of 1814 without feeling his interest for the emperor to be strong, and without perhaps being conscious of a latent wish that he may succeed. Our opinion is against him, our serious wish is of course for England; but the imagination has a sympathy of its own, and will not give place. We read about the great general—never greater than in that last emergency—showing resources of genius that seem almost infinite, and that assuredly have never been surpassed, yet vanquished, yielding to the power of circumstances, to the combined force of adversaries, each of whom singly he out-matches in strength, and all of whom together he surpasses in majesty and in mind. Something of the same sort of interest belongs to the Satan of the first two books of *Paradise Lost*. We know that he will be vanquished; his name is not a recom-mendation. Still we do not take the same interest in them that we do in him; our sympathies, our fancy, are on his side.

Perhaps much of this was inevitable; yet what a defect it is! especially what a defect in Milton's own view, and looked at with the stern realism with which he regarded it! Suppose that the author of evil in the universe were the most attractive being in it; suppose that the source of all sin were the origin of all interest to us!

John Milton 1859

In the most exciting parts of Wordsworth—and these sonnets are not very exciting—you always feel, you never forget, that what you have before you is the excitement of a recluse. There is nothing of the stir of life; nothing of the *brawl* of the world. But Milton, though always a scholar by trade, though solitary in old age, was through life intent on great affairs, lived close to great scenes, watched a revolution, and if not an actor in it, was at least secretary to the actors. He was familiar—by daily experience and habitual sympathy—with the earnest debate of arduous questions, on which the life and death of the speakers certainly depended, on which the weal or woe of the country perhaps depended. He knew how profoundly the individual character of the speakers—their inner and real nature—modifies their opinion on such questions; he knew how surely that nature will appear in the expression of them. This great experience, fashioned by a fine imagination, gives to the debate of Satanic Council in Pandaemonium its reality and its life. It is a debate in the Long Parliament, and though the *theme* of *Paradise Lost* obliged Milton to side with the monarchical element in the universe, his old habits are often too much for him; and his real sympathy—the impetus and energy of his nature—side with the rebellious element. For the purposes of art this is much better.

Of a court, a poet can make but little; of a heaven, he can make very little; but of a courtly heaven, such as Milton conceived, he can make nothing at all. The idea of a court and the idea of a heaven are so radically different, that a distinct combination of them is always grotesque and often ludicrous. *Paradise Lost*, as a whole, is radically tainted by a vicious principle. It professes to justify the ways of God to man, to account for sin and death, and it tells you that the whole originated in a *political event*; in a court squabble as to a particular act of patronage and the due or undue promotion of an eldest son. Satan may have been wrong, but on Milton's theory he had an *arguable* case at least. There was something arbitrary in the promotion; there were little symptoms of a job; in *Paradise Lost* it is always clear that the devils are the weaker, but it is never clear that the angels are the better. Milton's sympathy and his imagination slip back to the Puritan rebels whom he loved, and desert the courtly angels whom he could not love, although he praised them. There is no wonder that Milton's hell is better than his heaven, for he hated officials and he loved rebels, for he employs his genius below, and accumulates his pedantry above. On the great debate in Pandaemonium all his genius is concentrated. . . .

Mr Pitt knew Belial's speech by heart, and Lord Macaulay has called it incomparable; and these judges of the oratorical art have well decided. A mean foreign policy cannot be better defended. Its sensibleness is effectually explained, and its tameness as much as possible disguised.

But we have not here to do with the excellence of Belial's policy, but with the excellence of his speech; and with that speech in a peculiar manner. This speech, taken with the few lines of description with which Milton introduces them, embodies, in as short a space as possible, with as much perfection as possible, the delineation of a type of character common at all times, dangerous in many times; sure to come to the surface in moments of difficulty, and never more dangerous than then. As Milton describes it, it is one among several *typical* characters which will ever have their place in great councils, which will ever be heard at important decisions, which are part of the characteristic and inalienable whole of this statesmanlike world. The debate in Pandaemonium is a debate among these typical characters at the greatest conceivable crisis, and with adjuncts of solemnity which no other situation could rival. It is the greatest *classical* triumph, the highest achievement of the *pure* style in English literature; it is the greatest description of the highest and most typical characters with the most choice circumstances and in the fewest words.

Art in English Poetry 1864

ARNOLD

If to our English race an inadequate sense for perfection of work is a real danger, if the discipline of respect for a high and flawless excellence is peculiarly needed by us, Milton is of all our gifted men the best lesson, the most salutary influence. In the sure and flawless perfection of his rhythm and diction he is as admirable as Virgil or Dante, and in this respect he is unique amongst us. No one else in English literature and art possesses the like distinction. . . .

That Milton, of all our English race, is by his diction and rhythm the one artist of the highest rank in the great style whom we have; this I take as requiring no discussion, this I take as certain.

The mighty power of poetry and art is generally admitted. But where the soul of this power, of this power at its best, chiefly resides, very many of us fail to see. It resides chiefly in the refining and elevation wrought in us by the high and rare excellence of the great style. We may feel the effect without being able to give ourselves clear account of its cause, but the thing is so. Now, no race needs the influence mentioned, the influences of refining and elevation, more than ours; and in poetry and art our grand source for them is Milton.

To what does he owe this supreme distinction? To nature first and foremost, to that bent of nature for inequality which to the worshippers of the average man is so unacceptable; to a gift, a divine favour. 'The older one grows,' says Goethe, 'the more one prizes natural gifts, because by no possibility can they be procured and stuck on.' Nature formed Milton to be a great poet. But what other poet has shown so sincere a sense of the grandeur of his vocation, and a moral effort so constant and sublime to make and keep himself worthy of it? The Milton of religious and political controversy, and perhaps of domestic life also, is not seldom disfigured by want of amenity, by acerbity. The Milton of poetry, on the other hand, is one of those great men 'who are modest'—to quote a fine remark of Leopardi—'who are modest, because they continually compare themselves, not with other men, but with that idea of the perfect which they have before their mind'. The Milton of poetry is the man, in his own magnificent phrase, of 'devout prayer to that Eternal Spirit that can enrich with all utterance and knowledge, and sends out his Seraphim with the hallowed fire of his altar, to touch and purify the lips of whom he pleases'. And finally, the Milton of poetry is, in his own words again, the man of 'industrious and select reading'. Continually he lived in companionship with high and rare excellence, with the great Hebrew poets and prophets, with the great poets of Greece and Rome. The Hebrew compositions were not in verse, and can be not inadequately represented by the grand, measured prose of our English Bible. The verse of the poets of Greece and Rome no translation can adequately reproduce. Prose cannot have the power of verse; verse-translation may give whatever of charm is in the soul and talent of the translator himself, but never the specific charm of the verse and poet translated. In our race are thousands of readers, presently there will be millions, who know not a word of Greek and Latin, and will never learn those languages. If this host of readers are ever to gain any sense of the power and charm of the great poets of antiquity, their way to gain it is not through translations of the ancients, but through the original poetry of Milton, who has the like power and charm, because he has the like great style.

Through Milton they may gain it, for, in conclusion, Milton is English; this master in the great style of the ancients is English . . . Milton has made the great style no longer an exotic here; he has made it an inmate amongst us, a leaven, and a power.

Milton 1888

RALEIGH

We are deceived by names; the more closely *Paradise Lost* is studied, the more does the hand of the author appear in every part. The epic poem, which in its natural form is a kind of cathedral for the ideas of a nation, is by him transformed into a chapel-of-ease for his own mind, a monument to his own genius and his own habits of thought. . . .

In Milton's poetry we find ourselves in a remote atmosphere; far indeed from the shrewd observation of daily life, farther even from that wonderful analysis of emotion which is the pastime of Shakespeare and Meredith. Beautiful figured writing and keen psychological observation of this kind are beside the purpose of Milton, and beyond his power.

For the time we must forgo the attempt to see into the life of things, and must accept in imagination our position as citizens in this strange majestic commonwealth of angels and men. . . .

In the poem itself signs are not wanting that Milton felt the terrible strain imposed upon him by the intense and prolonged abstraction of his theme—its unreality and superhuman elevation. Some of the comparisons that he chooses to illustrate scenes in Hell are taken from the incidents of simple rustic life, and by their contrasts with the lurid creatures of his imagination come like a draught of cold water to a traveller in a tropical waste of sand and thorns. It is almost as if the poet himself were oppressed by the suffocation of the atmosphere that he has created, and, gasping for breath, sought relief by summoning up to remembrance the sweet security of pastoral life. . . .

Paradise Lost will not bear—it could at no time, not even in the most theological of ages, have borne—the more searching tests of realism, of verisimilitude, and credibility. It is all the greater skill in the poet that by his careful handling of our imagination and feeling he actually does produce 'that willing suspension of disbelief for the moment which constitutes poetic faith'. The less it will endure the trial as a system or theory of the universe, the more wonderful does it appear as a work of art. By the most delicate skill of architecture this gigantic filamented structure has been raised into the air. It looks like some enchanted palace that has lighted on the ground for a moment, resting in its flight. It is really the product of the most elaborate and careful engineering science;

the strains and stresses put on every part of the material have been calculated and allowed for. The poise and balance are so minutely exact that it just stands, and no more. But that it should stand at all is the marvel, seeing that it is spanned on frail arches over the abyss of the impossible, the unnatural, and the grotesque.

Milton 1900

KER

There is another consideration. Various abstract forms have attraction for poets. One of the uses of such an enquiry as this, of an attempt like this to discriminate and define, is that it helps in distinguishing the motives of poets, and the influences that have swayed them in their work. Take for example the poetry of Milton. In Milton, if anywhere, we may hope to find the study and the accomplishment of poetical form. We do find it, and at the same time we discover the play in his mind of all sorts of abstract unbodied poetical forms, unsubstantial yet vital forces, that contribute to the completed unalterable work. He is haunted by poetical forms in all the different senses of the word. There is the abstract form of Tragedy. It is with him all his life—something distinct from his recollection of any particular Tragedy—an abstract scheme, which at last at the end of his life he succeeds in filling up. *Samson Agonistes* has many meanings; among other things it is the repetition or the expression of a certain form with which Milton's mind was occupied and to which he attached great value. Part of the zest of writing the poem was in giving embodiment to an abstract ideal form.

So also in *Paradise Lost*. It was perhaps specially characteristic of Milton's age—of the literature and literary men of his age—to be devoted to these abstract forms. (It is not necessary to ask at present whether this was a weakness or not.) Many foolish people entertained this view: but also Milton held it, and his epics are written in order to carry out the principles of epic poetry; they have other motives, but this is one of them. Milton was influenced by all the epic poets whom he had read, but he was also influenced by something in their poetry to which none of them could exclusively lay claim—by the abstract or ideal pattern which he recognised behind and above their particular exemplifications of it, and which he believed in as something permanent and universal.

Form and Style in Poetry   1914–15

ELIOT

The comparative study of English versification at various periods is a large tract of unwritten history. To make a study of blank verse alone would be to elicit some curious conclusions. It would show, I believe, that blank verse within Shakespeare's lifetime was more highly developed, that it became the vehicle of more varied and more intense feeling than it has ever conveyed since; and that after the erection of the Chinese Wall of Milton, blank verse suffered not only arrest but retrogression.

Christopher Marlowe   1918

Milton's celestial and infernal regions are large but insufficiently furnished apartments filled by heavy conversation; and one remarks about the Puritan mythology its thinness.

William Blake   1920

While it must be admitted that Milton is a very great poet indeed, it is something of a puzzle to decide in what his greatness consists. On analysis, the marks against him appear both more numerous and more significant than the marks to his credit. As a man, he is antipathetic. Either from the moralist's point of view, or from the theologian's point of view, or from the psychologist's point of view, or from that of the political philosopher, or judging by the ordinary standards of likeableness in human beings, Milton is unsatisfactory. The doubts which I have to express about him are more serious than these. His greatness as a poet has been sufficiently celebrated, though I think largely for the wrong reasons, and without the proper reservations. His misdeeds as a poet have been called attention to, as by Mr Ezra Pound, but usually in passing. What seems to me necessary is to assert at the same time his greatness—in what he could do well he did better than any one else has ever done it—and the serious charges to be made against him, in respect of the deterioration—the peculiar kind of deterioration—to which he subjected the language . . .

There is a large class of persons, including some who appear in print as critics, who regard any censure upon a 'great' poet as a breach of the peace, as an act of wanton iconoclasm, or even hoodlumism. The kind of derogatory criticism that I have to make upon Milton is not intended for such persons, who cannot understand that it is more important, in some vital respects, to be a *good* poet than to be a *great* poet; and of what I have to say I consider that the only jury of judgement is that of the ablest poetical practitioners of my own time.

The most important fact about Milton, for my purposes, is his blindness. I do not mean that to go blind in middle life is itself enough to determine the whole nature of a man's poetry. Blindness must be considered in conjunction with Milton's personality and character, and the peculiar education which he received. It must also be considered in connexion with his devotion to, and expertness in, the art of music. Had Milton been a man of very keen senses—I mean of *all* the five senses—his blindness would not have mattered so much. But for a man whose sensuousness, such as it was, had been withered early by book-learning, and whose gifts were naturally aural, it mattered a great deal. It would seem, indeed, to have helped him to concentrate on what he could do best.

At no period is the visual imagination conspicuous in Milton's poetry. It would be as well to give a few illustrations of what I mean by visual imagination. From *Macbeth*:

> This guest of summer,
> The temple-haunting martlet, does approve
> By his loved mansionry that the heaven's breath
> Smells wooingly here: no jutty, frieze,
> Buttress, nor coign of vantage, but this bird
> Hath made his pendant bed and procreant cradle:

> Where they most breed and haunt, I have observed
> The air is delicate.

It may be observed that such an image, as well as another familiar quotation from a little later in the same play,

> Light thickens, and the crow
> Makes wing to the rooky wood

not only offer something to the eye, but, so to speak, to the common sense. I mean that they convey the feeling of being in a particular place at a particular time. The comparison with Shakespeare offers another indication of the peculiarity of Milton. With Shakespeare, far more than with any other poet in English, the combinations of words offer perpetual novelty; they enlarge the meaning of the individual words joined: thus 'procreant cradle', 'rooky wood'. In comparison, Milton's images do not give this sense of particularity, nor are the separate words developed in significance. His language is, if one may use the term without disparagement, *artificial* and *conventional*.

> O'er the smooth *enamelled* green . . .
> . . . paths of this drear wood
> The nodding horror of whose shady brows
> Threats the forlorn and wandering passenger.

('Shady brow' here is a diminution of the value of the two words from their use in the line from *Dr Faustus*

> Shadowing more beauty in their airy brows)

The imagery in *L'Allegro* and *Il Penseroso* is all general:

> While the ploughman near at hand,
> Whistles o'er the furrowed land,
> And the milkmaid singeth blithe,
> And the mower whets his scythe,
> And every shepherd tells his tale
> Under the hawthorn in the dale.

It is not a particular ploughman, milkmaid, and shepherd
that Milton sees (as Wordsworth might see them); the sensuous effect of these verses is entirely on the ear, and is joined
to the concepts of ploughman, milkmaid, and shepherd. Even
in his most mature work, Milton does not infuse new life into
the word, as Shakespeare does.

> The sun to me is dark
> And silent as the moon,
> When she deserts the night
> Hid in her vacant interlunar cave.

Here *interlunar* is certainly a stroke of genius, but is merely
combined with 'vacant' and 'cave', rather than giving and
receiving life from them. Thus it is not so unfair, as it might
at first appear, to say that Milton writes English like a dead
language. The criticism has been made with regard to his
involved syntax. But a tortuous style, when its peculiarity is
aimed at precision (as with Henry James), is not necessarily
a dead one; only when the complication is dictated by a demand
of verbal music, instead of by any demand of sense. . . .

A disadvantage of the rhetorical style appears to be, that a
dislocation takes place, through the hypertrophy of the
auditory imagination at the expense of the visual and tactile,
so that the inner meaning is separated from the surface, and
tends to become something occult, or at least without effect
upon the reader until fully understood. To extract everything
possible from *Paradise Lost*, it would seem necessary to read it
in two different ways, first solely for the sound, and second for
the sense. The full beauty of his long periods can hardly be
enjoyed while we are wrestling with the meaning as well;
and for the pleasure of the ear the meaning is hardly necessary,
except in so far as certain key-words indicate the emotional
tone of the passage. Now Shakespeare, or Dante, will bear
innumerable readings, but at each reading all the elements of
appreciation can be present. There is no interruption between
the surface that these poets present to you and the core. While,
therefore, I cannot pretend to have penetrated to any 'secret'

of these poets, I feel that such appreciation of their work as I am capable of points in the right direction; whereas I cannot feel that my appreciation of Milton leads anywhere outside of the mazes of sound. That, I feel, would be the matter for a separate study, like that of Blake's prophetic books; it might be well worth the trouble, but would have little to do with my interest in the poetry. So far as I perceive anything, it is a glimpse of a theology that I find in large part repellent, expressed through a mythology which would have better been left in the Book of Genesis, upon which Milton has not improved. There seems to me to be a division, in Milton, between the philosopher or theologian and the poet; and, for the latter, I suspect also that this concentration upon the auditory imagination leads to at least an occasional levity. I can enjoy the roll of

> . . . Cambalu, seat of Cathaian Can
> And Samarcand by Oxus, Temir's throne,
> To Paquin of Sinaean kings, and thence
> To Agra and Lahor of great Mogul
> Down to the golden Chersonese, or where
> The Persian in Ecbatan sate, or since
> In Hispahan, or where the Russian Ksar
> In Mosco, or the Sultan in Bizance,
> Turchestan-born . . .

and the rest of it, but I feel that this is not serious poetry, not poetry fully occupied about its business, but rather a solemn game. More often, admittedly, Milton uses proper names in moderation, to obtain the same effect of magnificence with them as does Marlowe—nowhere perhaps better than in the passage from *Lycidas*:

> Whether beyond the stormy Hebrides,
> Where thou perhaps under the whelming tide
> Visit'st the bottom of the monstrous world;
> Or whether thou to our moist vows deny'd,
> Sleep'st by the fable of Bellerus old,
> Where the great vision of the guarded Mount
> Looks toward Namancos and Bayona's hold

than which, for the single effect of grandeur of sound, there is nothing finer in poetry. . . .

But there are two attitudes both of which are necessary and right to adopt in considering the work of any poet. One is when we isolate him, when we try to understand the rules of his own game, adopt his own point of view: the other, perhaps less usual, is when we measure him by outside standards, most pertinently by the standards of language and of something called Poetry, in our own language and in the whole history of European literature. It is from the second point of view that my objections to Milton are made: it is from this point of view that we can go so far as to say that, although his work realizes superbly one important element in poetry, he may still be considered as having done damage to the English language from which it has not wholly recovered.

A Note on the Verse of John Milton   1936

The essence of the permanent censure of Milton is, I believe, to be found in Johnson's essay. This is not the place in which to examine certain particular and erroneous judgments of Johnson; to explain his condemnation of *Comus* and *Samson* as the application of dramatic canons which to us seem inapplicable; or to condone his dismissal of the versification of *Lycidas* by the specialisation, rather than the absence, of his sense of rhythm. Johnson's most important censure of Milton is contained in three paragraphs, which I must ask leave to quote in full.

[These three paragraphs are on p. 114 of this selection. They begin 'Through all his greater works there prevails an uniform peculiarity of *Diction*' and end 'like other lovers, we find grace in its deformity']

This criticism seems to me substantially true: indeed, unless we accept it, I do not think we are in the way to appreciate the peculiar greatness of Milton. His style is not a *classic* style, in that it is not the elevation of a *common* style, by the final touch of genius, to greatness. It is, from the foundation, and in every particular, a personal style, not based upon common speech, or common prose, or direct communication of meaning. Of some great poetry one has difficulty in pronouncing just what it is, what infinitesimal touch, that has made all the difference from a plain statement which anyone could make; the slight transformation which, while it leaves a plain statement a plain statement, has always the maximal, never the minimal, alteration of ordinary language. Every distortion of construction, the foreign idiom, the use of a word in a foreign way or with the meaning of the foreign word from which it is derived rather than the accepted meaning in English, every idiosyncrasy is a particular act of violence which Milton has been the first to commit. There is no cliché, no poetic diction in the derogatory sense, but a perpetual sequence of original acts of lawlessness. Of all modern writers of verse, the nearest analogy seems to me to be Mallarmé, a much smaller poet, though still a great one. The personalities, the poetic theories of the two men could not have been more different; but in respect of the violence which they could do to language, and justify, there is a remote similarity. Milton's poetry is poetry at the farthest possible remove from prose; his prose seems to me too near to half-formed poetry to be good prose.

To say that the work of a poet is at the farthest possible remove from prose would once have struck me as condemnatory: it now seems to me simply, when we have to do with a Milton, the precision of its peculiar greatness. As a poet, Milton seems to me probably the greatest of all eccentrics. His work illustrates no general principles of good writing; the only principles of writing which it illustrates are such as are valid only for Milton himself to observe. . . .

I repeat that the remoteness of Milton's verse from ordinary speech, his invention of his own poetic language, seems to me one of the marks of his greatness. Other marks are his sense of structure, both in the general design of *Paradise Lost* and *Samson*, and in his syntax; and finally, and not least, his inerrancy, conscious or unconscious, in writing so as to make the best display of his talents, and the best concealment of his weaknesses.

The appropriateness of the subject of *Samson* is too obvious to expatiate upon: it was probably the one dramatic story out of which Milton could have made a masterpiece. But the complete suitability of *Paradise Lost* has not, I think, been so often remarked. It was surely an intuitive perception of what he could not do that arrested Milton's project of an epic on King Arthur. For one thing, he had little interest in, or understanding of, individual human beings. In *Paradise Lost* he was not called upon for any of that understanding which comes from an affectionate observation of men and women. But such an interest in human beings was not required—indeed its *absence* was a necessary condition—for the creation of his figures of Adam and Eve. These are not a man and woman such as any we know: if they were, they would not be Adam and Eve. They are the original *Man* and *Woman*, not types, but prototypes. They have the general characteristics of men and women, such that we can recognize, in the temptation and the fall, the first motions of the faults and virtues, the abjection and the nobility, of all their descendants. They have ordinary humanity to the right degree, and yet are not, and should not be, ordinary mortals. Were they more particularized they would be false, and if Milton had been more interested in humanity, he could not have created them. Other critics have remarked upon the exactness, without defect or exaggeration, with which Moloch, Belial, and Mammon, in the second book, speak according to the particular sin which each represents. It would not be suitable that the infernal powers should have, in the human sense, characters, for a character is always mixed; but in the hands of an inferior manipulator, they might easily have been reduced to *humours*.

The appropriateness of the material of *Paradise Lost* to the genius and limitations of Milton, is still more evident when we consider the visual imagery. I have already remarked, in a paper written some years ago, on Milton's weakness of visual observation, a weakness which I think was always present

—the effect of his blindness may have been rather to strengthen the compensatory qualities than to increase a fault which was already present. Mr Wilson Knight, who has devoted close study to recurrent imagery in poetry, has called attention to Milton's propensity towards images of engineering and mechanics; to me it seems that Milton is at his best in imagery suggestive of vast size, limitless space, abysmal depth, and light and darkness. No theme and no setting, other than that which he chose in *Paradise Lost*, could have given him such scope for the kind of imagery in which he excelled, or made less demand upon those powers of visual imagination which were in him defective.

Most of the absurdities and inconsistencies to which Johnson calls attention, and which, so far as they can justly be isolated in this way, he properly condemns, will I think appear in a more correct proportion if we consider them in relation to this general judgment. I do not think that we should attempt to *see* very clearly any scene that Milton depicts: it should be accepted as a shifting phantasmagoria. To complain, because we first find the arch-fiend 'chain'd on the burning lake', and in a minute or two see him making his way to the shore, is to expect a kind of consistency which the world to which Milton has introduced us does not require. . . .

Bridges catalogues the systematic irregularities which give perpetual variety to Milton's verse, and I can find no fault with his analysis. But however interesting these analyses are, I do not think that it is by such means that we gain an appreciation of the peculiar rhythm of a poet. It seems to me also that Milton's verse is especially refractory to yielding up its secrets to examination of the single line. For his verse is not formed in this way. It is the period, the sentence and still more the paragraph, that is the unit of Milton's verse; and emphasis on the line structure is the minimum necessary to provide a counter-pattern to the period structure. It is only in the period that the wave-length of Milton's verse is to be found: it is his ability to give a perfect and unique pattern to every paragraph, such that the full beauty of the line is found in its context, and his ability to work in larger musical units than any other poet—

that is to me the most conclusive evidence of Milton's supreme mastery. The peculiar feeling, almost a physical sensation of a breathless leap, communicated by Milton's long periods, and by his alone, is impossible to procure from rhymed verse. Indeed, this mastery is more conclusive evidence of his intellectual power, than is his grasp of any *ideas* that he borrowed or invented. To be able to control so many words at once is the token of a mind of most exceptional energy.

Milton II   1947

WILLIAMS

The general opposition resolved itself into four statements: (i) that Milton was a bad man; (ii) that Milton was, especially, a proud man and was continually writing approvingly about his own pride (Blake's incorrect epigram—that Milton 'was of the devil's party without knowing it'—was generally used here); (iii) that Milton's verse is hard, sonorous, and insensitive; (iv) that Milton's subject was remote and uninteresting. This being almost exactly what the orthodox party had been, for centuries, saying with admiration, they were quite helpless when they found it said with contempt. The solemn rituals in praise of Milton were suddenly profaned by a change of accent, but the choruses had not altered; what then were the pious worshippers to do?

There had been, of course, another possibility all along; it may be put very briefly by saying that Milton was not a fool. The peculiar ignorance of Christian doctrine which distinguished most of the academic Chairs and of the unacademic journalists who had been hymning Milton had not prevented them from arguing about the subtle theological point of the Nature of the Divine Son in *Paradise Lost*. The peculiar opposition to high speculations on the nature of chastity felt in both academic and unacademic circles had prevented any serious appreciation of that great miracle of the transmutation of the flesh proposed in *Comus*. And the peculiar ignorance of morals also felt everywhere had enabled both circles to assume that Milton might be proud and yet that he might not at the same time believe that pride was wrong and foolish. It was never thought that, if he sinned, he might repent, and that his repentance might be written as high in his poetry as, after another manner, Dante's in his. Finally, it was not supposed in either of those circles, that Satan could be supposed to be Satan, and therefore a tempter; that Christ (in *Paradise Regained*) could be supposed to hold human culture a poor thing in comparison with the salvation of the soul; or that Samson, in the last great poem, could in fact reach a point of humility at which he could bring himself occasionally to protest like Job against the apparent dealings of God with the soul.

I have said nothing here against the explicit denial to Milton of any drama or of any humanity. Those denials, as well as the others, had been consecrated by custom and a false *pietas*. Yet there was no need for them. The great and sensitive poetry of that august genius had escaped his admirers. 'Milton,' said Landor, 'wrote English like a learned language'; no one had thought it worth while to learn it as a living language. All *Paradise Lost* was supposed to be an image of pride; and yet much of *Paradise Lost* can be felt to revolve, laughingly and harmoniously, round the solemn and helpless image of pride. To discuss this in full would need a volume. All that can be done here is to dwell on a few chief points in the discussion of *Paradise Lost*, with one or two comments on the other poems. And we may begin with *Comus*.

Comus is a kind of philosophical ballet. Comus himself is, no doubt, a black enchanter, but he talks the most beautiful poetry, and he does not seriously interrupt the dance of the three young creatures opposed to him, with their heavenly attendant: there is a particular evasion of violence (when Comus is 'driven in'). But what is this ritual ballet about? It is about an attempted outrage on a Mystery. The mystery which Comus desires to profane is the Mystery of Chastity. It is no use trying to deal with *Comus* and omitting chastity; *Hamlet* without the Prince would be an exciting melodrama compared to the result of that other eviction. Chastity (not only, though perhaps chiefly, that particular form of it which is Virginity;

'it will be observed that Sabrina, the chaste goddess, is particularly favourable to herds and shepherd life) is the means, in *Comus*, by which all evils are defeated, the flesh is transmuted, and a very high and particular Joy ensured. It may be true that we ourselves do not believe that to be so, but our disbelief is largely as habitual as our admiration of *Comus*. That is why it has been possible to admire *Comus* without any serious realization of the mystery of chastity, in spite of John Milton.

> To him that dares
> Arm his profane tongue with contemptuous words
> Against the Sun-clad power of Chastity,
> Fain would I something say, yet to what end?

And that, as one may say, is that. Comus is a fool in these matters, and

> worthy that thou should'st not know
> More happiness than is thy present lot.

But the Lady and her brothers and the Attendant Spirit and Sabrina do know. They know that Chastity is the guardian and protector of fruitfulness, that Temperance is the means of intense Joy. In their eyes Comus, by refusing to admit the general principle of things and to be obedient to it, is foolishly and sinfully limiting the nature of Joy. He prefers drunkenness to the taste of wine and promiscuousness to sensitiveness. He knows nothing about that other power which can make the flesh itself immortal; he prefers to sit about in sepulchres. Let him, cries the whole lovely dance.

Obedience then and Joy are the knowledge, in their degree, of those three Youths of *Comus*. And *Paradise Lost*, following long after, did not forget its prelude. It dealt with the same subject, but differently. Obedience, in the longer poem, is no longer that of a particular devotion to a particular law; it is the proper order of the universe in relation to a universal law, the law of self-abnegation in love. This, like chastity, is a mystery, but a mystery so simple that only the two sublimely innocent figures of Adam and Eve—beautiful, august, pure, and lucid—are able to express it; they, and the glowing fires of the celestial hierarchy; they, and beyond them the passionate deity of the Divine Son. It is not only a law—something that ought to be obeyed—but a fact—something that obeys and is obeyed. There remains, nevertheless, the possibility of disobedience to the law, of revolt against the fact. That disobedience depends on choice; and it is that choice on which the poem concentrates.

Comus had not gone so far. There is challenge there but no analysis of choice. Indeed, that is a problem which has been very rarely attacked in English verse. Generally the poets have confined themselves, sooner or later, to showing the decision; and certainly the actual motion of the will in its pure essence is inconceivable by the human imagination. Even Shakespeare, in *Macbeth*, when he reached that point, disguised it; Macbeth is half-determined; he asks if he will be safe; and when he is assured of safety he finds that he is wholly determined. But the actual decision is not there. . . .

Introduction to the English Poems of John Milton 1940

Dryden

Dryden's critical fortunes have on the whole been very equable. Apart from a short period in the early eighteenth century when the rising brilliance of Pope overshadowed him, there has been general agreement that he is a great, though a limited, poet. His historical position as the chief initiator of the classical period in English poetry has always been recognized; and it has also been generally felt that he was superior to all his successors in the classical style, with the possible exception of Pope. If Arnold pushed him a little lower, Mr Eliot has raised him a little higher than his usual place. But when he sinks again, as he will, he will not sink very far—only to a position among the most secure if not the most glorious.

A great deal of Dryden criticism takes the form of comparisons between him and Pope, and it has been difficult to decide whether these passages should be placed here or in the section of Pope criticism. I have tried to divide them justly and equally.

DRYDEN

Fanciful poetry and music, used with moderation, are good; but men who are wholly given over to either of them, are commonly as full of whimsies as diseased and splenetic men can be. Their heads are continually hot, and they have the same elevation of fancy sober, which men of sense have when they drink. So wine used moderately does not take away the judgment, but used continually debauches men's understandings, and turns them into sots, making their heads continually hot by accident, as the others are by nature; so, mere poets

157

and mere musicians are as sottish as mere drunkards are, who live in a continual mist, without seeing or judging any thing clearly.

A man should be learned in several sciences, and should have a reasonable, philosophical, and in some measure a mathematical head, to be a complete and excellent poet; and besides this, should have experience in all sorts of humours and manners of men; should be thoroughly skilled in conversation, and should have a great knowledge of mankind in general.

> Postscript to *The Notes and Observations on the Empress*
> *of Morocco* 1674

If anything of mine is good, it is my Mac-Fleckno; and I shall value myself the more on it, because it is the first piece of ridicule written in heroics.

> Reported by Pope in *Spence's Anecdotes*

. . . when it was in debate at Will's Coffee-house, what character he would have with posterity, he said, with a sullen modesty, 'I believe they will allow me to be a good versifier.'

> *Oldmixon, Essay on Criticism* 1728

ADDISON

But see where artful Dryden next appears,
Grown old in rhyme, but charming ev'n in years.
Great Dryden next, whose tuneful muse affords
The sweetest numbers, and the fittest words.
Whether in comic sounds or tragic airs
She forms her voice, she moves our smiles or tears.
If satire of heroic strains she writes,
Her hero pleases and her satire bites.
From her no harsh unartful numbers fall,
She wears all dresses, and she charms in all.

> *An Account of the Greatest English Poets* 1694

CONGREVE

I may venture to say in general Terms, that no Man hath written in our Language so much, and so various Matter, and in so various Manners, so well. Another thing I may say peculiar to him; which is, that his Parts did not decline with his Years: But that he was an improving Writer to his last, even to near seventy Years of Age; improving even in Fire and Imagination, as well as in Judgement. Witness his *Ode on St. Cecilia's Day*, and his *Fables*, his latest Performances. . . .

His Versification and his Numbers he could learn of no Body: For he first profess'd those Talents in Perfection in our Tongue. And they who have best succeeded in them since his Time, have been indebted to his Example; and the more they have been able to imitate him, the better they have succeeded.

As his Style in Prose is always specifically different from his Style in Poetry; so, on the other hand, in his Poems, his Diction is, where-ever his Subject requires it, so sublimely, and so truly Poetical, that its Essence, like that of pure Gold, cannot be destroy'd. Take his Verses, and divest them of their Rhimes, disjoint them in their Numbers, transpose their Expressions, make what Arrangement and Disposition you please of his Words, yet shall there Eternally be Poetry, and something which will be found incapable of being resolv'd into absolute Prose: An incontestable Characteristick of a truly poetical Genius.

Preface to Tonson's Edition 1715

DENNIS

. . . my departed friend, whom I infinitely esteemed when living for the solidity of his thought, for the spring and the warmth and the beautiful turn of it; for the power and variety and fulness of his harmony; for the purity, the perspicuity, the energy of his expression; and, whenever these great qualities are required, for the pomp and solemnity and majesty of his style.

Letter to Tonson 1715

POPE

Dryden always uses proper language, lively, natural, and fitted to the subject, it is scarce ever too high or too low; never, perhaps, except in his plays.

Spence's Anecdotes 1743

Waller was smooth; but Dryden taught to join
The varying verse, the full-resounding line,
The long majestick march, and energy divine.

Imitations of Horace: To Augustus 1737

JOHNSON

In a general survey of Dryden's labours he appears to have had a mind very comprehensive by nature, and much enriched with acquired knowledge. His compositions are the effects of a vigorous genius operating upon large materials.

The power that predominated in his intellectual operations was rather strong reason than quick sensibility. Upon all occasions that were presented he studied rather than felt, and produced sentiments not such as Nature enforces, but meditation supplies. With the simple and elemental passions, as they spring separate in the mind, he seems not much acquainted and seldom describes them but as they are complicated by the various relations of society and confused in the tumults and agitations of life. . . .

Dryden's was not one of the 'gentle bosoms'; Love, as it subsists in itself, with no tendency but to the person loved and wishing only for correspondent kindness, such love as shuts out all other interest, the Love of the Golden Age, was too soft and subtle to put his faculties in motion. He hardly conceived it but in its turbulent effervescence with some other desires; when it was inflamed by rivalry or obstructed by difficulties; when it invigorated ambition or exasperated revenge.

He is therefore, with all his variety of excellence, not often pathetick; and had so little sensibility of the power of effusions purely natural that he did not esteem them in others . . . he could more easily fill the ear with some splendid novelty than awaken those ideas that slumber in the heart.

The favourite exercise of his mind was ratiocination; and that argument might not be too soon at an end, he delighted to talk of liberty and necessity, destiny and contingence; these he discusses in the language of the school with so much profundity that the terms which he uses are not always understood. It is indeed learning, but learning out of place.

When once he had engaged himself in disputation, thoughts flowed in on either side: he was now no longer at a loss; he had always objections and solutions at command. . . .

Next to argument, his delight was in wild and daring sallies of sentiment, in the irregular and excentrick violence of wit. He delighted to tread upon the brink of meaning, where light and darkness begin to mingle; to approach the precipice of absurdity, and hover over the abyss of unideal vacancy. This inclination sometimes produced nonsense, which he knew, as

> Move swiftly, sun, and fly a lover's pace,
> Leave weeks and months behind thee in thy race.

>   Amariel flies . . .
> To guard thee from the demons of the air;
> My flaming sword above them to display,
> All keen, and ground upon the edge of day.

And sometimes it issued in absurdities, of which perhaps he was not conscious:

> Then we upon our orb's last verge shall go,
> And see the ocean leaning on the sky;
> From thence our rolling neighbours we shall know,
> And on the lunar world securely pry.

F

These lines have no meaning; but may we not say, in imitation of Cowley on another book:

'Tis so like *sense* 'twill serve the turn as well? . . .

He descends to display his knowledge with pedantick ostentation; as when, in translating Virgil, he says, 'tack to the larboard'—and 'veer starboard'; and talks, in another work, of 'virtue spooming before the wind'. . . .

He had a vanity, unworthy of his abilities, to show, as may be suspected, the rank of the company with whom he lived, by the use of French words, which had then crept into conversation; such as *fraicheur* for *coolness*, *fougue* for *turbulence*, and a few more, none of which the language has incorporated or retained. They continue only where they stood first, perpetual warnings to future innovators.

These are his faults of affectation; his faults of negligence are beyond recital. Such is the unevenness of his compositions that ten lines are seldom found together without something of which the reader is ashamed. Dryden was no rigid judge of his own pages; he seldom struggled after supreme excellence, but snatched in haste what was within his reach; and when he could content others, was himself contented. He did not keep present to his mind an idea of pure perfection; nor compare his works, such as they were, with what they might be made. He knew to whom he should be opposed. He had more musick than Waller, more vigour than Denham, and more nature than Cowley; and from his contemporaries he was in no danger. Standing therefore in the highest place he had no care to rise by contending with himself; but while there was no name above his own was willing to enjoy fame on the easiest terms.

He was no lover of labour. What he thought sufficient he did not stop to make better, and allowed himself to leave many parts unfinished, in confidence that the good lines would overbalance the bad. What he had once written he dismissed from his thoughts; and, I believe, there is no example to be found of any correction or improvement made by him after publication. The hastiness of his productions might be the effect of necessity; but his subsequent neglect could hardly have any other cause than impatience of study. . . .

Of Dryden's works it was said by Pope that 'he could select from them better specimens of every mode of poetry than any other English writer could supply'. Perhaps no nation ever produced a writer that enriched his language with such variety of models. To him we owe the improvement, perhaps the completion of our metre, the refinement of our language, and much of the correctness of our sentiments. By him we were taught 'sapere et fari', to think naturally and express forcibly. Though Davies has reasoned in rhyme before him, it may be perhaps maintained that he was the first who joined argument with poetry. He shewed us the true bounds of a translator's liberty. What was said of Rome, adorned by Augustus, may be applied by an easy metaphor to English poetry embellished by Dryden, 'lateritiam invenit, marmoream reliquit', he found it brick, and he left it marble.

Life of Dryden 1779

BEATTIE

Dryden's verse, though often faulty, has a grace, and a spirit, peculiar to itself. That of Pope is more correct, and perhaps upon the whole more harmonious; but it is in general more languid, and less diversified. Pope's numbers are sweet but elaborate; and our sense of their energy is in some degree interrupted by our attention to the art displayed in their contexture: Dryden's are natural and free; and, while they communicate their own sprightly motion to the spirits of the reader, hurry him along with a gentle and pleasing violence, without giving him time either to animadvert on their faults, or to analyse their beauties. Pope excels in solemnity of sound; Dryden, in an easy melody, and boundless variety of rhythm. In this last respect I think I could prove, that he is superior to all other English poets, Milton himself not excepted. Till Dryden appeared, none of our writers in rhime of that last century approached in any measure to Fairfax and Spenser. Of Waller, it can only be said that he is not harsh; of Denham and Cowley, if a few couplets were struck out of their works, we could not say so much. But in Dryden's hands, the English rhiming couplet assumed a new form; and seems hardly susceptible of any further improvement. One of the greatest poets of this century, the late and much-lamented Mr Gray of Cambridge, modestly declared to me, that if there was in his own numbers any thing that deserved approbation, he had learned it all from Dryden.

Critics have often stated a comparison between Dryden and Pope, as poets of the same order, and who differed only in *degree* of merit. But, in my opinion, the merit of the one differs considerably in *kind* from that of the other. Both were happy in a sound judgement and most comprehensive mind. Wit, and humour, and learning too, they seem to have possessed in equal measure; or, if Dryden may be thought to have gone deeper in the sciences, Pope must be allowed to have been the greater adept in the arts. The diversities in point of correctness and delicacy, which arose from their different ways of life, I do not now insist upon. But, setting those aside, if Dryden founds any claim of preference on the originality of his manner, we shall venture to affirm, that Pope may found a similar claim, and with equal justice, on the perfection of his taste; and that, if the critical writings of the first are more voluminous, those of the second are more judicious; if Dryden's inventions are more diversified, those of Pope are more regular, and more important. Pope's style may be thought to have less simplicity, less vivacity, and less of the purity of the mother-tongue; but it is at the same time more uniformly elevated, and less debased by vulgarism, than that of his great master—and the superior variety that animates the numbers of the latter, will perhaps be found to be compensated by the steadier and more majestic modulation of the former. Thus far their merits would appear to be pretty equally balanced. But if the opinion of those critics be true, who hold that the highest regions of Parnassus are appropriated to pathos and sublimity, Dryden must after all confess, that he has never ascended so far as his illustrious imitator: there being nothing in the writings of the first so deeply pathetic as the *Epistle of Eloisa*, or the *Elegy on the*

Unfortunate Lady; nor so uniformly sublime as the *Essay on Man*, or the *Pastoral of the Messiah*. This last is indeed but a selection and imitation of a choice passage; but it bespeaks a power of imitation, and a taste in selection, that Dryden does not seem to have possessed. To all which may I not be permitted to add, what I think I could prove, that the pathos of Homer is frequently improved by Pope, and that of Virgil very frequently debased by Dryden.

The writings of Dryden are stamped with originality, but are not always the better for that circumstance. Pope is an imitator professedly, and of choice; but to most of those whom he copies he is at least equal, and to many of them superior. . . . In the lyric style, he was no match for Dryden: but when he copies the manner of Virgil, and borrows the thoughts of Isaiah, Pope is superior not only to himself, but to almost all other poets.

On Poetry and Music   1776

COWPER

But I admire Dryden most, who has succeeded by mere dint of genius, and in spite of a laziness and a carelessness almost peculiar to himself. His faults are numberless, and so are his beauties. His faults are those of a great man, and his beauties are such (at least sometimes) as Pope with all his touching and retouching could never equal.

Letter to Unwin   5th January 1782

WORDSWORTH

I was much pleased to hear of your engagement with Dryden; not that he is, as a *Poet*, any great favourite of mine. I admire his talents and *Genius* greatly, but he is not a poetical genius. The only qualities I can find in Dryden that are *essentially* poetical are a certain ardour and impetuosity of mind with an excellent ear: it may seem strange that I do not add to this great command of language, too, as it is most

desirable that a Poet should possess, or rather, that he should
not be without; but it is not language that is in the high sense
of the word poetical, being neither of the imagination nor of
the passions; I mean of the amiable, the ennobling, of the
intense passions; I do not mean to say that there is nothing
of this in Dryden, but as little, I think, as is possible, considering how much he has written. You will easily understand
my meaning when I refer to his versification of *Palamon and
Arcite*, as contrasted with the language of Chaucer. Dryden
has neither a tender heart nor a lofty sense of moral dignity:
where his language is poetically impassioned, it is mostly
upon unpleasing subjects; such as the follies, vices, and crimes
of classes of men or of individuals. That his cannot be the
language of imagination must have necessarily followed from
this, that there is not a single image from Nature in the whole
body of his works; and in his translation from Virgil, whenever
Virgil can be fairly said to have his *eye* upon his object, Dryden
always spoils the passage. . . .

Letter to Scott　1805

SCOTT

The distinguishing characteristic of Dryden's genius seems
to have been the power of reasoning and of expressing the
result in appropriate language. This may seem slender praise;
yet those were the talents that led Bacon into the recesses of
philosophy, and conducted Newton to the cabinet of nature.
The prose works of Dryden bear repeated evidence to his
philosophical powers. His philosophy was not indeed of a
formed and systematic character; for he is often contented to
leave the path of argument which must have conducted him to
the fountain of truth, and to resort with indolence or indifference to the leaky cisterns which had been hewn out by
former critics. But where his pride or his taste are interested, he
shows evidently, that it was not deficiency in the power of
systematizing, but want of time and patience necessary to
form a system, which occasioned the discrepancy that we
often notice in his critical and philological disquisitions. This

power of ratiocination, of investigating, of discovering, and appreciating that which is really excellent, if accompanied with the necessary command of fanciful illustration, and elegant expression, is the most interesting quality which can be possessed by a poet. It must indeed have a share in the composition of everything that is truly estimable in the fine arts, as well as in philosophy. Nothing is so easily attained as the power of presenting the extrinsic qualities of fine painting, fine music, or fine poetry; the beauty of colour and outline, the combination of notes, the melody of versification, may be imitated by artists of mediocrity; and many will view, hear or peruse their performances, without being able to discover positively why they should not, since composed according to all the rules, afford pleasure equal to those of Raphael, Handel, or Dryden. The deficiency lies in the vivifying spirit, which like *alcohol*, may be reduced to the same principle in all the fine arts, though it assumes such varied qualities from the mode in which it is exerted or combined. Of this power of intellect, Dryden seems to have possessed almost an exuberant share, combined, as usual, with the faculty of correcting his own conceptions, by observing human nature, the practical and experimental philosophy as well of poetry as of ethics or physics. The early habits of Dryden's education and poetical studies gave his researches somewhat too much of a metaphysical character; and it was a consequence of his mental acuteness, that his dramatic personages often philosophized or reasoned, when they ought only to have felt. The more lofty, the fiercer, the more ambitious feelings, seem also to have been his favourite studies. Perhaps the analytical mode in which he exercised his studies of human life, tended to confine his observation to the more energetic feelings of pride, anger, ambition, and other high-toned passions.

Life of Dryden 1808

JEFFREY

The result seemed at one time suspended on the will of Dryden—in whose individual person the genius of the English and of the French schools of literature may be said to have maintained a protracted struggle. But the evil principle prevailed! Carried by the original bent of his genius, and his familiarity with our older models, to the cultivation of our native style, to which he might have imparted more steadiness and correctness—for in force and in sweetness it was already matchless—he was unluckily seduced by the attractions of fashion, and the dazzling of the dear wit and gay rhetoric in which it delighted, to lend his powerful aid to the new corruptions and refinements; and, in fact, to prostitute his great gifts for the purposes of party rage or licentious ribaldry.

Review of Scott's Swift 1816

HAZLITT

Dryden and Pope are the great masters of the artificial style of poetry in our language, as the poets of whom I have already treated, Chaucer, Spenser, Shakspeare, and Milton, were of the natural; and though this artificial style is generally and very justly acknowledged to be inferior to the other, yet those who stand at the head of that class, ought, perhaps, to rank higher than those who occupy an inferior place in a superior class. They have a clear and independent claim upon our gratitude, as having produced a kind and degree of excellence which existed equally nowhere else . . .

Dryden was a better prose-writer, and a bolder and more varied versifier than Pope. He was a more vigorous thinker, a more correct and logical declaimer, and had more of what may be called strength of mind than Pope; but he had not the same refinement and delicacy of feeling. Dryden's eloquence and spirit were possessed in a higher degree by others, and in nearly the same degree by Pope himself; but that by which Pope was distinguished, was an essence which he alone possessed, and of incomparable value on that sole account. Dryden's *Epistles* are excellent, but inferior to Pope's, though they appear (particularly the admirable one to Congreve) to have been the model on which the latter formed his. His *Satires* are better than Pope's. His *Absalom and Achitophel* is superior, both in force of invective and discrimination of character, to any thing of Pope's in the same way. The character of Achitophel is very fine; and breathes, if not a sincere love for virtue, a strong spirit of indignation against vice.

Mac Flecknoe is the origin of the idea of the *Dunciad*; but it is less elaborately constructed, less feeble, and less heavy. The difference between Pope's satirical portraits and Dryden's, appears to be this in a good measure, that Dryden seems to grapple with his antagonists, and to describe real persons; Pope seems to refine upon them in his own mind, and to make them out just what he pleases, till they are not real characters, but the mere driveling effusions of his spleen and malice. Pope describes the thing, and then goes on describing his own description till he loses himself in verbal repetitions. Dryden recurs to the object often, takes fresh sittings of nature, and gives us new strokes of character as well as of his pencil. . . .

Lectures on the English Poets   1818

Dryden stands nearly at the head of the second class of English poets, *viz.* the *artificial*, or those who describe the mixed modes of artificial life, and convey general precepts and abstract ideas. He had invention in the plan of his *Satires*, very little fancy, not much wit, no humour, immense strength of character, elegance, masterly ease, indignant contempt approaching to the sublime, not a particle of tenderness, but eloquent declamation, the perfection of uncorrupted English style, and of sounding, vehement, varied versification. The *Alexander's Feast*, his *Fables* and *Satires*, are his standard and lasting works.

A Critical List of Authors   1824

COLERIDGE

. . . Yet Cowley *was* a Poet, which, with all my unfeigned admiration of his vigorous sense, his agile logical wit, and his high excellencies of diction and metre, is more than (in the *strict* use of the term, Poet) I can conscientiously say of

Dryden. Only if Pope was a *Poet*, as Lord Byron swears, then Dryden, I admit, was a very *great* Poet.

Marginalia in Pepys 1825?

You will find this a good gage or criterion of genius—whether it progresses and evolves, or only spins upon itself. Take Dryden's Achitophel and Zimri—Shaftesbury and Buckingham; every line adds to or modifies the character, which is, as it were, a-building up to the last verse; whereas, in Pope's Timon, &c., the first two or three couplets contain all the pith of the character, and the twenty or thirty lines that follow are so much evidence or proof of overt acts of jealousy, or pride, or whatever it may be that is satirised.

Table Talk   August 6, 1832

Dryden's genius was of the sort which catches fire by its own motion; his chariot wheels *get* hot by driving fast.

Table Talk   November 1, 1833

MACAULAY

The first rank in poetry was beyond his reach; but he challenged and secured the most honourable place in the second. His imagination resembled the wings of an ostrich. It enabled him to run, though not to soar. When he attempted the highest flights, he became ridiculous; but, while he remained in a lower region, he out-stripped all competitors. . . .

The general soundness and healthfulness of his mental constitution, his information of vast superficies though of small volume, his wit scarcely inferior to that of the most distinguished followers of Donne, could not save him from disgraceful failure as a rival of Shakspeare, but raised him far above the level of Boileau. His command of language was immense. With him died the secret of the old poetical diction of England—the art of producing rich effects by familiar words.

In the following century, it was as completely lost as the Gothic method of painting glass, and was but poorly supplied by the laborious and tesselated imitations of Mason and Gray. On the other hand, he was the first writer under whose skilful management the scientific vocabulary fell into natural and pleasing verse. In this department, he succeeded as completely as his contemporary Gibbons succeeded in the similar enterprise of carving the most delicate flowers from heart of oak. The toughest and most knotty parts of language became ductile at his touch. His versification in the same manner, while it gave the first model of that neatness and precision which the following generation esteemed so highly, exhibited, at the same time, the last examples of nobleness, freedom, variety of pause, and cadence. His tragedies in rhyme, however worthless in themselves, had at least served the purpose of nonsense-verses; they had taught him all the arts of melody which the heroic couplet admits. For bombast, his prevailing vice, his new subjects gave little opportunity; his better taste gradually discarded it.

He possessed, as we have said, in a pre-eminent degree, the power of reasoning in verse; and this power was now peculiarly useful to him. His logic is by no means uniformly sound. On points of criticism, he always reasons ingeniously; and, when he is disposed to be honest, correctly. But the theological and political questions which he undertook to treat in verse were precisely those which he understood least. His arguments, therefore, are often worthless. But the manner in which they are stated is beyond all praise. The style is transparent. The topics follow each other in the happiest order. The objections are drawn up in such a manner that the whole fire of the reply may be brought to bear on them. The circumlocutions which are substituted for technical phrases are clear, neat, and exact. The illustrations at once adorn and elucidate the reasoning. The sparkling epigrams of Cowley, and the simple garrulity of the burlesque poets of Italy, are alternately employed, in the happiest manner, to give effect to what is obvious, or clearness to what is obscure. . . .

But he was perpetually acting against his better knowledge.

His sins were sins against light. He trusted that what was bad would be pardoned for the sake of what was good. What was good, he took no pains to make better. He was not, like most persons who rise to eminence, dissatisfied even with his best productions. He had set up no unattainable standard of perfection, the contemplation of which might at once improve and mortify him. His path was not attended by an unapproachable mirage of excellence, for ever receding, and for ever pursued. He was not disgusted by the negligence of others; and he extended the same toleration to himself. His mind was of a slovenly character—fond of splendour, but indifferent to neatness. Hence most of his writings exhibit the sluttish magnificence of a Russian noble, all vermin and diamonds, dirty linen and inestimable sables. Those faults which spring from affectation, time and thought in a great measure removed from his poems. But his carelessness he retained to the last. If towards the close of his life he less frequently went wrong from negligence, it was only because long habits of composition rendered it more easy to go right . . .

He may, on the whole, be pronounced to have been a man possessed of splendid talents, which he often abused, and of a sound judgment, the admonitions of which he often neglected; a man who succeeded only in an inferior department of his art, but who, in that department, succeeded pre-eminently; and who with a more independent spirit, a more anxious desire of excellence, and more respect for himself, would, in his own walk, have attained to absolute perfection.

John Dryden   1828

SOUTHEY

The age from Dryden to Pope is the worst age of English poetry.

Dryden himself lowered its tone, even while he improved the style of versification. He never aimed at any high mark. His good sense prevented him from over-valuing himself, and aspiring to become eminent either as a sublime or a pathetic poet. When he wrote for popular applause, he thought of the

public with the Romish priests, *populus vult decipi et deci-
pietur*; he knew that, on the stage, bombast might pass for
poetry, as tinsel served for gold; and confessing that there were
passages in his tragedies which called vengeance upon him for
their extravagance, and which he repented of among his sins,
he said, 'All I can say for those passages, is that I knew they
were bad enough to please, even when I wrote them.' In satire,
on the contrary, he felt his strength; and in that legislative or
didactic strain wherein he excelled all predecessors in his own
language, he has not been excelled by any who have followed
him. In this he addressed himself exclusively to the understanding; there was nothing for the imagination, nothing for
the feelings. But there was no mannerism in his style that could
be aped, no mechanism that could be discovered and imitated,
no artifices that could be copied, and not many of those
expressions and turns of phrase which they who mistake memory for invention might add to their stock of common places.
His ease, and vigour, and perspicuity were not attainable by
imitative talents.

Life of Cowper 1836

LANDOR

Chatting on deck was Dryden too,
The Bacon of the rhyming crew;
None ever crost our mystic sea
More richly stored with thought than he;
Tho' never tender nor sublime,
He wrestles with and conquers Time.

To Wordsworth 1846

. . . *St. Cecilia's* music-book is interlined with epigrams;
and *Alexander's Feast* smells of gin at second-hand, with true
Briton fiddlers full of native *talent* in the orchestra.

Imaginary Conversation between Southey and Landor
1846

DE QUINCEY

I admire Pope in the very highest degree; but I admire him as a pyrotechnic artist for producing brilliant and evanescent effects out of elements that have hardly a moment's life within them. There is a flash and a startling explosion, then there is a dazzling coruscation, all purple and gold; the eye aches under the suddenness of a display that, springing like a burning arrow out of darkness, rushes back into darkness with arrowy speed, and in a moment all is over. Like festal shows, or the hurrying music of such shows,

It *was*, and it is not.

Untruly, therefore, was it ever fancied of Pope, that he belonged by his classification to the family of the Drydens. Dryden had within him a principle of continuity which was not satisfied without lingering upon his own thoughts, brooding over them, and oftentimes pursuing them through their unlinkings with the *sequaciousness* (pardon a Coleridgian word) that belongs to some process of creative nature, such as the unfolding of a flower. But Pope was all jets and tongues of flame; all showers of scintillation and sparkle. Dryden followed, genially, an impulse of his healthy nature. Pope obeyed, spasmodically, an over-mastering febrile paroxysm.

Lord Carlisle on Pope 1851

ANON

The *Religio Laici* and the *Hind and the Panther* are the religious or argumentative poems of Dryden, as the *Absalom* and the *Medal* are instances of his political and literary satire. Viewed in relation to his earlier writings, these poems impress us with the ease with which his mind struck out new courses of thought, as its springs were gently touched by the agency of external events—and the grace with which the painter of an artificial and sensuous society rose to the dignity of the Christian philosopher. Dryden had already founded the satirical literature of his country. He had remained the almost undisputed master of the stage through a long period of general emulation. He had written the finest lyric verses of which that age could boast, and he was destined yet to write some of the finest lyric verses which the English language to this day possesses. Nor did it require the natural exhaustion of one train of ideas to develop another equally original and comprehensive. It is true that the period of life at which he first essayed his theological poetry was congenial to earnest reflection; as it was truly and beautifully written a century after Dryden's day, that

> The clouds which gather round the setting sun
> Do take a sober colouring from an eye
> That hath kept watch o'er man's mortality.

But the circumstances of his writings show that those writings were not generally suggested by the successive dominance of single phases of thought, exhibited in an ordinary course of mental progress. The springs of his imagination were essentially objective, as those of the imagination of Milton and of Byron were altogether subjective. They were almost invariably called into play by the artificial action of political events, which could not have presented a more than casual coincidence with the intrinsic action of the mental system. The varied talents of which Dryden gave proof at different periods of his life must, therefore, have been, for the most part, perpetually coexistent; and those circumstances which may be construed, in some degree, as his moral degradation, were his intellectual glory.

The Edinburgh Review 1855

LOWELL

His contemporary, Dr Heylin, said of French cooks, that 'their trade was not to feed the belly, but the palate'. Dryden was a great while in learning this secret, as available in good writing as in cookery. He strove after it, but his thoroughly

English nature, to the last, would too easily content itself with serving up the honest beef of his thought, without regard to daintiness of flavor in the dressing of it. Of the best English poetry, it might be said that it is understanding aerated by imagination. In Dryden, the solid part too often refused to mix kindly with the leaven, either remaining lumpish or rising to a hasty puffiness. Grace and lightness were with him much more a laborious achievement than a natural gift, and it is all the more remarkable that he should so often have attained to what seems such an easy perfection in both. Always a hasty writer, he was long in forming his style, and to the last was apt to snatch the readiest word rather than wait for the fittest. He was not wholly and unconsciously poet, but a thinker who sometimes lost himself on enchanted ground and was trans-figured by its touch. This preponderance in him of the reason-ing over the intuitive faculties, the one always there, the other flashing in when you least expect it, accounts for that inequality and even incongruousness in his writing which makes one revise one's judgement at every tenth page. . . .

Was he, then, a great poet? Hardly, in the narrowest definition. But he was a strong thinker who sometimes carried common sense to a height where it catches the light of a diviner air, and warmed reason till it had wellnigh the illuminating property of intuition. Certainly he is not, like Spenser, the poets' poet, but other men have also their rights. Even the Philistine is a man and a brother, and is entirely right so far as he sees. To demand more of him is to be unreasonable. And he sees, among other things, that a man who undertakes to write should first have a meaning perfectly defined to himself, and then should be able to set it forth clearly in the best words. This is precisely Dryden's praise, and amid the rickety senti-ment looming big through misty phrase which marks so much of modern literature, to read him is as bracing as a northwest wind. He blows the mind clear. In mind and manner his foremost quality is energy. In ripeness of mind and bluff heartiness of expression, he takes rank with the best. His phrase is always a short-cut to his sense, for his estate was too spacious for him to need that trick of winding the path of his thought about, and planting it out with clumps of epithet, by which the landscape-gardeners of literature give to a paltry half-acre the air of a park. In poetry, to be next-best is, in one sense, to be nothing; and yet to be among the first in any kind of writing, as Dryden certainly was, is to be one of a very small company. He had, beyond most, the gift of the right word. And if he does not, like one or two of the greatest masters of song, stir our sympathies by that indefinable aroma so magical in arousing the subtle associations of the soul, he has this in common with the few great writers, that the winged seeds of his thought embed themselves in the memory and germinate there.

John Dryden 1868

The judgment of our forefathers which assigned to Dryden the third or fourth place among English poets will not be corroborated by modern criticism. It would, indeed, be easy to frame, and to frame with unexceptionable correctness, a definition of poetry which should exclude, or nearly exclude, him from the right to be numbered among poets at all. Of imagination in the sensuous acceptation of the term he had little, in the higher acceptation of the term nothing. And if his genius is, to borrow an expression from Plato, without the power of the wing, it is almost equally deficient in most of those other qualities which constitute the essential distinction between poetry and rhetoric. It was neither finely touched nor finely tempered. It had little sense of the beautiful, of the pathetic, of the sublime, though it could juggle with their counterfeits. To say with Wordsworth that there is not a single image from Nature to be found in the whole body of his poetry would be to say what is not true; but it is true that such images are rare. The predominating power in Dryden was a robust, vigorous, and logical intellect, intensely active and extraordinarily versatile. In addition to this he possessed, or, to speak more properly, acquired, a singularly fine ear for the rhythm of verse, and a plastic mastery over our language, such as few even of the Classics of our poetry have attained. What these powers could effect they effected to the full. They placed him in the front rank of rhetorical poets. They enabled him to rival Lucretius in didactic poetry, Lucan in epic, and Juvenal in satire. If they could not supply what Nature had denied him, they supplied its semblance. There is in Dryden's poetry, and especially in his lyrical poetry, a vehemence and energy, a rapidity of movement and a fertility and vividness of imagery, which is sometimes difficult to distinguish from the expression of that emotional and spiritual exaltation which constitutes genuine enthusiasm. But genuine enthusiasm is not there. *Alexander's Feast* is a consummate example of what a combination of all the qualities which enter into the composition of rhetorical masterpieces can effect. But it is nothing more. The moment we compare it, say, with Pindar's first Pythian Ode, its relation to true poetry becomes at once apparent It is the same when he attempts the pathetic and when he attempts the sublime. For the first he substitutes—as in the *Elegy on Oldham*, the *Ode on Mrs Anne Killigrew*, *Eleonora*, and the lines on Ossory in *Absalom and Achitophel*—elaborate eloquence; for the second, if he does not collapse in bombast, magnificence and pomp.

But when all deductions are made, how much must the most scrupulous criticism still leave to Dryden. As long as our literature endures, his genial energy, his happy unstinted talent, his incomparable power of style, can never fail to fascinate. It may be said with simple truth that what is best in his work is in our language the best of its kind. . . .

No one indeed, can contemplate without wonder the manifold energy of that vigorous and plastic genius, which added to our literature so much which is excellent, and so much which is admirable, and which elicited from one of the most fastidious of poets and critics the rapturous exhortation—to read Dryden—'and to be blind to all his faults!'

Dryden 1878

ARNOLD

Are Dryden and Pope poetical classics? Is the historic estimate, which represents them as such, and which has been so long established that it cannot easily give way, the real estimate? Wordsworth and Coleridge, as is well known, denied it; but the authority of Wordsworth and Coleridge does not weigh much with the young generation, and there are many signs to show that the eighteenth century and its judgments are coming in to favour again. Are the favourite poets of the eighteenth century classics?

It is impossible within my present limits to discuss the question fully. And what man of letters would not shrink from seeming to dispose dictatorially of the claims of two men who are, at any rate, such masters in letters as Dryden and Pope; two men of such admirable talent, both of them, and one of them, Dryden, a man, on all sides, of such energetic and genial power? And yet, if we are to gain the full benefit from poetry, we must have the real estimate of it. I cast about for some mode of arriving, in the present case, at such an estimate without offence. And perhaps the best way is to begin as it is easy to begin, with cordial praise.

When we find Chapman, the Elizabethan translator of Homer, expressing himself in his preface thus: 'Though truth in her very nakedness sits in so deep a pit, that from Gades to Aurora and Ganges few eyes can sound her, I hope yet those few here will so discover and confirm that, the date being out of her darkness in this morning of our poet, he shall now gird his temples with the sun'—we pronounce that such a prose is intolerable. When we find Milton writing: 'And long it was not after, when I was confirmed in this opinion, that he, who would not be frustrate of his hope to write well hereafter in laudable things, ought himself to be a true poem'—we pronounce that such a prose has its own grandeur, but that it is obsolete and inconvenient. But when we find Dryden telling us: 'What Virgil wrote in the vigour of his age, in plenty and at ease, I have undertaken to translate in my declining years; struggling with wants, oppressed with sickness, curbed in my genius, liable to be misconstrued in all I write'—then we exclaim that here at last we have the true English prose, a prose such as we would all gladly use if we only knew how. Yet Dryden was Milton's contemporary.

. . . A fit prose was a necessity; but it was impossible that
a fit prose should establish itself amongst us without some
touch of frost to the imaginative life of the soul. The needful
qualities for a fit prose are regularity, uniformity, precision,
balance. The men of letters, whose destiny it may be to bring
their nation to the attainment of a fit prose, must of necessity,
whether they work in prose or in verse, give a predominating,
an almost exclusive attention to the qualities of regularity,
uniformity, precision, balance. But an almost exclusive attention to these qualities involves some repression and silencing
of poetry.

We are to regard Dryden as the puissant and glorious
founder, Pope as the splendid high priest, of our age of prose
and reason, of our excellent and indispensable eighteenth
century. For the purposes of their mission and destiny their
poetry, like their prose, is admirable. Do you ask me whether
Dryden's verse, take it almost where you will, is not good?

> A milk-white Hind, immortal and unchanged,
> Fed on the lawns and in the forest ranged.

I answer: Admirable for the purposes of the inaugurator of an
age of prose and reason. Do you ask me whether Pope's verse,
take it almost where you will, is not good?

> To Hounslow Heath I point, and Banstead Down;
> Thence comes your mutton, and these chicks my own.

I answer: Admirable for the purposes of the high priest of an
age of prose and reason. But do you ask me whether such verse
proceeds from men with an adequate poetic criticism of life,
from men whose criticism of life has a high seriousness, or
even, without that high seriousness, has poetic largeness, freedom, insight, benignity? Do you ask me whether the application of ideas to life in the verse of these men, often a powerful
application, no doubt, is a powerful *poetic* application? Do
you ask me whether the poetry of these men has either the

matter or the inseparable manner of such an adequate poetic criticism; whether it has the accent of

> Absent thee from felicity awhile . . .

or of

> And what is else not to be overcome . . .

or of

> O martyr sounded in virginitee!

I answer: It has not and cannot have them; it is the poetry of the builders of an age of prose and reason. Though they may write in verse, though they may in a certain sense be masters of the art of versification, Dryden and Pope are not classics of our poetry, they are classics of our prose.

The Study of Poetry 1880

SWINBURNE

Among his forefathers and successors of the giant brood, Jonson has excelled him in weighty wealth and Byron has equalled him in spontaneous versatility of genius; but Dryden at his best is a surer workman of a trustier hand than either. And however unequal in his lyric touch, he has been but comparatively overpraised for the consummate force and swift felicity of his labours in the middle region of that line. He is the undisputed lord of lyrical rhetoric: he wins his way and makes his points with the easy and mighty touch of a sovereign orator. All the great effects of eloquence are his to command at the slightest wave of his hand in summons: all these, and something more, which is part of his indefinable birthright as a poet. Very few poets have had any mentionable measure of the gifts most proper and fruitful to the art of noble oratory, which all were his alike in such fruitful and imperial affluence; though many have had more of those which are more especially proper to their art, and to that art alone. To sum up, we may revert to the distinction already drawn between the Olympian and the Titanic orders of men. There was little enough of the godlike in Dryden's composition; but, once more, what a man was this giant, and what a giant was this man!

A Century of English Poetry 1880

ELIOT

If the prospect of delight be wanting (which alone justifies the perusal of poetry) we may let the reputation of Dryden sleep in the manuals of literature. To those who are genuinely insensible of his genius (and these are probably the majority of living readers of poetry) we can only oppose illustrations of the following proposition: that their insensibility does not merely signify indifference to satire and wit, but lack of perception of qualities not confined to satire and wit and present in the work of other poets whom these persons feel that they understand. To those whose taste in poetry is formed entirely upon the English poetry of the nineteenth century—to the majority—it is difficult to explain or excuse Dryden: the twentieth century is still the nineteenth, although it may in time acquire its own character. The nineteenth century had, like every other, limited tastes and peculiar fashions; and, like every other, it was unaware of its own limitations. Its tastes and fashions had no place for Dryden; yet Dryden is one of the tests of a catholic appreciation of poetry. . . .

With regard to Dryden, therefore, we can say this much. Our taste in English poetry has been largely founded upon a partial perception of the value of Shakespeare and Milton, a perception which dwells upon sublimity of theme and action. Shakespeare had a great deal more; he had nearly everything to satisfy our various desires for poetry. The point is that the depreciation or neglect of Dryden is not due to the fact that his work is not poetry, but to a prejudice that the material, the feelings, out of which he built is not poetic. . . .

It would be truer to say, indeed, even in the form of the unpersuasive paradox, that Dryden is distinguished principally by his *poetic* ability. We prize him, as we do Mallarmé, for what he made of his material. Our estimate is only in part the appreciation of ingenuity: in the end the result *is* poetry. Much of Dryden's unique merit consists in his ability to make the small into the great, the prosaic into the poetic, the trivial into the magnificent. In this he differs not only from Milton, who required a canvas of the largest size, but from Pope, who required one of the smallest. If you compare any satiric 'character' of Pope with one of Dryden, you will see that the method and intention are widely divergent. When Pope alters, he diminishes; he is a master of miniature. The singular skill of his portrait of Addison, for example, in the *Epistle to Arbuthnot*, depends upon the justice and reserve, the apparent determination not to exaggerate. The genius of Pope is not for caricature. But the effect of the portraits of Dryden is to transform the object into something greater. . . .

> A fiery soul, which working out its way,
> Fretted the pigmy body to decay:
> And o'er informed the tenement of clay.

These lines are not merely a magnificent tribute. They create the object which they contemplate. Dryden is, in fact, much nearer to the master of comic creation than to Pope. As in Jonson, the effect is far from laughter; the comic is the material, the result is poetry. . . .

Dryden, with all his intellect, had a commonplace mind. His powers were, we believe, wider, but no greater, than Milton's; he was confined by boundaries as impassable, though less strait. He bears a curious antithetical resemblance to Swinburne. Swinburne was also a master of words, but Swinburne's words are all suggestions and no denotation; if they suggest nothing, it is because they suggest too much. Dryden's words, on the other hand, are precise, they state immensely, but their suggestiveness is often nothing.

> That short dark passage to a future state;
> That melancholy riddle of a breath,
> That something, or that nothing, after death,

is a riddle, but not melancholy enough, in Dryden's splendid verse. The question, which has certainly been waiting, may justly be asked: whether, without this which Dryden lacks, verse can be poetry? What is man to decide what poetry is? Dryden's use of language is not, like that of Swinburne, weakening and demoralizing. . . .

Dryden lacked what his master Jonson possessed, a large and unique view of life; he lacked insight, he lacked profundity. But where Dryden fails to satisfy, the nineteenth century does not satisfy us either; and where that century has condemned him, it is itself condemned. In the next revolution of taste it is possible that poets may turn to the study of Dryden. He remains one of those who have set standards for English verse which it is desperate to ignore.

John Dryden 1922

Pope

The critics of Pope have always been torn between their admiration for his brilliant virtues, and their recognition of his narrow limitations. It was only during his lifetime that the former prevailed so far as to reduce nearly all criticism to mere adulation —there was nothing in this period, indeed, which seemed to deserve a place in this book. Little more than ten years after his death, Joseph Warton found the courage to speak of the limitations, and since then a steady discussion has gone on. In the early nineteenth century, Wordsworth, Bowles, and others saw more of the limitations; while Byron, Campbell, and their allies saw more of the merits of Pope's poetry. The controversy which raged acutely for a few years went on reverberating down the century, and I suppose it still continues.

POPE

The things that I have written fastest have always pleased most. I wrote the *Essay on Criticism* fast, for I had digested all the matter in prose before I began upon it in verse. *The Rape of the Lock* was written fast: all the machinery, you know, was added afterwards; and the making that, and what was published before, hit so well together is, I think, one of the greatest proofs of judgment of any thing I ever did. . . .

About 15 I got acquainted with Mr. Walsh: he encouraged me much, and used to tell me that there was one way left of excelling; for though we had several great poets, we never had any one great poet that was correct, and he desired me to make that my study and aim. . . .

I learned versification chiefly from Dryden's works, who

has improved it much beyond any of our former poets, and would probably have brought it to its perfection, had he not been unhappily obliged to write so often in haste. . . .

I would have my things in merciful hands. I am in no concern whether people should say this is writ well or ill; but that this is writ with a good design. 'He has writ in the cause of virtue, and done some thing to mend people's morals,' is the only commendation I long for. . . .

I have followed *that* (the significance of the numbers, and the adapting them to the sense) much more even than Dryden, and much oftener than any one minds it; particularly in the translation of Homer, when it was not necessary to do so, and in the *Dunciad* often; and indeed in all my poems. . . .

The great rule of verse is—to be musical: this other is only a secondary consideration, and should not jar too much with the former.

Spence's Anecdotes

SPENCE

If that be the case, I beg pardon, says Antiphaus: Were I the greatest enemy in the world to mere harmony, and the stated returns and gingle of syllables; I should be one of the first among the admirers of sound, whenever it is made serviceable to nature and true sense. That is the art (says Philypsus) and the mastery for which I particularly admire Mr Pope: It is he who took up that great Rule of the *sound's being a comment on the sense*, and enforced it beyond any of the criticks, who went before him. To this writer we chiefly owe the revival of the noble art of numbers; and the method of signifying motions, and actions, and all that vast variety of our passions, by *sounds*. In his incomparable *Essay on Criticism*, this writer has given us the best advices, and interwoven the most beautiful examples into them, in a manner that will always be admired. The first stanza, in his *Ode on St. Caecilia's Day*, is the fullest piece of this kind perhaps extant in any language: 'tis itself a perfect concert. In the translations of Homer, we find him very frequent, and very just, in the same

manner of expressing things: I call it so; and cou'd almost be
persuaded to think it a better way of expressing, than in the
common way of *words*. These have a sense affixt to them by
custom: while the other speaks by the ideas of things. That
is a flowing, variable help: this is the voice of nature, and a
sort of *universal* poetical *language*.

Mr Pope affords us infinite examples of this beauty in his
translation of the Odyssey; it would be endless to repeat them
all, or to admire them as they deserve. But amidst all this
variety, there is a single point, which I have observed more
than any of the rest: Whenever the poet is speaking of the
watry element, or any thing belonging to it, his management
of sounds is particularly frequent and beautiful. . . .

Words give us the bare ideas of things; but words, thus
managed, impress those ideas very strongly and sensibly upon
the mind. Do you not perceive the storm rising, *when the wild
winds whistle o'er the main*? and are you not in the midst of it
when *east, west, together roar, and south and north roll mountains to the shore*? Then we are hurried o'er the deep, and see
all the rocks and dangers of it:

> Dire Scylla there a scene of horror forms,
> And here Charybdis fills the sea with storms
> When the tide rushes from her rumbling caves,
> The rough rock roars, tumultuous boil the waves;
> They toss, they foam. . . .

The next moment, if the poet pleases (like the Daemon he
speaks of) he can make all as gentle and serene, as it was before
rough and boisterous.

> Sunk are at once the winds: the air above,
> And waves below, at once forget to move:
> Some Daemon calm'd the air, and smooth'd the deep,
> Hush'd the loud winds, and charm'd the waves to sleep.

Did you ever see a more perfect calm? Yet, smooth and
hush'd as these lines are, you may easily perceive a difference

between the description of a still sea, and the easy, beautiful current of a river.

> Smooth flows the gentle stream with wanton pride,
> And in soft mazes rolls a silver tide.

How happy is the hand of the poet, and what a command has he of nature, to make the numbers of his verse speak his sentiments! Thus to paint even sounds; and to draw by measures what does not come under the power of the pencil!

An Essay on Mr Pope's Odyssey   Evening III

[It is relevant to the understanding of this passage to quote Spence's description of his two disputants:

'The inlarged genius of Philypsus always led him to dwell upon the most beautified parts of a poem with the greatest pleasure: while Antiphaus, who has a very clear head, and has given much into a strict way of thinking, is taken most with just descriptions, and plain natural ideas: the one was so possess'd with the pleasure which he felt from fine thoughts and warm expressions, that he did not take a full satisfaction in low beauty, and simple representations of nature; the other, on the contrary, had such an aversion to glitterings and elevation, that he was distasted at any the least appearance of either. If the latter was perhaps too much prejudiced for the ancients, from the purity and justness which we find in most of their works; Philypsus had his foible too, and was sometimes caught by the flourish and colouring of the moderns. In a word, if Philypsus wou'd sometimes contemn a point as low and mean, tho' in reality proper enough, and naturally express'd; Antiphaus in his turn, might happen now and then to blame a passage which requir'd a good degree of ornament, as being too glaring and artificial.' *Evening I.*

The dialogue proceeds on the basis that Philypsus has a natural inclination to admire Pope, Antiphaus an equally

natural inclination to find fault with him—and this assump-
tion is more revealing than anything Spence says outright]

WARTON

Dear Sir,

Permit me to break into your retirement, the residence
of virtue and literature, and to trouble you with a few reflections
on the merits and real character of an admired author, and
on other collateral subjects of criticism, that will naturally
arise in the course of such an enquiry. No love of singularity, no
affectation of paradoxical opinions, gave rise to the following
work. I revere the memory of Pope, I respect and honour his
abilities; but I do not think him at the head of his profession.
In other words, in that species of poetry wherein Pope excelled,
he is superior to all mankind: and I only say, that this species
of poetry is not the most excellent one of the art.

We do not, it should seem, sufficiently attend to the difference there is, betwixt a Man of Wit, a Man of Sense, and a
True Poet. Donne and Swift were undoubtedly men of wit,
and men of sense: but what traces have they left of Pure Poetry?
It is remarkable, that Dryden says of Donne: He was the greatest wit, tho' not the greatest poet of this nation. Fontenelle
and La Motte are entitled to the former character; but what
can they urge to gain the latter? Which of these characters is
the most valuable and useful, is entirely out of the question:
all I plead for, is, to have their several provinces kept distinct
from each other; and to impress on the reader, that a clear
head, and acute understanding are not sufficient, alone, to
make a Poet; that the most solid observations on human life,
expressed with the utmost elegance and brevity, are Morality,
and not Poetry; that the Epistles of Boileau in Rhyme, are no
more poetical, than the Characters of La Bruyère in Prose;
and that it is a creative and glowing Imagination, 'acer spiritus
ac vis', and that alone, that can stamp a writer with this exalted
and very uncommon character, which so few possess, and of
which so few can properly judge. . . .

The Sublime and the Pathetic are the two chief nerves of

The romantic premise early

all genuine poesy. What is there transcendently Sublime or Pathetic in Pope? In his works there is indeed, 'nihil inane, nihil arcessitum; . . . puro tamen fonti quam magno flumini proprior'; as the excellent Quintilian remarks of Lysias. And because I am perhaps unwilling to speak out in plain English, I will adopt the following passage of Voltaire, which, in my opinion, as exactly characterizes Pope as it does his model Boileau, for whom it was originally designed. '*Incapable peut-être du sublime qui élève l'âme, et du sentiment qui l'attendrit, mais fait pour éclairer ceux à qui la nature accorda l'un et l'autre, laborieux, sévère, précis, pur, harmonieux, il devint, enfin, le poéte de la Raison.*'

Our English poets may, I think, be disposed in four different classes and degrees. In the first class, I would place, our only three sublime and pathetic poets; Spenser, Shakespeare, Milton. In the second class should be ranked, such as possessed the true poetical genius, in a more moderate degree, but who had noble talents for moral, ethical, and panegyrical poesy. At the head of these are Dryden, Prior, Addison, Cowley, Waller, Garth, Fenton, Gay, Denham, Parnell. In the third class may be placed, men of wit, of elegant taste, and lively fancy in describing familiar life, tho' not the higher scenes of poetry. Here may be numbered, Butler, Swift, Rochester, Donne, Dorset, Oldham. In the fourth class, the mere versifiers, however smooth and mellifluous some of them may be thought, should be disposed. Such as Pitt, Sandys, Fairfax, Broome, Buckingham, Lansdown. This enumeration is not intended as a complete catalogue of writers, and in their proper order, but only to mark out briefly the different species of our celebrated authors. In which of these classes Pope deserves to be placed, the following work is intended to determine.

Concludes — *Essay on the Genius and Writings of Pope:*
"next to Milton and *The Dedication 1756*
just above Dryden" JOHNSON

With such faculties, and such dispositions, he excelled every other writer in *poetical prudence*; he wrote in such a manner as might expose him to few hazards. He used almost always the same fabrick of verse; and, indeed, by those few essays which he made of any other, he did not enlarge his reputation. Of this uniformity, the certain consequence was readiness and dexterity. By perpetual practice, language had in his mind a systematical arrangement; having always the same use for words, he had words so selected and combined as to be ready at his call. This increase of facility he confessed himself to have perceived in the progress of his translation. . . .

He professed to have learned his poetry from Dryden, whom, whenever an opportunity was presented, he praised through his whole life with unvaried liberality; and perhaps his character may receive some illustration, if he be compared with his master.

Integrity of understanding and nicety of discernment were not allotted in a less proportion to Dryden than to Pope. The rectitude of Dryden's mind was sufficiently shown by the dimission of his poetical prejudices, and the rejection of unnatural thoughts and rugged numbers. But Dryden never desired to apply all the judgment that he had. He wrote, and professed to write, merely for the people; and when he pleased others, he contented himself. He spent no time in struggles to rouse latent powers; he never attempted to make that better which was already good, nor often to mend what he must have known to be faulty. He wrote, as he tells us, with very little consideration; when occasion or necessity called upon him, he poured out what the present moment happened to supply, and, when once it had passed the press, ejected it from his mind; for when he had no pecuniary interest, he had no further solicitude.

Pope was not content to satisfy; he desired to excel, and therefore always endeavoured to do his best: he did not court the candour, but dared the judgment of his reader, and, expecting no indulgence from others, he shewed none to himself. He examined lines and words with minute punctilious observation, and retouched every part with indefatigable diligence, till he had left nothing to be forgiven. . . . It will seldom be found that he altered without adding clearness, elegance, or vigour. Pope had perhaps the judgment of Dryden; but Dryden certainly wanted the diligence of Pope.

In acquired knowledge, the superiority must be allowed to Dryden, whose education was more scholastick, and who before he became an author had been allowed more time for study, with better means of information. His mind has a larger range, and he collects his images and illustrations from a more extensive circumference of science. Dryden knew more of man in his general nature, and Pope, in his local manners. The notions of Dryden were formed by comprehensive speculation, and those of Pope by minute attention. There is more dignity in the knowledge of Dryden, and more certainty in that of Pope. . . .

Of genius, that power which constitutes a poet; that quality without which judgment is cold and knowledge is inert; that energy which collects, combines, amplifies, and animates; the superiority must, with some hesitation, be allowed to Dryden. It is not to be inferred that of this poetical vigour Pope had only a little, because Dryden had more; for every other writer since Milton must give place to Pope; and even of Dryden it must be said, that if he has brighter paragraphs, he has not better poems. Dryden's performances were always hasty, either excited by some external occasion, or extorted by domestick necessity; he composed without consideration, and published without correction. What his mind could supply at call, or gather in one excursion, was all that he sought, and all that he gave. The dilatory caution of Pope enabled him to condense his sentiments, to multiply his images, and to accumulate all that study might produce, or chance might supply. If the flights of Dryden therefore are higher, Pope continues longer on the wing. If of Dryden's fire the blaze is brighter, of Pope's the heat is more regular and constant. Dryden often surpasses expectation, and Pope never falls below it. Dryden is read with frequent astonishment, and Pope with perpetual delight.

Life of Pope 1781

BOWLES

In what has been said, I have avoided the introduction of picturesque description; that is, accurate representations from *external objects* of Nature: but if the premises laid down in the commencement of these Reflections are true, no one can stand pre-eminent as a great Poet, unless he has not only a heart susceptible of the most pathetic or most exalted feelings of Nature, but an eye *attentive to*, and *familiar with*, every external appearance that she may exhibit, in every change of season, every variation of light and shade, every rock, every tree, every leaf, in her solitary places. He who has not an eye to observe these, and who cannot with a glance distinguish every diversity of hue in her variety of beauties, must so far be deficient in one of the essential qualities of a Poet.

Here Pope, from infirmities, and from physical causes, was particularly deficient. When he left his own laurel circus at Twickenham, he was lifted into his chariot or his barge; and with weak eyes, and tottering strength, it is physically impossible he could be a *descriptive* Bard. Where description has been introduced among his Poems, as far as his observation could go, he excelled; more could not be expected. In the descriptions of the Cloister, as far as could be gained by books, or suggested by imagination, he was eminently successful; but even here, perhaps, he only proved that he could not go far: and

> The streams that shine between the hills,
> The grotts that echo to the tinkling rills,

were possibly *transcripts* of what he could most easily *transcribe*—his own views and scenery.

But how different, how minute is his description, when he describes what he is master of: for instance, the game of Ombre, in the *Rape of the Lock*? This is from *artificial life*; and with artificial life, from his infirmities, he must have been chiefly conversant: But if he had been gifted with the same powers of observing outward Nature, I have no doubt he would have

G

evinced as much accuracy in describing the appropriate and peculiar beauties, such as Nature exhibits in the Forest where he lived, as he was able to describe, in a manner so novel, and with colours so vivid, a Game of Cards. . . .

When he left these regions, to unite the most exquisite machinery of fancy with the descriptions of *artificial life*, *The Rape of the Lock* will, first and last, present itself—a composition, as Johnson justly observes, the 'most elegant, the most airy', of all his Works; a composition, to which it will be in vain to compare anything of the kind. He stands alone, unrivalled, and possibly never to be rivalled. All Pope's successful labour of correct and musical versification, all his talents of accurate description, though in an inferior province of Poetry, are here consummately displayed; and as far as artificial life, that is, Manners, not Passions, are capable of being rendered poetical, they are here rendered so, by the fancy, the propriety, the elegance, and the poetic beauty of the Sylphic machinery.

This 'delightful' Poem, as I have said, appears to stand conspicuous and beautiful, in that medium where Fancy begins to leave Nature, and *approximates to local manners*. The Muse has, indeed, no longer her great characteristic attributes, pathos or sublimity; but she appears so interesting, that we almost doubt whether the garb of elegant refinement is not as captivating, as the most beautiful appearances of Nature.

After what I have taken the liberty of suggesting, I hope I shall be excused if I say a few words respecting Pope's versification. . . . That Pope has made the versification of English couplets infinitely more smooth, I will readily allow. . . . For myself, I mean merely to say, that I should think it the extreme arrogance of folly to make my own ear the criterion of music; but I cannot help thinking, that Dryden, and of later days Cowper, are much more *harmonious* in their general versification, than Pope. . . . Whoever candidly compares these Writers together, unless his ear be habituated to a *certain recurrence of pauses* at the end of a line, will not (though he will give the highest praise for compactness, skill, precision, and force, to the *undivided Couplets* of Pope, *separately* considered), will not, I think, assent to the position, that in versification, 'what he found brick-work, he left marble'.

In variety, and in variety *only*, let it be remembered, I think Pope deficient.

Observations on the Poetic Character of Pope 1806

The anger of Swift was general; the spleen of Pope particular: one was disgusted with the *nature of man*; the other piqued and offended by individuals, confining his animosity to the small circle of those who offended him. Swift, politically speaking, was disappointed that the high post in society, to which, from his talents, he thought himself entitled to aspire, was early wrested from the grasp of his ambition. Pope, attaining a situation, though a private one, much higher than he could have expected, chiefly felt offended when his intellectual superiority was disputed.

Neither had reason to complain; but the acrimony of Swift was directed against man and society; the spleen of Pope against the individuals, Phillips, and Dennis, Lord Fanny, and Lady Mary, &c. &c.

Life and Writings of Pope 1806

WORDSWORTH

The arts by which Pope, soon afterwards, contrived to procure to himself a more general and a higher reputation than perhaps any English poet ever attained during his lifetime, are known to the judicious. And as well known is it to them that the undue exertion of these arts is the cause why Pope has for some time held a rank in literature to which, if he had not been seduced by an over-love of immediate popularity, and had confided more in his native genius, he never could have descended. He bewitched the nation by his melody, and dazzled it by his polished style, and was himself blinded by his own success. Having wandered from humanity in his *Eclogues*, with boyish inexperience, the praise which these

compositions obtained tempted him into a belief that nature
was not to be trusted, at least in pastoral poetry.

Essay Supplementary to the Preface   1815

KEATS

                         Yes, a schism
Nurtured by foppery and barbarism,
Made great Apollo blush for this his land.
Men were thought wise who could not understand
His glories: with a puling infant's force
They sway'd about upon a rocking horse,
And thought it Pegasus. Ah dismal soul'd!
The winds of heaven blew, the ocean roll'd
Its gathering waves—ye felt it not. The blue
Bared its eternal bosom, and the dew
Of summer nights collected still to make
The morning precious: beauty was awake!
Why were ye not awake? But ye were dead
To things ye knew not of—were closely wed
To musty laws lined out with wretched rule
And compass vile: so that ye taught a school
Of dolts to smooth, inlay, and clip, and fit,
Till, like the certain wands of Jacob's wit,
Their verses tallied. Easy was the task:
A thousand handicraftsmen wore the mask
Of Poesy. Ill-fated, impious race!
That blasphemed the bright Lyrist to his face,
And did not know it—no, they went about,
Holding a poor decrepid standard out
Mark'd with most flimsy mottos, and in large
The name of one Boileau!

Sleep and Poetry   1817

[This appears to be the piece which Lord Byron took as
'abuse of Pope'; and is included here on his authority, though
its scope is rather wider]

BYRON

There will be found as comfortable metaphysics, and ten times more poetry in the *Essay on Man*, than in the *Excursion*. If you search for passion, where is it to be found stronger than in the epistle from *Eloisa to Abelard*, or in *Palamon and Arcite*? Do you wish for invention, imagination, sublimity, character? seek them in *The Rape of the Lock*, the *Fables* of Dryden, the *Ode on Saint Cecilia's Day*, and *Absalom and Achitophel*: you will discover in these two poets only, all for which you must ransack innumerable metres, and God only knows how many *writers* of the day, without finding a tittle of the same qualities—with the addition, too, of wit, of which the latter have none. . . . I will say nothing of the harmony of Pope and Dryden in comparison, for there is not a living poet (except Rogers, Gifford, Campbell, and Crabbe) who can write an heroic couplet. The fact is, that the exquisite beauty of their versification has withdrawn the public attention from their other excellences, as the vulgar eye will rest more upon the splendour of the uniform than the quality of the troops. It is this very harmony, particularly in Pope, which has raised the vulgar and atrocious cant against him—because his versification is perfect, it is assumed that it is his only perfection; because his truths are so clear, it is asserted that he has no invention; and because he is always intelligible, it is taken for granted that he is the 'Poet of Reason', as if this was a reason for his being no poet. Taking passage for passage, I will undertake to cite more lines teeming with *imagination* from Pope than from any *two* living poets, be they who they may. To take an instance at random from a species of composition not very favourable to imagination—Satire: set down the character of Sporus, with all the wonderful play of fancy which is scattered over it. . . .

Now, mark the images separately and arithmetically:

1. The thing of *silk*
2. *Curd* of *ass's* milk

   3. The *butterfly*
   4. The *wheel*
   5. Bug with gilded wings
   6. *Painted* child of dirt
   7. Whose *buzz*
   8. Well-bred *spaniels*
   9. *Shallow streams run dimpling*
  10. *Florid* impotence
  11. *Prompter. Puppet squeaks*
  12. *The ear of Eve*
  13. *Familiar toad*
  14. *Half froth, half venom, spits* himself abroad
  15. *Fop* at the *toilet*
  16. *Flatterer* at the *board*
  17. *Amphibious* thing
  18. Now *trips a lady*
  19. Now *struts a lord*
  20. A *cherub's* face
  21. A *reptile* all the rest
  22. The *Rabbins*
  23. Pride that *licks the dust*

Now, is there a line of all the passage without the most forcible imagery (for his purpose)? Look at the *variety*—at the *poetry* of the passage—at the *imagination*: there is hardly a line from which a painting might not be made, and *is*. But this is nothing in comparison with his higher passages in the *Essay on Man*, and many of his other poems, serious and comic. There never was such an unjust outcry in this world as that which these fellows are trying against Pope.

> *Observations upon an Article in Blackwood's Magazine*,
> 1819: the last part from *Letter to Murray*   1821

They support Pope, I see, in the *Quarterly*. Let them continue to do so: it is a Sin and a Shame, and a *damnation* to think that *Pope*!! should require it—but he does. Those

miserable mountebanks of the day, the poets, disgrace themselves and deny God, in running down Pope, the most *faultless*
of Poets, and almost of men. . . .

He is the moral poet of all civilisation; and as such, let us
hope that he will one day be the national poet of all mankind.
He is the only poet that never shocks; the only poet whose
faultlessness has been made his reproach. Cast your eye over
his productions; consider their extent, and contemplate their
variety—pastoral, passion, mock heroic, translation, satire,
ethics—all excellent, and often perfect. If his great charm be
his *melody* how comes it that foreigners adore him even in their
diluted translations?

Letters and Journals   1830

HAZLITT

The question, whether Pope was a poet, has hardly yet
been settled, and is hardly worth settling; for if he was not a
great poet, he must have been a great prose-writer, that is,
he was a great writer of some sort. He was a man of exquisite
faculties, and of the most refined taste; and as he chose verse
(the most obvious distinction of poetry) as the vehicle to express
his ideas, he has generally passed for a poet, and a good one.
If, indeed, by a great poet, we mean one who gives the utmost
grandeur to our conceptions of nature, or the utmost force
to the passions of the heart, Pope was not in this sense a great
poet; for the bent, the characteristic power of his mind, lay
the clean contrary way; namely, in representing things as they
appear to the indifferent observer, stripped of prejudice and
passion, as in his Critical Essays; or in representing them in the
most contemptible and insignificant point of view, as in his
Satires; or in clothing the little with mock-dignity, as in his
poems of Fancy; or in adorning the trivial incidents and
familiar relations of life with the utmost elegance of expression,
and all the flattering illusions of friendship or self-love, as in
his Epistles. He was not then distinguished as a poet of lofty
enthusiasm, of strong imagination, with a passionate sense of

the beauties of nature, or a deep insight into the workings
of the heart; but he was a wit, and a critic, a man of sense, of
observation, and the world, with a keen relish for the elegances
of art, or of nature when embellished by art, a quick tact for
propriety of thought and manners as established by the forms
and customs of society, a refined sympathy with the sentiments and habitudes of human life, as he felt them within the
little circle of his family and friends. He was in a word, the
poet, not of nature, but of art; and the distinction between the
two, as well as I can make it out, is this: The poet of nature
is one who, from the elements of beauty, of power, and of
passion in his own breast, sympathises with whatever is
beautiful, and grand, and impassioned in nature, in its simple
majesty, in its immediate appeal to the senses, to the thoughts
and hearts of all men; so that the poet of nature, by the truth,
and depth, and harmony of his mind, may be said to hold
communion with the very soul of nature; to be identified
with and to foreknow and to record the feelings of all men at
all times and places, as they are liable to the same impressions; and to exert the same power over the minds of his
readers, that nature does. He sees things in their eternal beauty,
for he sees them as they are; he feels them in their universal
interest, for he feels them as they affect the first principles
of his and our common nature. . . .

Pope was not assuredly a poet of this class, or in the first
rank of it. He saw nature only dressed by art; he judged of
beauty by fashion; he sought for truth in the opinions of the
world; he judged of the feelings of others by his own. The
capacious soul of Shakspeare had an intuitive and mighty
sympathy with whatever could enter into the heart of man in
all possible circumstances: Pope had an exact knowledge of
all that he himself loved or hated, wished or wanted. Milton
has winged his daring flight from heaven to earth, through
Chaos and old Night. Pope's muse never wandered with
safety, but from his library to his grotto, or from his grotto into his library back again. His mind dwelt with greater pleasure
on his own garden, than on the garden of Eden; he could
describe the faultless whole-length mirror that reflected his

own person, better than the smooth surface of the lake that reflects the face of heaven—a piece of cut glass or a pair of paste buckles with more brilliance and effect, than a thousand dew-drops glittering in the sun. He would be more delighted with a patent lamp, than with 'the pale reflex of Cynthia's brow', that fills the skies with its soft silent lustre, that trembles through the cottage window, and cheers the watchful mariner on the lonely wave. In short, he was the poet of personality and of polished life. That which was nearest to him, was the greatest; the fashion of the day bore sway in his mind over the immutable law of nature. He preferred the artificial to the natural in external objects, because he had a stronger fellow-feeling with the self-love of the maker or proprietor of a gewgaw, than admiration of that which was interesting to all mankind. He preferred the artificial to the natural in passion, because the involuntary and uncalculating impulses of the one hurried him away with a force and vehemence with which he could not grapple; while he could trifle with the conventional and superficial modification of mere sentiment at will, laugh at or admire, put them on or off like a masquerade-dress, make much or little of them, indulge them for a longer or a shorter time, as he pleased; and because while they amused his fancy and exercised his ingenuity, they never once disturbed his vanity, his levity, or indifference. His mind was the antithesis of strength and grandeur; its power was the power of indifference. He had none of the enthusiasm of poetry; he was in poetry what the sceptic is in religion.

It cannot be denied, that his chief excellence lay more in diminishing, than in aggrandizing objects; in checking, not in encouraging our enthusiasm; in sneering at the extravagances of fancy or passion, instead of giving a loose to them; in describing a row of pins and needles, rather than the embattled spears of Greeks and Trojans; in penning a lampoon or a compliment, and in praising Martha Blount. . . .

His Muse was on a peace-establishment, and grew somewhat effeminate by long ease and indulgence. He lived in the smiles of fortune, and basked in the favour of the great. In his smooth and polished verse we meet with no prodigies of

G*

nature, but with miracles of wit; the thunders of his pen are whispered flatteries; its forked lightnings pointed sarcasms; for 'the gnarled oak', he gives us 'the soft myrtle': for rocks, and seas, and mountains, artificial grass-plats, gravel-walks, and tinkling rills; for earthquakes and tempests, the breaking of a flower-pot, or the fall of a china jar; for the tug and war of the elements, or the deadly strife of the passions, we have

> Calm contemplation and poetic ease.

Yet within this retired and narrow circle how much, and that how exquisite, was contained! What discrimination, what wit, what delicacy, what fancy, what lurking spleen, what elegance of thought, what pampered refinement of sentiment! . . .

There is a cant in the present day about genius, as every thing in poetry: there was a cant in the time of Pope about sense, as performing all sorts of wonders. It was a kind of watchword, the shibboleth of a critical party of the day. As a proof of the exclusive attention which it occupied in their minds, it is remarkable that in the *Essay on Criticism* (not a very long poem) there are no less than half a score successive couplets rhyming to the word *sense*. . . .

I have mentioned this the more for the sake of those critics who are bigotted idolisers of our author, chiefly on the score of his correctness. These persons seem to be of opinion that 'there is but one perfect writer, even Pope'. This is, however, a mistake: his excellence is by no means faultlessness. If he had no great faults, he is full of little errors. His grammatical construction is often lame and imperfect. . . .

And shall we cut ourselves off from beauties like these with a theory? Shall we shut up our books, and seal up our senses, to please the dull spite and inordinate vanity of those 'who have eyes, but they see not—ears, but they hear not—and understandings, but they understand not'—and go about asking our blind guides, whether Pope was a poet or not? It will never do.

Lectures on the English Poets 1818

COLERIDGE

In Massinger, as in all our poets before Dryden, in order to make harmonious verse in the reading, it is absolutely necessary that the meaning should be understood—when the meaning is once seen, then the harmony is perfect. Whereas in Pope and in most of the writers who followed in his school, it is the mechanical metre which determines the sense. . . .

Lectures of 1818

. . . Pope's *Essay on Man* . . . mere metrical good sense and wit. . . .

Notes on Selden's Table Talk 1836

His (Claudian's) power of pleasingly reproducing the same thought in different language is remarkable, as it is in Pope.

Table Talk 1833

Among those with whom I conversed, there were, of course, very many who had formed their taste and their notions of poetry from the writings of Pope and his followers; or, to speak more generally, in that school of French poetry, condensed and invigorated by English understanding, which had predominated from the last century. I was not blind to the merits of this school; yet, as from inexperience of the world, and consequent want of sympathy with the general subjects of these poems, they gave me little pleasure, I doubtless undervalued the kind, and, with the presumption of youth, withheld from its masters the legitimate name of poets. I saw that the excellence of this kind consisted in just and acute observations of men and manners in an artificial state of society, as its matter and substance; and, in the logic of wit, conveyed in smooth and strong epigrammatic couplets as its form. Even when the subject was addressed to the fancy or the intellect, as in the *Rape of the Lock*, or the *Essay on Man*; nay, when it was a consecutive narration, as in that astonishing product of matchless talent and ingenuity, Pope's *Translation of the Iliad*; still a point was looked for at the end of each second line, and the whole was as it were a sorites, or, if I may exchange a logical for a grammatical metaphor, a conjunction disjunctive of epigrams. Meantime the matter and diction seemed to me characterized not so much by poetic thoughts, as by thoughts translated into the language of poetry. . . . I was, at that early period, led to a conjecture which, many years afterwards, was recalled to me from the same thought having been started in conversation, but far more ably, and developed more fully, by Mr Wordsworth, namely, that this style of poetry, which I have characterized above as translations of prose thoughts into poetic language, had been kept up by, if it did not wholly arise from, the custom of writing Latin verses, and the great importance attached to these exercises in our public schools.

Biographia Literaria   1817

CAMPBELL

If his contemporaries forgot other poets in admiring him, let him not be robbed of his just fame on pretence that a part of it was superfluous. The public ear was long fatigued with repetitions of his manner; but if we place ourselves in the situation of those to whom his brilliancy, succinctness, and animation were wholly new, we cannot wonder at their being captivated to the fondest admiration. In order to do justice to Pope, we should forget his imitators, if that were possible; but it is easier to remember than to forget by an effort—to acquire associations than to shake them off. Every one may recollect how often the most beautiful air has palled upon the ear, and grown insipid from being played or sung by vulgar musicians. It is the same thing with regard to Pope's versification. That his peculiar rhythm and manner are the very best in the whole range of our poetry need not be asserted. He has a gracefully peculiar manner, though it is not calculated to be an universal one; and where, indeed, shall we find the style of poetry that could be pronounced an exclusive model for every

composer? His pauses have little variety, and his phrases are
too much weighed in the balance of antithesis. But let us look
to the spirit that points his antithesis, and to the rapid precision
of his thoughts, and we shall forgive him for being too anti-
thetic and sententious. . . .

Mr Bowles . . . lays great stress upon the argument, that
Pope's images are drawn from art more than from nature.
That Pope was neither so insensible to the beauties of nature,
nor so indistinct in describing them as to forfeit the character
of a genuine poet, is what I mean to urge, without exaggerating
his picturesqueness. But before speaking of that quality in his
writings, I would beg leave to observe, in the first place, that
the faculty by which a poet luminously describes objects of art
is essentially the same faculty which enables him to be a faith-
ful describer of simple nature; in the second place, that nature
and art are to a greater degree relative terms in poetical description than is generally recollected; and, thirdly, that artificial objects and manners are of so much importance in fiction,
as to make the exquisite description of them no less characteristic of genius than the description of simple physical appearances. . . . Why then try Pope, or any other poet, exclusively by
his powers of describing inanimate phenomena? Nature, in
the wide and proper sense of the word, means life in all its
circumstances—nature moral as well as external. . . .

Pope's discrimination lay in the lights and shades of human
manners, which are at least as interesting as those of rocks and
leaves. In moral eloquence he is for ever *densus et instans sibi*.
The mind of a poet employed in concentrating such lines as
these descriptive of creative power, which

> Builds life on death, on change duration founds,
> And bids th'eternal wheels to know their rounds,

might well be excused for not descending to the minutely
picturesque. The vindictive personality of his satire is a fault
of the man, and not of the poet. But his wit is not all his charm.
He glows with passion in the *Epistle of Eloisa*, and displays
a lofty feeling, much above that of the satirist and the man of

the world, in his *Prologue to Cato,* and his *Epistle to Lord Oxford.* I know not how to designate the possessor of such gifts but by the name of a genuine poet.

Essay on the English Poets 1819

SOUTHEY

The age of Pope was the golden age of poets—but it was the pinchbeck age of poetry. They flourished in the sunshine of public and private patronage; the art meantime was debased, and it continued to be so as long as Pope continued lord of the ascendant. More injury was not done to the taste of his countrymen by Marino in Italy, nor by Gongora in Spain, than by Pope in England. The mischief was effected not by his satirical and moral pieces, for these entitle him to the highest place among the poets of his class; it was by his Homer. There have been other versions as unfaithful; but none were ever so well executed in as bad a style; and no other work in the language so greatly vitiated the diction of English poetry. Common readers (and the majority must always be such) will always be taken by glittering faults, as larks are caught by bits of looking-glass: and in this meretricious translation, the passages that were most unlike the original, which were most untrue to nature, and therefore most false in taste, were precisely those which were most applauded, and on which critic after critic dwelt with one cuckoo note of admiration. They who found nothing imitable in Dryden, could imitate this. The art of poetry, or rather the art of versification, which was now the same thing, was made easy to the meanest capacity. . . .

. . . it is a noticeable fact, that of all the poets in the intermediate half-century, not one who attained to any distinction which he has since held, or is likely to hold, was of the school of Pope. That school has produced versifiers in abundance, but no poet. No man of genius, nor even of original talents acknowledged his supremacy, while his authority was paramount with the public and its blind guides.

Life of Cowper 1836

DE QUINCEY

It is an error equally gross, and an error in which Pope himself participated, that his plume of distinction from preceding poets consisted in *correctness*. Correctness in what? Think of the admirable qualifications for settling the scale of such critical distinctions which that man must have had who turned out upon this vast world the single oracular word 'correctness' to shift for itself, and explain its own meaning to all generations. Did he mean logical correctness in maturing and connecting thoughts? But of all poets that have practised reasoning in verse, Pope is the one most inconsequential in the deduction of his thoughts, and the most severely distressed in any effort to effect or to explain the dependency of their parts. There are not ten consecutive lines in Pope unaffected by this infirmity. All his thinking proceeded by insulated and discontinuous jets; and the only resource for *him*, or chance of even seeming correctness, lay in the liberty of stringing his aphoristic thoughts like pearls, having no relation to each other but that of contiguity. To *set* them like diamonds was for Pope to risk distraction; to systematize was ruin. On the other hand, if this elliptical word *correctness*, for elliptical it must be until its subject of control is assigned, is to be understood with such a complimentary qualification as would restrict it to Pope's use of *language*, that construction is even more untenable than the other—more conspicuously untenable—for many are they who have erred by illogical thinking, or by distracted evolution of thoughts: but rare is the man amongst classical writers in any language who has disfigured his meaning more remarkably than Pope by imperfect expressions. We do not speak of plebeian phrases, of exotic phrases, of slang, from which Pope was not free, though *more* free than many of his contemporaries. From vulgarism indeed he was shielded, though imperfectly, by the aristocratic society he kept: *they* being right, *he* was right: and he erred only in the cases where they misled him: for even the refinement of that age was oftentimes coarse and vulgar. His grammar, indeed, is often vicious;

preterites and participles he constantly confounds, and regi-
sters this class of blunders for ever by the cast-iron index of
rhymes that never *can* mend. But worse than this mode of
viciousness is his syntax, which is so bad as to darken his
meaning at times, and at other times to defeat it. But these
were errors cleaving to his times; and it would be unfair to
exact from Pope a better quality of diction than belonged to
his contemporaries. Still it is indisputable that a better model
of diction and of grammar prevailed a century before Pope.
In Spenser, in Shakespeare, in the Bible of King James's
reign, and in Milton, there are very few grammatical errors.
But Pope's defect in language was almost peculiar to himself.
It lay in an inability, nursed doubtless by indolence, to carry
out and perfect the expression of the thought he wishes to
communicate. The language does not realize the idea: it
simply suggests or hints it. Thus, to give a single illustration:

> Know, God and Nature only are the same:
> In man the judgement shoots at flying game.

The first line one would naturally construe into this: that God
and Nature were in harmony, whilst all other objects were
scattered into incoherency by difference and disunion. Not at
all; it means nothing of the kind; but that God and Nature
only are exempted from the infirmities of change. *They* only
continue uniform and self-consistent. This *might* mislead many
readers; but the second line *must* do so: for who would not
understand the syntax to be, that the judgement, as it exists
in man, shoots at flying game? But, in fact, the meaning is,
that the judgement, in aiming its calculations at man, aims at
an object that is still on the wing, and never for a moment
stationary. We give this as a specimen of a fault in diction, the
very worst amongst all that are possible; to write bad grammar
or colloquial slang does not necessarily obscure the sense; but a
fault like this is a treachery, and hides the true meaning under
the cloud of a conundrum: nay worse; for even a conundrum
has fixed conditions for determining its solution, but this sort
of mutilated expression is left to the solutions of conjecture. . . .

The *Satires* of Pope, and what under another name *are* satires, viz. his *Moral Epistles*, offer a second variety of evidence to his voluptuous indolence. They offend against philosophic truth more heavily than the *Essay on Man*; but not in the same way. The *Essay on Man* sins chiefly by want of central principle, and by want therefore of all coherency amongst the separate thoughts. But taken *as* separate thoughts, viewed in the light of fragments and brilliant aphorisms, the majority of the passages have a mode of truth; not of truth central and coherent, but of truth angular and splintered. The *Satires*, on the other hand, were of false origin. They arose in a sense of talent for caustic effects, unsupported by any satiric heart, Pope had neither the malice (except in the most fugitive form), which thirsts for leaving wounds, nor, on the other hand, the deep moral indignation which burns in men whom Providence has from time to time armed with scourges for cleansing the sanctuaries of truth or justice. He was contented enough with society as he found it: bad it might be, but it was good enough for *him*: and it was the merest self-delusion if at any moment the instinct of glorying in his satiric mission (the *magnificabo apostolatum meum*) persuaded him that in *his* case it might be said: *Facit indignatio versum*. The indignation of Juvenal was not always very noble in its origin, or pure in its purpose: it was sometimes mean in its quality, false in its direction, extravagant in its expression: but it was tremendous in the roll of its thunders, and as withering as the scowl of a Mephistopheles. Pope having no such internal principle of wrath boiling in his breast, being really (if one must speak the truth) in the most pacific and charitable frame of mind towards all scoundrels whatever, except such as might take it into their heads to injure a particular Twickenham grotto, was unavoidably a hypocrite of the first magnitude when he affected (or sometimes really conceited himself) to be in a dreadful passion with offenders as a body. It provokes fits of laughter, in a man who knows Pope's real nature, to watch him in the process of brewing the storm that spontaneously will not come; whistling, like a mariner, for a wind to fill his satiric sails; and pumping up into his face hideous grimaces in order to appear convulsed with histrionic rage. Pope should have been counselled never to write satire, except on those evenings when he was suffering horribly from indigestion. By this means the indignation would have been ready-made. The rancour against all mankind would have been sincere; and there would have needed to be no extra expense in getting up the steam. As it is, the short puffs of anger, the uneasy snorts of fury in Pope's satires, give one painfully the feeling of a locomotive-engine with unsound lungs. Passion of any kind may become in some degree ludicrous, when disproportioned to its exciting occasions. But it is never entirely ludicrous, until it is self-betrayed as counterfeit. Sudden collapses of the manufactured wrath, sudden oblivion of the criminal, announce Pope's as *always* counterfeit. . . .

. . . as regards Pope's position, it may seem odd—but it is not so—that a man's social position should overrule his intellect. The scriptural denunciation of riches, as a snare to any man that is striving to rise above worldly views, applies not at all less to the intellect, and to any man seeking to ascend by some aerial arch of flight above ordinary intellectual efforts. Riches are fatal to those continuities of energy without which there is no success of that magnitude. Pope had £800 a year. *That* seems not so much. No, certainly not, supposing a wife and six children: but by accident Pope had no wife and no children. He was luxuriously at his ease: and this accident of his position in life fell in with a constitutional infirmity that predisposed him to indolence. Even his religious faith, by shutting him out from those public employments which else his great friends would have been too happy to obtain for him, aided his idleness, or sometimes invested it with a false character of conscientious self-denial. He cherished his religion too certainly as a plea for idleness. The result of all this was, that in his habits of thinking and of study (if *study* we can call a style of reading so desultory as *his*) Pope became a pure *dilettante*; in his intellectual eclecticism he was a mere epicure, toying with the delicacies and varieties of literature; revelling in the first bloom of moral speculations, but sated immediately; fastidiously retreating from all that threatened labour, or that exacted continuous attention; fathoming, throughout all his vagrancies among books, no foundation; filling up no chasms; and with all his fertility of thought expanding no germs of new life.

This career of luxurious indolence was the result of early luck which made it possible, and of bodily constitution which made it tempting. And when we remember his youthful introduction to the highest circles in the metropolis, where he never lost his footing, we cannot wonder that, without any sufficient motive for resistance, he should have sunk passively under his constitutional propensities, and should have fluttered amongst the flowerbeds of literature or philosophy far more in the character of a libertine butterfly for casual enjoyment, than of a hard-working bee pursuing a premeditated purpose.

Such a character, strengthened by such a situation, would at any rate have disqualified Pope for composing a work severely philosophic, or where philosophy did more than throw a coloured light of pensiveness upon some sentimental subject. If it were necessary that the philosophy should enter substantially into the very texture of the poem, furnishing its interest and prescribing its movement, in that case Pope's combining and theorizing faculty would have shrunk as from the labour of building a pyramid. And woe to him where it did *not*, as really happened in the case of the *Essay on Man*. For his faculty of execution was under an absolute necessity of shrinking in horror from the enormous details of such an enterprise to which so rashly he had pledged himself. He was sure to find himself, as find himself he did, landed in the most dreadful embarrassment upon reviewing his own work. A work which, when finished, was not even begun; whose arches wanted their key-stones; whose parts had no coherency; and whose pillars, in the very moment of being thrown open to public view, were already crumbling into ruins. . . .

Alexander Pope 1848

That Pope is to be classed as an inferior poet, has arisen purely from a confusion between the departments of poetry which he cultivated and the merit of his culture. The first place must undoubtedly be given for ever—it cannot be refused —to the impassioned movements of the tragic, and to the majestic movements of the epic muse. We cannot alter the relations of things out of favour to an individual. But in his own department, whether higher or lower, that man is supreme who has not yet been surpassed; and such a man is Pope. . . .

Not for superior correctness, but for qualities the very same as belong to his most distinguished brethren, is Pope to be considered a great poet; for impassioned thinking, powerful description, pathetic reflection, brilliant narration. His characteristic difference is simply that he carried these powers into a different field, and moved chiefly through the social paths of men, and viewed their characters as operating through their manners.

Encyclopedia Britannica 1842

RUSKIN

I have brought my little volume of Pope's poems with me; which I shall read carefully. I hardly know which is most remarkable, the magnificent power and precision of mind, or the miserable corruption of the entire element in which it is educated, and the flatterings, falsenesses, affectations, and indecencies which divert the purpose and waste the strength of the writer, while his natural perception of truth and his carefully acquired knowledge of humanity still render his works of inestimable value. I see he was first educated by a Roman Catholic, and then in *Twickenham* classicism. I am glad to find my term is exactly what I wanted it to be. Pope is the purest example, as well as the highest, of the Cockney classic.

Letter 1851

And of yet greater importance is it deeply to know that every beauty possessed by the language of a nation is significant of the innermost laws of its being. . . . All great languages invariably utter great things, and command them; they cannot be mimicked because it is not only vocal but vital; and you can only learn to speak as these men spoke, by becoming what these men were.

Now for direct confirmation of this, I want you to think over the relation of expression to character in two great masters of the absolute art of language, Virgil and Pope. You are perhaps surprised at the last name; and indeed you have in English much higher grasp and melody of language from more passionate minds, but you have nothing else, in its range, so perfect . . . the serene and just benevolence which placed Pope, in his theology, two centuries in advance of his time, and enabled him to sum the law of noble life in two lines which, so far as I know, are the most complete, the most concise, and the most lofty expression of moral temper existing in English words:

> Never elated, while one man's oppress'd;
> Never dejected, while another's bless'd.

I wish you also to remember these lines of Pope, and to make yourselves entirely masters of his system of ethics; because, putting Shakespeare aside as rather the world's than ours, I hold Pope to be the most perfect representative we have, since Chaucer, of the true English mind; and I think the *Dunciad* is the most absolutely chiselled and monumental work 'exacted' in our country. You will find, as you study Pope, that he has expressed for you, in the strictest language, and within the briefest limits, every law of art, of criticism, of economy, of policy, and, finally, of a benevolence, humble, rational, and resigned, contented with its allotted share of life, and trusting the problem of its salvation to Him in whose hand lies that of the universe.

Lectures on Art   1870

SIR LESLIE STEPHEN

Pope was governed by the instantaneous feeling. His emotion came in sudden jets and gushes, instead of a continuous stream. The same peculiarity deprives his poetry of continuous harmony or profound unity of conception. His lively sense of form and proportion enables him indeed to fill up a simple framework (generally of borrowed design) with an eye to general effect, as in *The Rape of the Lock* or the first *Dunciad*. But even there his flight is short; and when a poem should be governed by the evolution of some profound principle or complex mood of sentiment, he becomes incoherent and perplexed. But on the other hand he can perceive admirably all that can be seen at a glance from a single point of view. Though he could not be continuous, he could return again and again to the same point; he could polish, correct, eliminate superfluities, and compress his meaning more and more closely, till he has constructed short passages of imperishable excellence. This microscopic attention to fragments sometimes injures the connexion, and often involves a mutilation of construction. He corrects and prunes too closely. He could, he says, in reference to the Essay on Man, put things more briefly in verse than in prose; one reason being that he could take liberties of this kind not permitted in prose writing. But the injury is compensated by the singular terseness and vivacity of his best style. Scarcely anyone, as is often remarked, has left so large a proportion of quotable phrases, and indeed, to the present he survives chiefly by the current coinage of that kind which bears his image and superscription. . . .

One point remains to be briefly noticed. The virtue on which Pope prided himself was correctness; and I have interpreted this to mean the quality which is gained by incessant labour, guided by quick feeling, and always under the strict supervision of common sense. The next literary revolution led to a depreciation of this quality. Warton (like Macaulay long afterwards) argued that in a higher sense, the Elizabethan poets were really as correct as Pope. Their poetry embodied a higher and more complex law, though it neglected the narrow cut-and-dried precepts recognized in the Queen Anne period. The new school came to express too undiscriminating a contempt for the whole theory and practice of Pope and his followers. Pope, said Cowper, and a thousand critics have echoed his words:

> Made poetry a mere mechanic art
> And every warbler had his tune by heart.

Without discussing the wider question, I may here briefly remark that this judgment, taken absolutely, gives a very false impression of Pope's artistic quality. Pope is undoubtedly monotonous. Except in one or two lyrics, such as the *Ode on St. Cecilia's Day*, which must be reckoned amongst his utter failures, he invariably employed the same metre. The discontinuity of his style, and the strict rules which he adopted, tend to disintegrate his poems. They are a series of brilliant passages, often of brilliant couplets, stuck together in a conglomerate; and as the inferior connecting matter decays, the interstices open and allow the whole to fall into ruin. To read a series of such couplets, each complete in itself, and each so constructed as to allow of a very small variety of form, is naturally to receive an impression of monotony. Pope's antitheses fall into a few common forms, which are repeated over and over again, and seem to copy each other. And, in a sense, such work can be very easily imitated. . . . making full allowance for Pope's monotony, and the tiresome prominence of certain mechanical effects, we must, I think, admit that he has after all succeeded in doing with unsurpassable excellence what innumerable rivals have failed to do as well. The explanation is—if the phrase explains anything—that he was a man of genius, or that he brought to a task, not of the highest class, a keenness of sensibility, a conscientious desire to do his very best, and a capacity for taking pains with his work, which enabled him to be as indisputably the first in his own peculiar line, as our greatest men have been in far more lofty undertakings.

Alexander Pope   1880

LYTTON STRACHEY

Pope, we are told, was not only without 'high seriousness'; he lacked no less an 'adequate poetic criticism of life'. What does this mean? The phrase is ambiguous; it signifies at once too much and too little. If we are to understand—as the context seems to imply—that, in Matthew Arnold's opinion, no poetic criticism of life can be adequate unless it possesses largeness, freedom, and benignity, we must certainly agree that Pope's poetic criticism of life was far from adequate; for his way of writing was neither large nor free, and there was nothing benignant about him. But the words will bear another interpretation; and in this sense it may turn out that Pope's poetic criticism of life was adequate to an extraordinary degree.

Let us examine for a moment the technical instrument which Pope used—I mean the heroic couplet. . . .

Perhaps the most characteristic of all the elements in the couplet is antithesis. Ordinary regularity demands that the sense should end with every line—that was a prime necessity; but a more scrupulous symmetry would require something more —a division of the line itself into two halves, whose meanings should correspond. And yet a further refinement was possible: each half might be again divided, and the corresponding divisions in the two halves might be so arranged as to balance each other. The force of neatness could no further go; and thus the most completely evolved type of the heroic line is one composed of four main words arranged in pairs, so as to form a double antithesis.

Willing to wound, and yet afraid to strike

is an example of such a line, and Pope's poems are full of them. With astonishing ingenuity he builds up these exquisite structures, in which the parts are so cunningly placed that they seem to interlock spontaneously, and, while they are all formed on a similar model, are yet so subtly adjusted that they produce a fresh pleasure as each one appears. But that is not all. Pope was preeminently a satirist. He was naturally drawn to the contemplation of human beings, their conduct in society, their characters, their motives, their destinies; and the feelings which these contemplations aroused in him were those of scorn and hatred. Civilisation illuminated by animosity—such was his theme; such was the passionate and complicated material from which he wove his patterns of balanced precision and polished clarity. Antithesis penetrates below the structure; it permeates the whole conception of his work. Fundamental opposites clash, and are reconciled. The profundities of persons, the futilities of existence, the rage and spite of genius— these things are mixed together, and presented to our eyes in the shape of a Chinese box. The essence of all art is the accomplishment of the impossible. This cannot be done, we say; and it *is* done. What has happened? A magician has waved his wand. It is impossible that Pope should convey to us his withering sense of the wretchedness and emptiness of the fate of old women in society, in five lines, each containing four words, arranged in pairs, so as to form a double antithesis. But the magician waves his wand, and there it is:

> See how the world its veterans rewards!
> A youth of frolics, an old age of cards;
> Fair to no purpose, artful to no end,
> Young without lovers, old without a friend;
> A fop their passion, but their prize a sot;
> Alive ridiculous, and dead forgot!

And now, perhaps, we have discovered what may truly be said to have been Pope's 'poetic criticism of life'. His poetic criticism of life was, simply and solely, the heroic couplet.

Pope 1925

EMPSON

I think myself, in the following border-line case, that I am describing the attitude of Pope, but such an analysis would have achieved its object if it described the attitude only of the majority of his readers. It is that description of a great eighteenth-century mansion in which Pope is apparently concerned only to make its grandeur seem vulgar and stupid.

his building is a town,
His pond an ocean, his parterre a down.
Who but must laugh, the master when he sees,
A puny insect, shuddering at a breeze.

My lord advances, with majestic mien,
Smit with the mighty pleasure to be seen.

But hark, the chiming clocks to dinner call;
A hundred footsteps scrape the marble hall:

Is this a dinner? this a genial room?
No, 'tis a temple, and a hecatomb.

(*Moral Essays*, iv)

All this is great fun; but before concluding that Pope's better judgment really disapproved of the splendour that he evidently envied, one must remember the saying that as Augustus found Rome, so Dryden found English 'brick, and left it marble'; that the Augustans minded about architecture and what Augustus did; that a great part of the assurance and solidity of their attitude to life depended on solid contemporary evidences of national glory. When Pope prophesies the destruction of the building his language takes on a grandeur which reflects back and transfigures it:

Another age shall see the golden ear
Embrown the slope, and nod on the parterre,
Deep harvest bury all his pride has planned,
And laughing Ceres reassume the land.

These lines seem to me to convey what is called an intuitive intimacy with nature; one is made to see a cornfield as something superb and as old as humanity, and breaking down dykes irresistibly, like the sea. But, of course, it *embrowns* as with further, more universal, *gilding*, and *nods on the parterre* like a duchess; common things are made dignified by a mutual comparison which entirely depends on the dignity of the

Canons. The glory is a national rather than a personal one; democracy will *bury* the oligarch; but the national glory is now centred in the oligarch; and if the whole people has been made great, it is through the greatness of the Duke of Chandos.

This seems to me rather a curious example of the mutual comparison which elevates both parties; in this case, it is the admiration latent in a sneer which becomes available as a source of energy for these subsidiary uses: and also an example of how the Wordsworthian feeling for nature can be called forth not by an isolated and moping interest in nature on her own account, but by a conception of nature in terms of human politics. I hope, at any rate, you agree with me that the lines convey this sort of sympathy intensely; that there is some sense of the immensity of harvest through a whole country; that the relief with which the cripple for a moment identifies himself with something so strong and generous gives these two couplets an extraordinary scale. . . .

A much fainter example of the sort of ambiguity in question is supplied by one of Pope's great passages about dowagers, which possesses in a high degree the sensuous beauty that is supposed to have been beyond his powers:

> As hags hold sabbats, not for joy but spite,
> So these their merry miserable night;
> So round and round the ghosts of beauty glide,
> And haunt the places where their honour died.
> See how the world its veterans rewards!
> A youth of frolics, an old age of cards;
> Fair to no purpose, artful to no end,
> Young without lovers, old without a friend;
> A fop their passion, but their prize a sot;
> Alive ridiculous, and dead forgot!

(Essay on Women, Ep. II 245)

An impression of febrile and uncontrollable hatred is given to the terrible climax of this passage by the flat, indifferent little words, *fop*, *sot*, which, if they are to fill out the line, to give it weight, as its meaning and position demand, cannot be dropped with the analytical contempt with which they appear on the printed page; must be hurled at a person conceived as in front of you, to whom you know they are intolerable. Never was the couplet more of a rocking-horse if each line is considered separately; but all the inertia of this flatness is needed to give him strength; never was the couplet given more delicacy of modulation than is here imposed by the mere weight and passion of the sense conveyed. What is so compelling about the passage is the combination within it of two sharply distinguished states of mind; the finicking precision with which the subject-matter is handled; the pity, bitterness, and terror with which the subject-matter must be conceived.

Seven Types of Ambiguity 1930

Gray and Collins

It is curious that two poets who never formed together a 'school', who never even knew each other, should be so closely linked in critical history.

Yet it is quite right. Not so much because a mere calculation of their similarities and dissimilarities would show a surplus of the former, as because they both reacted against the dominant 'school of Pope' at very much the same time and in the same general direction. This is already quite clearly recognised in the critical battles which accompanied the new movement of poetry at the beginning of the nineteenth century. Gray and Collins are generally admired together, and generally by the enemies of Pope and Byron.

During this period, Gray was the dominant partner. Indeed the defence of Gray against Dr Johnson became almost a genre of criticism in itself. To more modern tastes, however, Collins appears to be more acceptable.

But it doesn't much matter which is preferred in the comparison; what matters is that the habit of comparing them one way or the other does keep them in close association. Once completely separated, each would probably slip from the attention of the ordinary reader—and it would be a pity.

GRAY

As to the matter of style, I have this to say: the language of the age is never the language of poetry; except among the French, whose verse, where the thought or image does not support it, differs in nothing from prose. Our poetry, on the contrary, has a language peculiar to itself; to which almost

every one, that has written, has added something by enriching
it with foreign idioms and derivatives: nay sometimes words of
their own composition or invention. Shakespeare and Milton
have been great creators in this way; and no one more licentious
than Pope or Dryden, who perpetually borrow expressions
from the former. . . .

Letter to West 1742

It is a sentiment that very universally prevails, that poetry
is a light kind of reading, which one takes up only for a little
amusement, and that therefore it should be so perspicuous as
not to require a second reading. This sentiment would bear
hard on some of your best things, and on all Gray's except
his 'Churchyard Elegy', *which*, he *told me, with a good deal of
acrimony, owed its popularity entirely to the subject, and that
the public would have received it as well if it had been written
in prose.*

Letter of Dr J. Gregory to Dr Beattie 1766

Have you seen the Works of two young Authors, a Mr.
Warton and a Mr. Collins, both Writers of Odes? it is odd
enough, but each is the half of a considerable Man, & one the
counterpart of the other. The first has but little Invention,
very poetical choice of Expression, & a good Ear, the second,
a fine fancy, model'd upon the Antique, a bad Ear, great
Variety of Words, & Images with no Choice at all. They both
deserve to last some years, but will not.

Letter to Wharton 1746

GOLDSMITH

It is by no means our design to detract from the merit
of our author's present attempt: we would only intimate that
an English poet—'one whom the Muse has *marked for her
own*', could produce a more luxuriant bloom of flowers by
cultivating such as are natives of the soil, than by endeavouring

to force the exotics of another climate: or, to speak without a metaphor, such a genius as Mr Gray might give more pleasure, and acquire a larger portion of fame, if, instead of being an imitator, he did justice to his talents, and ventured to be more original. These two Odes, it must be confessed, breathe much of the spirit of Pindar, but then they have caught the seeming obscurity, the sudden transitions, and hazardous epithets of his mighty master; all which, though evidently intended for beauties, will, probably, be regarded as blemishes by the generality of his readers.

Review of Gray's Odes 1757

LANGHORNE

If a luxuriance of imagination, a wild sublimity of fancy, and a felicity of expression so extraordinary, that it might be supposed to be suggested by some superior power, rather than to be the effect of human judgment, or capacity—if these are allowed to constitute the excellence of lyric poetry, the Author of the Odes descriptive and allegorical, will indisputably bear away the palm from all his Competitors in that province of his Muse. . . .

The Ode on the poetical Character is so extremely wild and exorbitant, that it seems to have been written wholly during the tyranny of the imagination. Some, however, there are whose congenial spirits may keep pace with the Poet in his most excentric flights, and from some of his casual strokes may catch those sublime ideas which, like him, they have experienced, but have never been able to express—Some, to whom Fancy

The cest of amplest power *has* given;
To *whom* the godlike gift assigns,
To gaze her visions wild, and feel unmix'd her flame.

But poetry so entirely abstracted, can only be entertaining to the few. . . .

It is with peculiar pleasure that we do this justice to a Poet who was too great to be popular, and whose genius was neglected, because it was above the common taste.

The Monthly Review 1764

ANON

All that we find new in this collection is, *The Fatal Sisters*, an ode, the *Descent of Odin*, an ode, and the *Triumphs of Owen*, a fragment. These turn chiefly on the dark *diableries* of the Gothic times, and if to be mysterious and to be sublime be the same thing, these deep-wrought performances must undoubtedly be deemed so. For our part, we shall for ever regret the departure of Mr Gray's muse from that elegantly-moral simplicity she assumed in the Country Church-yard.

The Monthly Review 1768

COWPER

I have been reading Gray's works, and think him the only poet since Shakespeare entitled to the character of sublime. Perhaps you will remember that I once had a different opinion of him. I was prejudiced. He did not belong to our Thursday society, and was an Eton man, which lowered him prodigiously in our esteem.

Letter to Hill 1777

JOHNSON

Gray's Poetry is now to be considered; and I hope not to be looked on as an enemy to his name, if I confess that I contemplate it with less pleasure than his life.

His *Ode on Spring* has something poetical, both in the language and the thought; but the language is too luxuriant, and the thoughts have nothing new. . . .

The poem on the *Cat* was doubtless by its author considered as a trifle, but it is not a happy trifle. . . .

The *Prospect of Eton College* suggests nothing to Gray, which every beholder does not equally think and feel. His supplication to father *Thames*, to tell him who drives the hoop or tosses the ball, is useless and puerile. Father *Thames* has no better means of knowing than himself. . . .

I am one of those that are willing to be pleased, and therefore would gladly find the meaning of the first stanza of *The Progress of Poetry*. . . .

I do not see that *The Bard* promotes any truth, moral or political.

These odes are marked by glittering accumulations of ungraceful ornaments; they strike, rather than please; the images are magnified by affectation; the language is laboured into harshness. The mind of the writer seems to work with unnatural violence. *Double double, toil and trouble*. He has a kind of strutting dignity, and is tall by walking on tiptoe. His art and his struggle are too visible, and there is too little appearance of ease and nature.

To say that he has no beauties, would be unjust: a man like him, of great learning and great industry, could not but produce something valuable. When he pleases best, it can only be said that a good design was ill directed.

His translations of Northern and Welsh poetry deserve praise; the imagery is preserved, perhaps improved; but the language is unlike the language of other poets.

In the character of his *Elegy* I rejoice to concur with the common reader; for by the common sense of readers uncorrupted with literary prejudices, after all the refinement of subtilty and the dogmatism of learning, must be finally decided all claim to poetical honours. The *Church-yard* abounds with images which find a mirror in every mind, and with sentiments to which every bosom returns an echo. The four stanzas beginning *Yet even these bones*, are to me original: I have never seen the notions in any other place; yet he that reads them here, persuades himself that he has always felt them. Had Gray written often thus, it had been vain to blame, and useless to praise him.

Life of Gray   1781

H

. . . the grandeur of wildness, and the novelty of extravagance, were always desired by him, but were not always attained. Yet as diligence is never wholly lost, if his efforts
sometimes caused harshness and obscurity, they likewise produced in happier moments sublimity and splendour. This idea
which he had formed of excellence, led him to oriental fictions
and allegorical imagery; and perhaps, while he was intent upon
description, he did not sufficiently cultivate sentiment. His
poems are the productions of a mind not deficient in fire, nor
unfurnished with knowledge either of books or life, but somewhat obstructed in its progress by deviation in quest of mistaken beauties. . . . his diction was often harsh, unskilfully
laboured, and injudiciously selected. He affected the obsolete
when it was not worthy of revival; and he puts his words out
of the common order, seeming to think, with some later candidates for fame, that not to write prose is certainly to write
poetry. His lines commonly are of slow motion, clogged and
impeded with clusters of consonants. As men are often esteemed
who cannot be loved, so the poetry of Collins may sometimes
extort praise when it gives little pleasure.

Life of Collins 1781

POTTER

The wild and romantic scenery, the strength of conception,
the boldness of the figures, the terrible sublimity, the solemn
spirit of prophecy, and the animated glow of visions of glory
render the Bard 'the finest Ode in the world'. The language of
Gray is always pure, peculiarly compact and nervous, ever
appropriated to his subject; when that is gay and smiling, his
diction is elegant and glittering; in the sober reflections of
saintly melancholy it is grave and solemn; and it rises with an
elevated dignity along with the boldest flights of his sublime
imagination; and his numbers, regulated by a fine taste and a
nice ear, have through all their various modulations a rich
and copious harmony. . . .

What could induce Dr Johnson, who as a good man might
be expected to favour goodness, as a scholar to be candid to a

man of learning, to attack this excellent person and poet with
such outrage and indecency, we can only conjecture from
this observation, 'there must be a certain sympathy between
the book and the reader to create a good liking'. Now it is
certain that the Critic has nothing of this sympathy, no portion
nor sense of that *vivida vis animi*, that etherial flame which
animates the poet; he is therefore as little qualified to judge
of these works of imagination, as the shivering inhabitant of
the caverns of the North to form an idea of the glowing sun
that flames over the plains of Chili.

*An Inquiry into some Passages of Dr Johnson's Lives
of the Poets* 1783

WAKEFIELD

After so particular an illustration of the beauties of this
Ode, it will not be amiss to take some notice of Dr Johnson's
animadversions on it. If a vigorous understanding, a comprehensive knowledge, and a capacity of sound judgement, were
sufficient qualifications for a work of genuine criticism, no man
was ever better furnished than he for such an undertaking. But
a certain inelegance of taste, a frigid churlishness of temper,
unsubdued and unqualified by that melting sensibility, that
divine enthusiasm of soul, which are essential to a hearty relish
of poetical composition; and, above all, an invidious depravity
of mind, warped by the most unmanly prejudices, and operating in an unrelenting antipathy to contemporary merit, too
often counteracted and corrupted the other virtues of his
intellect. Nor am I under any apprehension of being charged
with an unjustifiable partiality in this opinion of him, when I
make no scruple to declare, that, notwithstanding some very
exceptionable passages, infinitely disgraceful both to his
understanding and his heart, I esteem his *Lives of the English
Poets* to be the noblest specimen of entertaining and solid
criticism, that modern times have produced; well worthy of
ranking on the same shelf with the most distinguished of the
ancients, *Aristotle* and *Quintilian*. . . .

Mr Gray's extensive learning, which was of the politest

kind, and his accurate judgement, gave his poetry that perfect finish which leaves it in this respect without a rival. I could soon show this superiority by scrutinizing any poem, that should be proposed, with the same minuteness which has examined his, without any consciousness of palliating or correcting faults, in the course of the preceding observations. *Collins*—

Had fortune smil'd propitious as his Muse—

would have been the only contemporary capable of attaining the excellence of *Mr Gray*. His natural powers, his enthusiasm, and his feelings, seem to have qualified him for all that is sublime and beautiful in poetry. If I might be allowed the presumption of making one alteration only, I would oppose four stanzas in his verses on the *Death of Thomson* to any passage on a similar subject that ever was written.

Notes to the Poems of Gray   1786

WORDSWORTH

... Gray ... was at the head of those who, by their reasonings, have attempted to widen the space of separation betwixt Prose and Metrical composition, and was more than any other man curiously elaborate in the structure of his own poetic diction. ...

Preface to Lyrical Ballads   1800

BERDMORE

While I am conversing with you, who are neither deaf, nor blind, I am tempted to enter more deeply into the examination of this astonishing performance [*The Bard*]; which I shall consider in rather a new light. Every reader is struck with the wildness of the scenery—the grandeur and sublimity of thought—the boldness of imagery—the fire and enthusiasm which animate the ode throughout. Let me now more particularly call your attention to the highly figurative and majestic diction, which pervades the whole, involved in that awful obscurity, so suited to the occasion, and characteristically belonging to the language of prophecy. This obscurity has, I know, been objected to by men of some note, who must surely have considered the subject very superficially, as a defect; for which, they say, while it sheds so much darkness over the whole composition, as to preclude from the view of the disappointed reader almost all its beauties, no merit in other respects, however great and transcendent, can compensate. For myself, I have no scruple in confessing, that this very obscurity, so much condemned by judges of this description, has always appeared in my eye a distinguishing excellence of the poem. The tissue woven with bloody hands by the Bard, in concert with the spectres of his murdered brethren,

The winding sheet of Edward's race,

on which were to be traced their impending misfortunes, has in it something tremendously sublime, analogous to the emblematical images, under which are usually conveyed the prophetic denunciations of divine wrath in the sacred writings: of these every one feels the effect. In the same sublime strain the descendents of Edward are in succession designated, not by name, but by some mystic allusion; under which the figures assume a more terrific appearance, from the mist which is gathered round them. The tragical fate which severally awaits them, is denounced under the representation of some terrible image, encompassed with almost impenetrable darkness, impressing on the mind a dreadful foreboding of future calamity, the more alarming, as its nature, extent, and effect are unknown and undefined.

Specimens of Literary Resemblance   1801

COLERIDGE

He thought Collins had more genius than Gray, who was a singular instance of a man of taste, poetic feeling, and fancy, without imagination.

Table Talk 1811

I think there is something very majestic in Gray's *Installation Ode*; but as to the *Bard* and the rest of his lyrics, I must say I think them frigid and artificial. There is more real lyric feeling in Cotton's *Ode on Winter*.

Table Talk 1833

MITFORD

About ten years before this time, the Odes of Collins were published, and received with the most unmerited neglect. The public had been so long delighted with the wit and satire of Pope, had formed their taste so much on his manner of versification, and had been so accustomed to dwell upon the neat, pointed, and energetic style of that finished writer, that they were but ill prepared to admire the beauties of the lofty and magnificent language, in which Collins arrayed his sublime conceptions; and which must have been tasteless to those, who but a few years before, had received the last book of the *Dunciad*, from the dying hands of their favourite poet; and who could not pass from wit, epigram, and satire, to the bold conceptions, and wild grandeur of a poet, who imitated with signal success, the sublime compositions of Aeschylus. The very works which have now raised Gray and Collins to the rank of our two greatest lyric poets, were either neglected, or ridiculed by their contemporaries; while, to appreciate the justness of their thoughts, the harmony of their numbers, and the splendid creations of their genius, was left for the mature and almost unerring decisions of time.

The Life of Gray 1814

Though the mind of Gray was peculiarly susceptible of the impressions of natural scenery, and though it had a very strong and forcible hold of his feelings; yet he has never made such descriptions the entire subject-matter of any poem; but seems rather to hasten from them to the moral which they suggest; to the excitement of serious feeling, or pathetic sentiment, or powerful and sublime emotion.

In a letter which he wrote to Dr Beattie, containing some criticisms on part of *The Minstrel*, he says: 'What weighs most with me, it will throw more of action, pathos, and interest into your design, which already abounds in reflection and sentiment. As to description, I have always thought that it made the most graceful ornament of poetry, but never ought to make the subject.'—The practice of Gray seems to coincide very correctly with his advice. He appears never to introduce natural description solely for its own sake, but always with some further tendency, to draw from it some moral reflection, or to make it an agreeable embellishment of action. Not one of his poems can be called purely descriptive: but they generally commence with a view of nature, as of the morning, in the *Ode to Vicissitude*, or of evening in the *Elegy*, which suggesting some natural reflections to the mind of the poet, while they pass away themselves, leave forcible impressions of the feelings which they have inspired, and the train of thought which they have generated in the mind. The reason that induced Gray to reject the two stanzas towards the conclusion of the *Elegy*,

> Him have we seen the green woodside along,
> While o'er the heath we hied, our labour done;
> Oft as the woodlark pip'd her farewell song,
> With wistful eyes pursue the setting sun . . .

and,

> There scatter'd oft, the earliest of the year,
> By hands unseen, are showers of violets found;
> The redbreast loves to build, and warble there,
> And little footsteps lightly print the ground! . . .

though almost unobjectionable in themselves, and indeed very beautiful, as pieces of description, probably was, lest the descriptive part, which retarded the action of this latter part of the poem, might offend by its length, and interrupt by unnecessary images, the simplicity and unity of the composition.

Essay on the Poetry of Gray 1814

MATHIAS

It was from his ear, so exquisitely fine and so musically formed; it was from the contemplation of the legitimate structure of a lyrical stanza, of the necessity of its regularity, and of the labour and of the polish which are required not only to perfect every verse, but every single expression in every verse; it was indeed from all these views combined, that Mr Gray revolted from the vapid, vague, and unmeaning effusions of writers who, refusing to submit to the indispensable laws of lyrical poetry, or from ignorance of them, called their own wildness, genius, and their contempt of rules originality. He fixed his attention on all the most finished models of Greece and of modern Italy, he seized and appropriated their specifick and their diversified merits, united their spirit, improved upon their metre, and then, in conformity with his great preconceived idea, he gave at once in lyrick poetry to every succeeding age the law, the precept, and the example. . . .

In all the variety of Mr Gray's extensive reading, it has been seen how large a portion of his attention was given to Plato. No man was ever more enchanted with 'Socratick sounds' than he was: yet in his poetry, and it is rather singular, none of those allusions are to be discovered, which Milton (whose fond and lingering steps are always to be traced in the grove of the philosopher) delighted to adopt in his earlier and more captivating compositions. Whence is this peculiarity? The sublimity of Gray was strictly lyrical; and the pathos of his poetry was drawn (eminently so in his *Elegy*) from the feelings of our common nature, from the trembling hopes of a suffering humanity, and from what he termed 'the grateful earnest of eternal peace'; and, whether in the sacred calm or in the fervour of his genius, Mr Gray generally avoided all that could in any sense be called metaphysical. . . .

Observations on the Writings and on the Character of
Mr Gray 1814

HAZLITT

I should conceive that Collins had a much greater poetical genius than Gray: he had more of that fine madness which is inseparable from it, of its turbid effervescence, of all that pushes it to the verge of agony or rapture. Gray's *Pindaric Odes* are, I believe, generally given up at present: they are stately and pedantic, a kind of methodical borrowed phrenzy. But I cannot so easily give up, nor will the world be in any haste to part with his *Elegy in a Country Church-yard*: it is one of the most classical productions that ever was penned by a refined and thoughtful mind, moralising on human life.

Lectures on the English Poets 1818

Collins is a writer of a very different stamp who had perhaps less general power of mind than Young; but he had that true *vivida vis*, that genuine inspiration, which alone can give birth to the highest efforts of poetry. He leaves stings in the minds of his readers, certain traces of thought and feelings which never wear out, because nature had left them in his own mind. He is the only one of the minor poets of whom, if he had lived, it cannot be said that he might not have done the greatest things. The germ is there. He is sometimes affected, unmeaning, and obscure; but he also catches rich glimpses of the bowers of Paradise, and has lofty aspirations after the highest seats of the Muses. With a great deal of tinsel and splendid patch-work, he has not been able to hide the solid sterling ore of genius. In his best works there is an attic simplicity, a pathos, and fervour of imagination, which make us the more lament that the efforts of his mind were at first depressed by neglect and pecuniary embarrassment, and at length buried in the gloom of an unconquerable and fatal malady. . . .

. . . perhaps his *Ode on the Poetical Character* is the best of all. A rich distilled perfume emanates from it like the breath of genius; a golden cloud envelops it; a honeyed paste of poetic diction encrusts it, like the candied coat of the auricula. His *Ode to Evening* shows equal genius in the images and versification. The sounds steal slowly over the ear, like the gradual coming on of evening itself. . . .

Lectures on the English Poets 1818

CAMPBELL

If his works often 'whisper whence they stole their balmy spoils', it is not from plagiarism, but from a sensibility that sought and selected the finest impressions of genius from other gifted minds. But still there is a higher appearance of culture than fertility, of acquisition than originality, in Gray. He is not that being of independent imagination, and native and creative spirit, of whom we should say, that he would have plunged into a flood of poetry had there been none to leap before him. Nor were his learned acquisitions turned to the very highest account. He was the architect of no poetical design of extensive or intricate compass. . . . The fault of his meaning, is to be latent, not indefinite or confused. When we give his beauties re-perusal and attention, they kindle and multiply to the view. The thread of association that conducts to his remote allusions, or that connects his abrupt transitions, ceases then to be invisible. His lyrical pieces are like paintings on glass, which must be placed in a strong light to give out the perfect radiance of their colouring.

Specimens 1819

Collins published his *Oriental Eclogues* while at college, and his lyrical poetry at the age of twenty-six. Those works will abide comparison with whatever Milton wrote under the age of thirty. If they have rather less exuberant wealth of genius, they exhibit more exquisite touches of pathos. Like

Milton, he leads us into the haunted ground of imagination; like him, he has the rich economy of expression haloed with thought, which by single or few words often hints entire pictures to the imagination. . . .

A cloud of obscurity sometimes rests on his highest conceptions, arising from the fineness of his associations, and the daring sweep of his allusions; but the shadow is transitory, and interferes very little with the light of his imagery, or the warmth of his feelings. The absence of even this speck of mysticism from his *Ode on the Passions* is perhaps the happy circumstance that secured it unbounded popularity. . . .

In his *Ode to Fear* he hints at his dramatic ambition, and he planned several tragedies. Had he lived to enjoy and adorn existence, it is not easy to conceive his sensitive spirit and harmonious ear descending to mediocrity in any path of poetry; yet it may be doubted if his mind had not a passion for the visionary and remote forms of imagination too strong and exclusive for the general purposes of the drama. His genius loved to breathe rather in the preternatural and ideal element of poetry, than in the atmosphere of imitation, which lies closest to real life; and his notions of poetical excellence, whatever vows he might address to the manners, were still tending to the vast, the undefinable and the abstract. Certainly, however, he carried sensibility and tenderness into the highest regions of abstracted thought; his enthusiasm spreads a glow even amongst 'the shadowy tribes of mind', and his allegory is as sensible to the heart as it is visible to the fancy.

Specimens 1819

BAGEHOT

Gray's *Elegy* describes a mood which Gray felt more than other men, but which most others, perhaps all others, feel too. It is more popular, perhaps, than any other English poem, because that sort of feeling is the most diffused of high feelings, and because Gray added to a singular nicety of fancy an habitual proneness to a *contemplative*—a discerning but un-biassed—meditation on death and on life. Other poets cannot hope for such success: a subject so popular, so grave, so wise, and yet so suitable to the writer's nature, is hardly to be found.

Estimations in Criticism   1864

SIR LESLIE STEPHEN

The want of harmony between Gray and his surroundings goes far to explain his singular want of fertility. In fact, we may say—without any want of respect for a venerable institution—that Gray could hardly have found a more uncongenial residence. Cambridge boasts of its poets; and a University may well be proud which has had, amongst many others, such inmates as Spenser, Milton, Dryden, Gray, Coleridge, Wordsworth, Byron, and Mr Tennyson. If a sceptic chooses to ask what share the University can claim in stimulating the genius of those illustrious men, the answer might be difficult. But, in any case, no poet except Gray loved his University well enough to become a resident. If it were not for Gray I should be inclined to guess that a poet don was a contradiction in terms. The reason is very obvious to anyone who has enjoyed the latter title. It is simply that no atmosphere can be conceived more calculated to stimulate that excessive fastidiousness which all but extinguished Gray's productive faculties. He might wrap himself in simple contempt for the ale-drinking vanity of the don. He could, in the old college slang, 'sport his oak' and despise their railings, and even the shouts of 'Fire!' of the worthy fellow-commoners. But a poet requires some sympathy and, if possible, some worshippers. The inner circle of Gray's intimates was naturally composed of men fastidious like himself, and all of them more or less critics by profession. The reflection would be forced upon his mind, whenever he thought of publishing, What will be thought of my poems by Provost Snape, and Mr Public-Orator Tunstall, and Asheton of Jesus, and those other luminaries whom Dr Parr commemorates? And undoubtedly their first thought would be to show their claim to literary excellence by picking holes in their friend's compositions. They would rejoice greatly when they could show that faculties sharpened by the detection of false qualities and slips of grammar in their pupils' Latin verses were equal to the discovery of solecisms and defective rhymes in the work of a living poet. Gray's extreme sensitiveness to all such quillets of criticsm is marked in every poem he wrote. Had he been forced to fight his way in literature he would have learnt to swallow his scruples and take the chance in a free give and take struggle for fame. In a country living he might have forgotten his tormentors and have married a wife to secure at least one thoroughly appreciative and intelligent admirer. But to be shut up in a small scholastic clique, however little he might respect their individual merits, to have the chat of combination rooms ever in his ears, to be worried by bands of professional critics at every turn, was as though a singing bird should build over a wasp nest. The *Elegy* and the *Odes* just struggled into existence, though much of them was written before he settled down as a resident; but Gray, like many another don of great abilities, finished but a minute fragment of the work of which he more or less contemplated the execution. The books contemplated but never carried out by men in his position would make a melancholy and extensive catalogue. The effect of these influences upon his work is palpable to every reader of Gray. No English poet has ever given more decisive proof that he shared the secret of clothing even an obvious thought in majestic and resounding language, which we naturally call Miltonic. . . .

Gray and his School 1879

ARNOLD

In a poet of such magnitude, how shall we explain his scantiness of production? Shall we explain it by saying that to make of Gray a poet of this magnitude is absurd; that his genius and resources were small, and that his production, therefore, was small also, but that the popularity of a single piece, the *Elegy*—a popularity due in great measure to the subject—created for Gray a reputation to which he has really no right? . . .

Gray himself, however, maintained that the *Elegy* was not his best work in poetry, and he was right. High as is the praise due to the *Elegy*, it is yet true that in other productions of Gray he exhibits poetical qualities even higher than those exhibited in the *Elegy*. He deserves, therefore, his extremely high reputation as a poet, although his critics and the public may not always have praised him with perfect judgment. We are brought back, then, to the question: How, in a poet so really considerable, are we to explain his scantiness of production? . . .

The reason, the indubitable reason as I cannot but think it, I have already given elsewhere. Gray, a born poet, fell upon an age of prose. He fell upon an age whose task was such as to call forth in general men's powers of understanding, wit and cleverness, rather than their deepest powers of mind and soul. As regards literary production, the task of the eighteenth century in England was not the poetic interpretation of the world, its task was to create a plain, clear, straightforward, efficient prose. Poetry obeyed the bent of mind requisite for the due fulfilment of this task of the century. It was intellectual, argumentative, ingenious; not seeing things in their truth and beauty, not interpretative. Gray, with the qualities of mind and soul of a genuine poet, was isolated in his century. Maintaining them and fortifying them by lofty studies, he yet could not fully educe and enjoy them; the want of a genial atmosphere, the failure of sympathy in his contemporaries, were too great. . . .

Gray's production was scanty, and scanty, as we have seen, it could not but be. Even what he produced is not always pure in diction, true in evolution. Still, with whatever drawbacks, he is alone, or almost alone (for Collins has something of the like merit) in his age. Gray said himself that 'the style he aimed at was extreme conciseness of expression, yet pure, perspicuous, and musical'. Compared, not with the work of the great masters of the golden ages of poetry, but with the poetry of his own contemporaries in general, Gray's may be said to have reached, in style, the excellence at which he aimed; while the evolution also of such a piece as his *Progress*